DAILY LIFE DURING
WORLD WAR I

The Greenwood Press "Daily Life Through History" Series

The Age of Sail
Dorothy Denneen Volo and James M. Volo

The Ancient Egyptians
Bob Brier and Hoyt Hobbs

The Ancient Greeks
Robert Garland

Ancient Mesopotamia
Karen Rhea Nemet-Nejat

The Ancient Romans
David Matz

The Aztecs: People of the Sun and Earth
David Carrasco with Scott Sessions

Chaucer's England
Jeffrey L. Singman and Will McLean

Civil War America
Dorothy Denneen Volo and James M. Volo

Colonial New England
Claudia Durst Johnson

Early Modern Japan
Louis G. Perez

18th-Century England
Kirstin Olsen

Elizabethan England
Jeffrey L. Singman

The Holocaust
Eve Nussbaum Soumerai and Carol D. Schulz

The Inca Empire
Michael A. Malpass

Maya Civilization
Robert J. Sharer

Medieval Europe
Jeffrey L. Singman

The Nineteenth Century American Frontier
Mary Ellen Jones

Renaissance Italy
Elizabeth S. Cohen and Thomas V. Cohen

The Spanish Inquisition
James M. Anderson

Traditional China: The Tang Dynasty
Charles Benn

The United States, 1920–1939: Decades of Promise and Pain
David E. Kyvig

The United States, 1940–1959: Shifting Worlds
Eugenia Kaledin

The United States, 1960–1990: Decades of Discord
Myron A. Marty

Victorian England
Sally Mitchell

DAILY LIFE DURING
WORLD WAR I

NEIL M. HEYMAN

The Greenwood Press "Daily Life Through History" Series

GREENWOOD PRESS
Westport, Connecticut • London

Library of Congress Cataloging-in-Publication Data

Heyman, Neil M.
    Daily life during World War I / Neil M. Heyman.
        p.   cm.—(The Greenwood Press "Daily life through history" series, ISSN 1080–4749)
    Includes bibliographical references and index.
    ISBN 0–313–31500–0 (alk. paper)
    1. World War, 1914–1918—Social aspects.   I. Title.   II. Series.
    D521.H427   2002
    940.3—dc21   2001058341

British Library Cataloguing in Publication Data is available.

Library of Congress Catalog Card Number: 2001058341
ISBN: 0–313–31500–0
ISSN: 1080–4749

First published in 2002

Greenwood Press, 88 Post Road West, Westport, CT 06881
An imprint of Greenwood Publishing Group, Inc.
www.greenwood.com

Printed in the United States of America

The paper used in this book complies with the
Permanent Paper Standard issued by the National
Information Standards Organization (Z39.48–1984).

10 9 8 7 6 5 4 3 2 1

For Professor Alvin Coox (1924–1999)

Contents

Acknowledgments

The topic of World War I is both fascinating and forbidding. The study of its social aspects is particularly complex as well as emotionally engaging. The author wishes to express his thanks for the help he has received in his effort to examine that challenging topic.

The College of Arts and Letters of San Diego State University granted me several leaves to pursue my research and writing and also provided me with the funds needed for essential travel. Professor Joanne Ferraro, my friend and colleague in the Department of History, has given invaluable advice and support throughout the project. An equally helpful friend, Larry Laufer, M.D., aided me with generous advice in coping with the medical issues raised by a study of life during World War I.

In my search for appropriate photographs, I received copious assistance at the Hoover Library Archives from Mr. Remy Squires. Mr. Ian Small of the Commonwealth War Graves Commission helped me in the same endeavor and from a much greater distance.

My thanks go as well to my editor, Barbara Rader, who has provided the ideal mixture of enthusiasm, curiosity, and informed criticism. And, as always, the deepest thanks to Brenda, Mark, and David.

The historical profession has many talented and energetic members. Some are also generous in encouraging and promoting the work of their younger colleagues. Professor Alvin Coox, a member of my department at San Diego State University and a distinguished scholar in Japanese military history, exemplified that kind of generosity. I dedicate this book to him in fond remembrance.

Chronology of Events

1914

June 28	Austrian Archduke Franz Ferdinand assassinated by Serbian nationalists in Sarajevo
July 23	Austrian ultimatum to Serbia
July 28	Austria-Hungary declares war on Serbia
August 1	Germany declares war on Russia
August 3	Germany declares war on France
August 4	Germany invades Belgium; Britain declares war on Germany
August 7	Lord Kitchener, British Secretary of State for War, calls for volunteers to expand the regular British army
August 23	Battle of Mons
August 28	Three German cruisers sunk by British navy near Helgoland
September 6–11	Battle of the Marne
September 22	German U-boat sinks three British cruisers off Dutch coast

October 20–November 22	First Battle of Ypres
October 27	German mine sinks British battleship *Audacious* off Irish coast
November 6	British males in Germany between the ages of seventeen and fifty-five are interned
December 16	German cruisers raid coast of eastern England
December 25	Troops on both sides participate in unofficial "Christmas truce"

1915

January	German airships begin to bomb targets in southern England; bread rationing starts in Germany
February	Typhus epidemic breaks out among Allied prisoners in Germany; France and Germany agree to exchange badly wounded prisoners
March	First German airship raids on Paris
April 13	German government authorizes Herbert Hoover to begin program to feed civilian population in German-occupied France
April 22	Second Battle of Ypres begins with German gas attack
May 7	German submarine sinks British liner *Lusitania* off coast of Ireland; in the aftermath, English mobs attack German businesses in London, and most German males in Britain are interned
May 9	French begin offensive in Artois
September 22	French begin offensive in Champagne
September 25–26	Battle of Loos
October	Food riots break out in Berlin
December 15	Douglas Haig named commander-in-chief of British Expeditionary Force

1916

February 21	Battle of Verdun begins
May 17	British government adopts conscription
May 22	Germany establishes War Food Office
May 31–June 1	Battle of Jutland
July 1	Battle of the Somme begins; the British Army's losses (20,000 killed, 40,000 wounded) are the worst suffered by any country in modern times in a single day
August	Hindenburg and Ludendorff take overall command of German war effort
September 15	British army fighting at the Somme puts tanks into combat for the first time
October	Occupation authorities begin to deport Belgians for war work in Germany
November 7	Woodrow Wilson reelected as president of the United States
November 28	Germans begin bombing targets in England using airplanes
December 2	German Reichstag passes Auxiliary Service Law (Hindenburg Program)
December 7	David Lloyd George becomes prime minister of Great Britain
December 12	General Robert Nivelle becomes commander-in-chief of French armies

1917

January–February	Onset of "turnip winter" in Germany following failure of potato crop
February 1	Germany renews unrestricted submarine warfare
March	Women join British army as members of WAACS (Women's Army Auxiliary Corps); American women join the United States Navy as "yeomanettes"; Germans conduct strategic withdrawal to strengthened Hindenburg line in anticipation of Allied attack

March 8–12	Revolution in Russia overthrows the monarchy and establishes republic led by moderate liberals
April 6	United States declares war on Germany
April 16	French offensive under General Nivelle begins with heavy losses
May 4	First American destroyers reach British waters for antisubmarine duty
May 17	Philippe Pétain replaces Nivelle in command of French army
May 18	Selective Service Act establishes conscription in the United States
May 19	Herbert Hoover becomes Food Administrator for the United States; French armies begin to mutiny
May 25	French and German authorities agree to exchange middle-aged prisoners of war who have been held for at least eighteen months
May 26	General John Pershing named commander of American Expeditionary Force (AEF)
June	Lord Rhonda assumes direction of British food supply
June 5	United States passes Espionage Act; first group of Americans register for draft
June 7	British explode giant mines to initiate attack at Messines Ridge near Ypres
July 4	American troops of the First Division, including professionals and recent volunteers, parade through Paris
July 20	Secretary of War Newton Baker draws the lottery numbers indicating first registered Americans to be called into military service
July 31	Third Battle of Ypres (Passchendaele) begins
August	French government takes control over nation's food supply

September	First American draftees begin training
November 2	American forces suffer first casualties in combat in France
November 7	November revolution in Russia brings Communist Party led by V.I. Lenin and Leon Trotsky to power
November 16	Georges Clemenceau becomes premier of France
December 18	American government begins to restrict use of grain to brewing beer and places limits on beer's alcohol

1918

January	Massive strikes break out in German munitions factories; French government institutes bread rationing; United States government takes control of nation's railroad system
January 8	President Wilson presents peace program based upon Fourteen Points
February 6	Parliament grants the vote to British women
March	Germans begin major offensive on western front; German long-range cannon fire shells into Paris from a distance of seventy-five miles; first American female telephone operators ("hello girls") arrive in France
Spring 1918–Spring 1919	Worldwide influenza epidemic
May	German air attacks on England cease; Americans go into combat at Château-Thierry
June 6	American Marines attack at Belleau Wood
July	British government takes control of most of the nation's food supply
August 8	British achieve decisive breakthrough against German lines near Amiens
August 9	German long-range artillery ends bombardment of Paris

August 13	United States Marines accept first women recruits
September 12	American offensive at St. Mihiel
September 16	General Allied offensive begins on western front; Americans attack in Meuse-Argonne sector
October 3	Germany appeals to President Woodrow Wilson for an armistice
October 21	Germany ends unrestricted submarine war
October 29	Mutiny breaks out in German navy at Kiel
November 3	German sailors' rebellion spreads to local civilian population
November 7	False news of Armistice appears in Allied countries
November 9	Kaiser Wilhelm II abdicates; Germany becomes a republic
November 10	Wilhelm goes into exile in Holland
November 11	Germans sign Armistice
November 12	German women receive the right to vote
December 1	American troops enter their zone of occupation in western Germany

1919

January 18	Paris Peace Conference begins
February	Last Allied prisoners from western front repatriated
June 28	Treaty of Versailles signed
October	Last German prisoners held by British repatriated
November 19	United States Senate rejects peace treaty

1920

| August 28 | American women receive the right to vote |

Autumn   Last German prisoners held by French re-
                                patriated

1921

August 25   United States signs separate peace with Ger-
                                many (Treaty of Berlin)

Introduction

In eight days, stretching from the close of July to the start of August 1914, the major powers of Europe—Austria-Hungary, Germany, Russia, France, and Great Britain—entered the conflict we know as World War I. The war's eventual scope and cost came to astonish many Europeans, but few of the Continent's statesmen or informed members of its various populations were completely surprised at the outbreak of hostilities.

The conflicts among these large and powerful states had deep roots. Many tensions stemmed from the emergence of a powerful nation at the center of the Continent. The victory of the German states, led by Otto von Bismarck's Prussia, over France in the Franco-Prussian War of 1870–71 produced a united Germany. It also created lasting tension between a suddenly humbled France and its newly potent neighbor. France's humiliation was sealed by the successful German demand for strategic border regions: the entire province of Alsace and a portion of Lorraine.

Germany's quick emergence as the leading power on the Continent also cast a shadow over British interests. The Germans took a leading role in international trade and colonial questions, bedrock issues for British statesmen. Especially when Germany intruded into the British sphere of interest in South Africa—Berlin openly sided with Britain's Boer opponents before and during the Boer War of 1899–1902—relations deteriorated sharply. Above other factors, Germany's construction of a world-class navy based upon battleships put the government in Berlin at loggerheads with its counterpart in London. Such a fleet containing the most powerful vessels of the era seemed destined to meet Britain's

Grand Fleet in the North Sea. The possibility that Germany might dominate the sea lanes around Britain, and thus imperil the island nation's food supply, made hostilities likely, if not actually inevitable.

The dangers caused by German ambitions were matched by intractable conflicts elsewhere. Austria-Hungary faced a hostile Russia as Ottoman Turkish power collapsed in the Balkans, creating a power vacuum that sucked in both countries. Austria-Hungary had compelling reasons to intervene here, fearing for its very existence as Balkan states like the Kingdom of Serbia grew larger at Turkey's expense. Populated by a dozen nationalities including Serbs, Austria-Hungary might collapse if its Serb population and the southern territories they inhabited broke away to join the Kingdom of Serbia. A nightmare scenario in Vienna pictured other discontent ethnic groups in Austria-Hungary emboldened to break away as well.

Russia stood equally ready to intervene in Balkan affairs. The giant Slavic power in eastern Europe had assumed the role of Serbia's patron and ally. Russia desired to assert its standing as a Great Power, and contesting Austria for influence in the Balkans was the most likely way in which to do so. Russia's religious and cultural ties to the Serbs, with whom they shared a devotion to Eastern Orthodox Christianity, augmented St. Petersburg's political interest in the region. Thus, no Austrian move could take place without risking a serious Russian response.

Crises in one area of Europe threatened to spread. The alliance systems developed in the prewar decades made localized conflict unlikely. So too did informal understandings that tied the security of one country to another. Thus, Austria-Hungary had a formal treaty tying it to Germany. France and Russia were similarly linked. But the rising German threat had made Great Britain a probable—if not yet a formal—ally for France and Russia.

And specific events in the decade prior to 1914 saw the tensions become harder and harder to manage. A bumptious Germany precipitated two crises—one in 1905, a second in 1911—over France's efforts to tighten its control of Morocco. The area was generally seen to be a French sphere of influence, but the Germans hoped to obstruct French policy and thus to assert their own role in international affairs. More specifically, the Germans were trying to sever the tie between Britain and France, isolating their hostile neighbor to the West. In both cases the effort backfired. In the earlier crisis, Britain provided diplomatic backing to France in the face of German pressure. The crisis begun in 1911 was the more dangerous of the two. By dispatching a gunboat to a Moroccan port, the Germans provoked an official British pledge to stand by France even in the face of war. A humiliated Germany found itself compelled to back away.

Starting in 1907, Balkan crises threatened to bring Russia and Austria-

Hungary into direct confrontation. Initiatives by Russian diplomats helped set off the two Balkan Wars of 1912–13, removing Turkey's control from all but a sliver of the Balkans. A series of international conferences worked out new borders for the states in the region. But a perilous instability persisted. The enmity of many Serbs toward Austria-Hungary was matched by the determination of a "war party" in Vienna to wipe the Kingdom of Serbia off the map.

The British and Germans made an effort to negotiate a limit to their naval arms race when Britain's Secretary of State for War, Richard Haldane, visited Berlin in 1912. Educated in Germany and fluent in the language, Haldane hoped to lessen tensions. Limiting naval construction might improve Anglo-German relations as well as lightening the crushing financial burden the naval arms race put on both countries. The mission failed, the naval race went on, and mutual suspicions deepened.

In this volatile atmosphere, a single unfortunate incident had the potential to set off a European war. The assassination of Archduke Franz Ferdinand, the heir to the throne of Austria-Hungary, at the hands of Serb nationalists on June 28, 1914, was the lighted match that set off the explosion. Austria-Hungary's ensuing determination to go to war with Serbia received German backing. Russia moved to defend Serbia. Vienna's ultimatum to the Kingdom of Serbia on July 23—an ultimatum the Austrians saw no reason to think the Serbs could accept—set off one declaration of war after another: Austria-Hungary against Serbia on July 28, Germany against Russia on August 1, Germany against France on August 3, Britain against Germany on August 4.

And what were the prospects for the war's participants who soon found themselves in deadly struggle on the western front and elsewhere? Decades of steady—often frenzied—industrial growth had equipped Germany, France, and Britain with the capability of waging war on an unprecedented scale. These countries could raise armies numbering millions of men. They could equip those men with almost limitless quantities of deadly weapons ranging from rifles and machine guns to artillery of unprecedented size and lethality. The scientists and technicians in all of these nations could be enlisted to conjure up new tools of destruction.

THE SCOPE OF THIS BOOK

This work examines what daily life was like during the fifty-two months of World War I. The need to put such a huge topic into manageable form has led to a focus on the western front and the major powers that fought there. That strip of territory stretching more than 400 miles from the coast of the English Channel to the Swiss border became the center stage of the entire conflict. The western front saw the most intense military carnage of the war, and events there stimulated vast change in Britain, France, and Germany. In the third year of the war, the United States joined in the conflict. Its efforts also centered on the western front.

The war was first of all a military event. The initial eight chapters look at the military experience of the various participants. They consider how armies were recruited and trained, the equipment they used, and the food they ate. Trench warfare was a way of life and also a series of huge, bloody military encounters, and the account here looks first at the routine of serving in the trenches, then examines the phenomenon of combat.

While the soldier in the trench is the most familiar figure on the western front, sailors in the navies of the belligerents worked closely in relationship to the fighting on land. The effort to close routes to the outside world to one's antagonist led to both the Allied blockade of Germany and the German submarine assault on Allied merchant shipping. Along with a consideration of what the war was like for seamen, the story of the western front points to the novel experience of the airmen. Airplanes and the men who flew them, hitherto no factor in warfare, grew in importance as the war went on.

A military view of the wartime needs to pass beyond the various military forces and their different battlefields. It also includes the medical system that cared for the conflict's numerous casualties and the smaller but important system each country set up to deal with the unexpected numbers of enemy prisoners the war brought into its hands. Women also played a role in military affairs. The work of the military nurse was the most predictable contribution a woman could offer. But other women served in supporting roles for the armed services. In Britain and then the United States, they actually entered the armed forces. The unprecedented sight of women in uniform—disturbing to some—showed how different a shape this conflict was taking compared to earlier wars.

The next chapters deal with the civilian's world. Life at home changed in myriad ways, even for those far from the actual fighting. The impact and flavor of the war seeped into every aspect of daily living—from the schoolchild's lesson to the fevered prosperity of a wartime economy. For some civilians, the war created a direct threat. The new instruments of combat—chiefly the submarine and the airplane but even heavy artillery—put civilian lives at risk in unprecedented fashion. Millions of Frenchmen (and Belgians as well) had a wartime experience dominated by oppressive foreign rule.

For everyone connected with the war, the food supply, taken for granted at least by those well-off in peacetime, now became, if not an obsession, at least a concern. For those in blockaded Germany, it did become an obsession. The average civilian had his most direct and painful tie to the expanding wartime governments when the government sought to control what he got to eat each day.

The traditional social role of women on the home front also saw the impact of the conflict. Women became a crucial source of labor for the wartime economy. The war transformed growing prewar concern over declining birthrates into concerted efforts to increase the birthrate in several countries. And women as the gender that did not have to go to fight attracted a level of criticism that permits a peek into the growing bitterness the war produced.

By the time the Armistice was signed on November 11, 1918, more than four million had perished fighting on the western front. Both those at the fighting front and those at home had to cope with the loss of a familiar face, all too often the loss of a loved one. The size of the losses, as well as the violence of death between 1914 and 1918, jolted societies in which death, a peaceful death in one's bed at home, had become the province of the elderly. Daily life for many during World War I meant coming to grips with bereavement.

Finally, when the war at last ended, it came with a surge of excitement in the victorious countries. But the mere declaration that hostilities were suspended only began to change the lives of the millions in the armed forces. Their wartime experience extended on until the military authorities who had possessed life and death power over them could be convinced—or compelled—to let them go home.

THE COURSE OF THE WAR

The war began in August 1914 with a massive German offensive on the western front. Kaiser Wilhelm's armies smashed through Belgium and northeastern France, and penetrated almost within sight of Paris. Like the commanders of Napoleon's armies in the previous century, the Germans hoped to destroy their opponent's armed forces in a single, gigantic campaign, to seize his capital, and to watch him sue for peace. They were not alone. The French also began the war with an offensive against German territory, portions of Lorraine the Germans had seized from France in 1871.

Neither plan worked. The French assault ended in bloody failure. A successful French and British counterattack halted the German advance. The rival armies raced northward to outflank the other side and to regain the initiative, but neither the Anglo-French nor the German forces could move fast enough to unhinge its enemy's defenses. By the close of 1914, the war on the western front had settled down to a confrontation between millions of soldiers, soon to be reinforced by millions more.

The conflict raged in eastern Europe as well and eventually spread to the coast of China, the islands of the Pacific, the Middle East, and Africa. Germany had to fight a sizable conflict on the eastern front against Russia. Nonetheless all three of the principal antagonists from central and western Europe—Britain, France, and Germany—gathered the bulk of their armed strength on the western front. Initially, the war at sea also ranged far from Europe, but it soon came to focus on the waters of the North Sea and the eastern Atlantic. As the combatants took to the air, the skies over northwestern Europe saw the greatest combat in this dimension too.

By the start of 1915, French offensives to expel the Germans from territory they had taken the previous autumn gave the western front its grisly character. The pattern became ominously clear. Huge infantry assaults, prepared by as much artillery fire as the attacker could muster, hurtled against the opponent's defensive line. Artillery fire presumably weakened the enemy's defenses—in this case German defenses—but it also attracted his attention and his reserves to the point of the attack. With defensive lines consisting of trenches protected by barbed wire and held by soldiers with quick firing rifles and machine guns, attacks failed. They produced little more than a grim list of casualties.

New weapons came into play as both sides grew impatient with the stalemate. Both sides employed poison gas starting in 1915, and the first tanks appeared on the battlefield in 1916. The airplane was transformed from a fragile reconnaissance tool to a part of a large aerial armada. Those squadrons began to contest the skies over the battlefield with an equally strong enemy air force. The Germans employed airships (zeppelins) in 1915, then bomber planes starting the next year to strike at their enemies' homelands. The Allies responded in kind.

The French experienced their greatest losses of the war in the futile infantry attacks of 1915. The year 1916 saw Germany and Britain suffer in a comparable way. The German high command under Field Marshal Erich von Falkenhayn put aside hopes for a breakthrough. In February 1916, its forces attacked the French salient (an exposed bulge in the battle line) at the historic city of Verdun. The Germans hoped to destroy France's armed forces and the nation's will to fight by inflicting intolerable losses on French forces compelled for political reasons to hold Verdun. Following eight months of combat on a titanic scale, both sides suffered comparably painful losses.

During that same year, the new British armies, formed by volunteers in the first part of the war, took the field at the Battle of the Somme in France. British leaders like Field Marshal Douglas Haig clung to the hope that enough artillery combined with an aggressive infantry assault could penetrate the enemy lines. Victory would come, Haig assumed, when his troops plunged into the enemy rear and began an unstoppable advance into Germany. Instead, the battle began with a massacre of British infantry by German machine-gun fire unprecedented even on the western front. Continuing the attack in order to wear down the enemy by attrition, Haig spilled even more British blood. The Germans died in huge numbers as well, but the front remained solid.

The year 1916 saw the admirals on both sides of the North Sea abandon the caution they had shown since the war's beginning. The British waited in vain for the German High Seas Fleet to sail out of port and set the stage for a new Trafalgar, the decisive naval victory on the high seas that the British inflicted on the French navy in October 1805. The Germans were equally disappointed that the British Grand Fleet conducted its blockade of German ports from a safe distance. Skirmishing in the North Sea produced only a frustrated stalemate, with the admirals showing a healthy respect for the potential of weapons like modern minefields and submarine-launched torpedoes. The clash of the two great battle fleets at Jutland at the close of May brought heavier British than German losses. But it was a singular event, unmatched at any later point in the war, and it left command of the ocean's surface in British hands.

Desperation for both sides became even more evident in 1917. The French began an offensive against the Germans in Champagne, spurred on by the optimism of their new army commander, General Georges Nivelle. The collapse of the Nivelle offensive in the face of skilled and determined German resistance plunged much of the French army into mutiny. French forces became the first—but not the last—on the western front to see discipline and fighting spirit collapse. A new commander, General Philippe Pétain, restored order to the army, but at the cost of suspending the bloody offensives that had been the sole hope for a quick victory.

The Germans also took desperate measures in the hope of quick success. The submarine, a novel weapon used for the first time in World War I, seemed to be the tool for victory at sea. By cutting Britain's food supply, most of which was imported, the submarines of the German navy could, it was hoped, produce the national victory the army had failed to attain. The submarine assault continued in ominous fashion throughout the war, but it showed it would not succeed by the close of 1917. Allied losses remained manageable, and the vital supply ships continued to cross the Atlantic. A variety of novel or distasteful measures— using naval convoys despite the opposition of aggressively minded naval commanders, rationing food despite the hardship it levied on much of the population—defeated the German lunge. The cost of the German effort was to bring the United States into the war. Woodrow Wilson's government had declared two years earlier that it would not tolerate an unlimited submarine war by the Germans.

Meanwhile, the British continued their hopeful offensives to break the German line and thereby to open the road to victory. A new offensive— this time around the northwestern Belgian city of Ypres—began in the dry weather of summer, and continued into the rains of fall. With the low-lying terrain transformed into a sea of mud, the British suffered some of their worst losses of the war in the Third Battle of Ypres (also known as Passchendaele)—and for negligible scraps of territory.

The final year of the war began with a massive German offensive. Hoping to defeat the French and British before large American forces could arrive, the German command team of Paul von Hindenburg and Erich Ludendorff struck a series of powerful blows from one end of the western front to the other. The Germans surged forward, crippling an entire British field army in the process. But ultimately the Allied lines held. By late summer, the morale of the German army began to crack. The huge, but untrained American army ground forward in the Meuse-Argonne sector around Verdun in northeastern France, while the French and especially the British conducted sweeping offensives that drove the Germans back toward their own border.

As Allied forces approached the German frontier, German desperation produced momentous military and political consequences. Ludendorff, the key figure in the German high command, called upon the political leaders of Germany to obtain an Armistice. Under the pressure of America's president Woodrow Wilson, before the Armistice the Germans moved to create a parliamentary system akin to that of Great Britain. But events outran anyone's intention. German admirals, seeking a final sea battle in the North Sea, ordered their High Seas Fleet to prepare for a final offensive, but long abused seamen rebelled against their officers and spread the message of revolt into Germany's civilian population.

As Germany's delegation to the Armistice talks traveled to meet Allied representatives at Compiègne in the first week of November, Germany plunged into revolution. Kaiser Wilhelm II reluctantly abdicated, a provisional republic was formed, and radical leaders like Karl Liebknecht prepared to move the revolution into a more sweeping phase. They envisioned a change that would not halt at the stage of a middle-class republic; instead, it would move on into a revolutionary workers' government akin to the one Russia had accepted in November of the previous year.

PART I

THE MILITARY WORLD

1

Recruitment and Training

Two of the combatants on the western front—Germany and France—entered the war with large, trained armies. Each had a system of conscription that drew a substantial portion of the nation's young men into military service each year. Besides filling the army with its permanent staff and recent draftees, the military system in Germany and France placed young men who had completed their years of service into reserve units. Reservists returned to active duty for a time each year, and they stood ready to be mobilized and to join the standing army in case of national emergency. These nations could send millions of more or less trained fighting men to the battlefront within weeks after declaring war.

In 1914, elaborate plans, based upon the thickening web of railroad lines in both Germany and France, put reservists in their depots, linked them to units of the standing army, and moved these forces rapidly toward the fighting front. At the same time, enthusiastic volunteers rushed to the colors in both Germany and France. As the war continued, the existing system of conscription went on working. Each year's passing saw the young men of military age drawn into the conflict.

In Britain, the situation was dramatically different. The British had a small volunteer army side by side with a large volunteer navy. Britain had no established way to augment the country's military ranks substantially. The Territorial Force—a British version of the American National Guard—combined with small army and navy reserve forces offered only a limited way of reinforcing the standing military. In short order, however, Britain launched a massive effort to bring in volunteers for a new army. And, as the war progressed, the argument over whether to resort to conscription—to imitate the system the continental powers had long ago adopted—resulted in a draft law in 1916.

The United States also differed from the large nations on the Continent. American armed forces consisted of a substantial navy and a minuscule army. The only highly trained troops prepared to fight were in the tiny Marine Corps, its total strength less than 16,000 men. Following in short order after the American entry into the war, the government established nationwide conscription. With little or no preparation, the United States set out to create an army of millions of men.

GERMANY'S ARMY

The men of the German standing army and ready reserves who went to war in August 1914 had served a peacetime apprenticeship as soldiers. The standing army of approximately 800,000 included the contingents of recruits who had been called up in the fall of 1912 and 1913. They were quickly augmented by regular reservists from the contingents called up from 1907 through 1911. To that group were added older reservists from a home guard organization, the *Landwehr*, men ranging up to the age of thirty-nine.

Germany's relatively large population had permitted the government to be selective in choosing those physically and politically desirable for military service. More than 65 percent of the army recruits in 1911 came from rural areas even though more than half the population lived in urban areas. Only 13 percent of recruits came from large or medium-sized towns. It was in the towns that groups the government considered of questionable loyalty like labor unions and the Social Democratic party were most evident.

All reservists were veterans of two years of active duty beginning when they were called up in the fall of their twentieth year. Former cavalrymen had undergone three years of active service. Segregated in barracks as recruits, all had been initiated into their new role as members of the armed forces. Ever-present sergeants, who normally served for twelve years on active duty, had turned the young men's minds and bodies toward military purposes. During their first six months in uniform, recruits had received the traditional training for novice soldiers: close order drill, instruction in marksmanship and caring for their rifles, and practice in route marching and maneuvering. That was followed by a period on active duty, then a return to civilian life. Mobilizing such reservists produced a fighting force of 2.9 million men in August 1914.[1] Although there was some resistance to the call-up, especially in rural communities where bringing in the harvest seemed a high priority, only an insignificant number of reservists failed to report for duty.

In a society where military values were celebrated, most young Germans apparently accepted their obligation to serve with equanimity. Recruiting for specific units was tied to a designated geographical area. An entire age group from a community entered the army at one time with the occasion marked by local festivities. It was possible to volunteer for a desirable unit, including one in which a father or older brother had done his active duty. An educated young man could obtain a reserve commission, with its attendant social prestige, after volunteering for a year in the ranks. But even for the mass of recruits who came from a less-privileged position, completion of military service was celebrated as a rite of passage.

The heavy dose of close order drill recruits received was designed to produce the *Kadavergehorsam* (corpselike obedience) necessary to react appropriately to orders in the stress of combat. There was no effort to make recruits serving for two or three years into skilled marksmen. The ability to fire in "concentrated, controlled bursts" in battlefield conditions was sufficient. On the other hand, German training stressed aggressiveness in time of danger: Infantrymen, equipped with "inner assertiveness" (in the words of the drill regulations of 1906) were expected to move forward even in the face of enemy fire. German training manuals reflected an awareness of modern firepower but demanded that well-trained soldiers surmount their fear and play their part in assaulting the enemy.[2]

Most of the German soldiers who went to war in August 1914 were in their mid-twenties. Only a few of their most senior leaders had seen combat in the Franco-Prussian War of 1870–71. A larger, but still limited group had participated in colonial campaigns against the indigenous population in Germany's African possessions. There was nothing like the pool of combat veterans to be found at all ranks of the French and British armies. Nonetheless, the average German soldier in 1914 "saw himself as part of an institution incorporating both the rectitude of certitude and a significant technical competence." German training had given the rank and file "both the psychological and the professional equipment to survive on the modern battlefield," and they served in an army that reinforced their enthusiasm by "at least the appearance of knowing what it was doing."[3] As heavy casualties emptied the ranks of the German army, men from younger and older age groups entered military service. Similarly, the officer corps began to look different. Even before the war, the growth of the army had necessitated opening the army's leadership group, hitherto dominated by aristocrats, to men of middle-class origin. That process continued, and, to find an additional source of combat leaders, senior noncommissioned officers took over an increasing degree of responsibility.

A German called to military service during the war received his introduction to army life at a regimental base. There his instructors came from two sources. They were either officers and sergeants who had been wounded and were recovering their health, or else the training cadre consisted of elderly veterans who had been recalled for such duties. Preparation for the ordeal of the trenches did not progress beyond close order drill, bayonet practice, and elementary maneuvering according to prewar manuals.

German units at the front found they had to conduct their own practical training. In order to initiate fresh replacements into the realities of trench warfare, combat divisions set up Field Recruit Depots back in Germany. The instructors at these camps were recent veterans of the fighting. But even the training at these installations suffered from the lack of space needed to replicate the trench systems of the western front.

A visiting Dutch journalist, J.M. de Beaufort, described the atmosphere of a training barracks he visited in Munich in 1916. After six weeks of instruction, recruits were performing every movement with "a mechanical precision in all their actions." Answering their officers, they shouted their responses "as if they had been addressed by a man standing half a mile off." When de Beaufort asked the German captain guiding him through the barracks for an explanation, he received the answer that such a practice taught recruits a degree of military alertness. "Many of the recruits, when they arrive at their depots, are 'mother's darlings,' speak softly and slowly, and are startled when you address them." The German declared that two weeks of training, including the shouted responses demanded by their instructors, changed "their manner of acting and thinking."[4]

FRANCE'S ARMY

French recruits likewise spent two or more years in barracks, starting between the ages of eighteen and twenty. The annual call-up produced little of the festive air it did in German life, and one historian has noted that for young Frenchmen, "obligatory military service was at best an interruption, at worst a serious strain on family economies."[5] The relatively small pool of French manpower liable for military service, which brought in only 250,000 to 300,000 recruits per year, had impelled the government to institute a three-year tour of active duty in 1913. Without a change, the French would have a standing army of only 540,000 to confront more than 800,000 Germans.

The army at the war's beginning included recruits called up in 1911, 1912, and 1913. Reservists from the call-ups between 1896 and 1910 joined them at once. By the end of the year, new recruits from the class of 1914 had been drawn into the army, and reservists from the classes of 1892 through 1895 had taken up arms as well.

Recruits and reservists alike had heard sergeants shout in their ears, walked long miles in practice marches, and repeatedly cleaned their rifles. In the view of most observers, the French army was less successful than the German military in removing civilian attitudes from its recruits. France had the recent memory of seeing its army defeated in the Franco-Prussian War of 1870–71. Moreover, the Dreyfus affair, in which a Jewish officer's superiors unjustly accused him of treason, made many in France view the army as a bigoted, corrupt, and anti-Republican body. A French infantry regiment mutinied in 1906 rather than repress a rebellion by wine growers, and the annual call-up of reserves for training during the following year saw thirty-six out of every hundred men neglect to report.

The absence of the *Kadavergehorsam* upon which the Germans prided themselves seemed visible in the unrest that took place in twenty French army garrisons in 1913. It erupted when troops learned that they were expected to serve three years rather than the earlier two-year obligation. Nonetheless, when called up from civilian life in 1914, only 1.3 percent of France's reservists—instead of the anticipated 13 percent—failed to join their units. Eventually 7.8 million Frenchmen performed wartime military service. This constituted about one-fifth of the country's total population.[6]

The Three-Year Law passed in 1913 specified that recruits were to spend their first year in closely supervised drills. As "soldiers in the ranks," they were expected only to master the "mechanics of movement." In their second year, they were to be trained for combat, learning the "special functions that might fall to a soldier on the field of battle." In the newly established third year, a number of conscripts were expected to earn promotion to the rank of corporal or sergeant.[7] This French prewar training stressed offensive action against the enemy in all circumstances. A photograph of the 1913 maneuvers showed a scene similar to a painting in 1877 with soldiers "fighting in the open country and running on hillsides to attack the enemy with fixed bayonets, urged on by their mounted officers." The training doctrine stressed the role of the infantry, downgraded usefulness of artillery, and denigrated defensive tactics.[8] According to the tactical rules of April 1914, the necessary assault that would bring victory "cannot be fulfilled except . . . with an enormous expenditure of physical and moral energy and with blood sacrifices."[9] All this prepared soldiers for war—but, as it happened, not for World War I.

Possibly the ferocious call for offensive action in all circumstances did not penetrate into the army's rank and file. In provincial garrisons far from the influence of the War Ministry, it may not have won over much of the officer corps. Nonetheless, in the years before 1914, such aggressive and experienced colonial commanders as Joseph Joffre, Charles Mangin, and François Franchet d'Esperey had attained influential roles in France's army. They pursued a rigidly offensive posture from the start of the war onward.

As the war took its toll on the army, its character inevitably changed. The pre-1914 corps of noncommissioned officers had been composed largely of professional soldiers. Wartime corporals and sergeants were now mainly former civilians. The French army in the century prior to 1914 had promoted able sergeants to officers' rank. Such promotions now became common. There was nothing novel about the case of the rising young academic Marc Bloch, twenty-eight years old and a sergeant of the reserve since 1907. After distinguished combat service starting in October 1914, he was promoted to lieutenant's rank in April 1916 and ended the war as a captain. The origins of some officers were even more modest. When generals like Charles Mangin sought to promote only those noncommissioned officers with a middle-class background, they found it impossible to maintain that standard. The country needed men to lead platoons and companies in combat. "Demographically inferior France simply could not afford the luxury of high-class barriers."[10]

THE ENTHUSIASM OF 1914

Most German men of military age were already in service or assigned to a reserve division. But still, keen young men flocked to the colors. Those who had been exempted, men whose reserve units had not yet been called up, and those below or even above military age rushed to volunteer. Although German newspaper reports spoke of more than a million such volunteers, in fact 185,000 young Germans volunteered during August 1914. They came from all social groups, including the working class, but the majority consisted of students, tradesmen, or businessmen.[11]

Long lines appeared outside the headquarters of divisions that had vacancies for recruits. One-half of the 32,000 students in Gymnasia, elite high schools preparing young men to enter universities, volunteered. In some cases, entire classes went off to war at the start of the conflict. One-half of Germany's university students probably did the same. A mixture of motives pushed many of these young volunteers to don a uniform at the war's start. For some, a sense of duty was paramount. But there was also peer pressure in well-off and educated families to join up. Others, especially from less privileged economic groups, found a position in the army appealing when the alternative was unemployment.

Peacetime's extended training period was not feasible for these men in the earliest stage of the war. Six weeks in the army sufficed to prepare recruits for the battle zone. Franz Blumenfeld, a law student at the University of Freiburg, rushed to join the German army in his university town in early August. He was afraid that going back to his home in

Hamburg would mean losing the opportunity for an early trip to the front. On September 23, he found himself on a troop train bound for northern France.[12]

Herbert Sulzbach, the son of a wealthy banking family in Frankfurt-am-Main, recorded in his diary for August 8 that he had been "unbelievably lucky" to be accepted into the 63rd (Frankfurt) Field Artillery Regiment. Fifteen hundred volunteers had tried to enter the unit in the first days of the war; only one out of seven had been accepted. He was off to the western front on September 2 after what he called "a bare four weeks' training."[13]

Alan Seeger was a young American who joined the French armed forces in mid-August. He received five weeks of training, then left for the front at the start of October. Placed just behind the battle line, Seeger and his unit were schooled in combat techniques, including mock battles with blank shells. By late October, his regiment was facing the enemy.[14]

BRITAIN'S ARMY

Britain had the smallest army among the great powers of Europe. Shielded behind a powerful navy, the country used its army primarily to defend a global empire. The army had a total strength of approximately 12,800 officers and 230,000 enlisted men,[15] but this small force had the best military skills on the European scene. Its officer corps drew upon the elite of British society: sons of the nobility and landed gentry, children of old military families, and the scions of ambitious professional men. Although enlisted men mainly originated in the ranks of the unskilled and the unemployed, they became highly trained. The majority signed up for a term of seven years of service (artillerymen served for six or eight years), and they received a rugged regimen of gymnastics, close order drill, and extensive marching. They showed their military proficiency most clearly on the rifle range. The average British rifleman, encouraged by a bonus for skill with his weapon, could fire fifteen accurately aimed shots within a minute at a target 300 yards away. A talented shooter could fire thirty such rounds.

A typical British battalion serving in India made a demanding annual march each spring of 200 miles from the steaming plains into the cooler, more rugged mountain regions. There it underwent an intensive period of training in skirmishing, maneuvering, and interunit communication. The officers, men, and horses of British artillery units practiced setting up a six-gun battery within three minutes. The cannon were up and firing before an opposing enemy unit could possibly respond. Reforms in the decade before 1914 had resulted in a pool of trained civilians—the Territorial Army—capable of reinforcing the regulars. This force was an amalgamation of locally raised units analogous to the American Na-

A British recruiting poster directed at men in the
Empire. Courtesy of the Hoover Institution Archives.

tional Guard. Its citizen soldiers, who numbered some 250,000 officers
and men at the start of the war,[16] drilled several times a week and attended an annual two-week summer camp for maneuvers. Even with
this supplement, the numbers in the British army could not match the
sizable armed forces of France or Germany.

The Minister of War, Field Marshal Horatio Kitchener, had the rare
insight in August 1914 to predict a long war. He planned to expand the
nation's armed forces by putting millions of men into a completely new
force. Kitchener's so-called "New Army" came to depend, at first, on
raising volunteers. He used his vast personal prestige and the sharp
sense of national crisis at the war's beginning to call on the country's
young men to enlist. They were to join newly formed divisions for either
three years or for the duration of the war. Meanwhile, the Territorial
Army expanded with its own set of volunteers.

For two years, the British army met its needs with these volunteers.

The number of voluntary recruits ebbed and flowed. Military crises in the first months of fighting spurred men to sign up. Enlistment surged, for example, when the British first met the German army at the Battle of Mons in August. They rose again in October and November, when bloody fighting at the Battle of Ypres almost wiped out the prewar professional force. But personal factors operated side by side with a sense of patriotic duty to impel a young man to enlist. A sense of adventure motivated some; the lack of employment in a depressed industry pulled others into the armed forces. Criminals got the opportunity to join up rather than face prison; noblemen's servants were instructed by their employers to don a uniform. Apparently able-bodied young men in mufti often found themselves accosted in the street to answer questions about their failure to join up. Young women offered a white feather, a symbol of cowardice, to those who appeared reluctant to face the Germans. Those same young men were likely to find themselves dismissed from their jobs with an admonition from their employers that the country's military needed their services.

The flood of volunteers outstripped the ability of army authorities to deal with them. The defining elements of joining a military force—being fed by the army, receiving a uniform and a weapon, being placed in a tent or a barracks—were conspicuous by their absence. Young men sometimes lived at home or in nearby civilian homes for months until training camps were established. A recruit drilling in civilian clothes— or in a blue uniform very different from the regulation khaki of a British soldier—was a common sight.

Some regiments had entry requirements based upon social background. Young men of privileged origins were permitted to join such posh units as the University and Public Schools Brigade. Local authorities raised many units, and these incorporated the population of a given area, a common workplace, or a common social background. Thus, civilian leaders in urban communities like Manchester, Liverpool, and Bristol encouraged young men to enlist in "Pals" battalions. The army promised that such recruits would remain together during their training and during their service in the field. No one seems to have considered how heavy casualties in such locally based units would devastate entire communities.

Local authorities sometimes provided shelter for the soldiers—and sometimes even the equipment they used during their early months in the army. Only at the start of 1915 did military authorities begin to bring the flood of volunteers under full control. Soldiers now underwent organized training. Marching, drill, and rifle training—the standard, elementary elements in transforming civilians into soldiers—became the common experience of recruits. Young men of privileged social circles initially provided the huge number of new officers required for an ex-

A recruiting poster calls on British women to send their men to war. Courtesy of the Hoover Institution Archives.

panded army. Senior officers assumed that a young man who had attended an elite public school like Eton or Winchester had the personal qualities and the leadership experience to become an acceptable junior officer with only a brief period of training.

By the winter of 1915–16, the flow of recruits to both the enlisted and commissioned ranks of the army was inadequate. After long debate and a series of half-measures, the British government turned to a system of conscription. A second change was the willingness to train new junior officers from wider social circles. Former enlisted men from the professional army were one such source. Wartime volunteers from the middle class or even the working class who had shown skill in combat likewise now qualified to become "temporary gentlemen."

Training took place both in Britain and at the front. Newly arrived troops received a period of time in base camps near the English Channel. The most infamous of these was the installation at Étaples ("eat apples" or "heel taps" to British soldiers who could not manage the French pronunciation). There, novice soldiers, as well as troops given "rest" from the front, performed a heavy schedule of drills and marching designed to establish or renew their physical condition for the trenches. Novice troops and newly commissioned officers went first to quiet sections of the front for a stint in the front lines.

THE UNITED STATES' ARMY

The armed forces of the United States, like those of Britain, consisted of a large navy and a minuscule army. A crisis with Mexico in 1916 had led the government to mobilize the National Guard, with the result that the army had a source of trained manpower with which it could double its size fairly quickly. The total strength of the regular army when the country entered the conflict was approximately 127,000 officers and men. The National Guard added 180,000 or so to the pool of trained men. Most of these citizen-soldiers had the experience of serving on the Mexican border.[17]

America's entry into the war sparked a wave of enlistments similar to those in Germany and Britain in 1914. William Langer, subsequently a distinguished American historian, was a young prep school teacher who answered a newspaper advertisement requesting enlistees for a unit of American army engineers. The vagaries of army assignments put him instead into Company E of the 1st Gas Regiment, a force entirely composed of volunteers: "a substantial number of transfers from the Regular army, several college graduates ... older men, young lads, mechanics, salesmen, and what not." Langer noted that thousands like him joined without being conscripted despite "the most detailed and realistic accounts of the murderous fighting on the Somme and around Verdun, to say nothing of the day-to-day agony of trench warfare." He attributed this to a combination of factors. Although those included outrage at Imperial Germany, a sense of adventure played an even greater part. "Here was our one great chance for excitement and risk," before settling down to safe and uneventful routine.[18]

Nonetheless, the government decided that only a system of national conscription could raise the vast army needed to fight in Europe. Federal authorities avoided the pitfalls of conscription during the Civil War. Local officials would administer the system this time, and no one would be permitted to hire a substitute to serve in his place. Volunteers like William Langer continued to sign up, but gradually enlisting was limited and, in August and September 1918, blocked entirely. The draft seemed to military authorities a more efficient way to provide new soldiers while not depriving the country of men in essential civilian occupations. All those taken into the military were told that their services were required

American soldiers in training form the Liberty Bell. Courtesy of the Hoover Institution Archives.

for the duration of the war. The draft provided 2,750,000 men, two-thirds the total number who served in the armed forces. Some 340,000 men were called up but refused to report as ordered.

On July 5, almost 10 million young men, aged twenty-one to thirty, were the first to register for the draft. Eventually another 13 million followed. Each man received a number indicating the order in which he had registered with his local draft board. On July 20, the secretary of the army drew numbers from a lottery bowl to determine which young men would be called to national service. Volunteers and draftees combined to make a total of more than 4 million men who served in the army with another half million in the navy and Marine Corps. Two million Americans served overseas, the vast majority in France.[19]

The first draftees—180,000 strong—for the new "National Army" were called up in September 1917. Two measures had set the stage for their arrival. In the months directly following America's entry into the war, the army had trained thousands of volunteers—many of them young college graduates—to serve as junior officers. Between mid-May and mid-August 1917, some 38,000 young men underwent an intensive course of training, which 27,000 survived to receive their commissions. These newly graduated lieutenants and those who completed subsequent courses provided the junior infantry and artillery commanders for the American Expeditionary Force (AEF). The courses also provided the vast majority of the captains: ninety-nine percent of the company commanders in the AEF had less than one year's time in uniform.

In a vast effort, the nation's construction industry produced sixteen huge encampments for the new army. The project was the greatest American building enterprise since the construction of the Panama Canal. During the conflict, 200,000 civilians worked to provide housing for the expanded military. Despite its greater resources, the United States faced many of the problems that had confronted Britain in housing and training an influx of recruits.

Men arrived at camps in which construction crews were still hammering nails. One unit of the New York National Guard had to remove tree stumps before it could comfortably occupy its new camp in South Carolina. National Guardsmen from the Midwest found that the year's cotton crop had not been completely harvested on land making up their encampment in Texas. A private in the Eightieth Division recalled that most of the men in his unit were still in civilian clothes and shoes in November 1917. During a visit by Secretary of War Newton Baker, men dressed in "summer underclothing, blue overalls, and civilian shoes, and no overcoat" passed by the cabinet member's reviewing stand.[20]

The divisions of the Regular Army were drained of personnel to provide a skeleton command staff for the expanded National Guard and the new divisions being raised by the draft. In order to bolster British and French morale, the United States War Department pulled together four regiments of the regular army to form a division for early shipment to France. The First Division arrived in time to send an infantry battalion marching through Paris on July 4 to the cheers of the city's population. This seemingly professional force, on closer examination, showed America's lack of preparation for combat against the Central Powers. Most of the division's enlisted men were recently enlisted raw recruits, its officers were reservists, and its mortar and artillery units had none of the weapons they needed for the battlefield.

Unlike the European belligerents on the western front, the United States was a nation with a large immigrant population. Approximately 18 percent of the recruits to the military were foreign-born, many of them without a sound command of English. Individual units took up the task

American soldiers learn to fight with the bayonet. Courtesy of the National Archives.

of teaching them the nation's language. As a chaplain in the Seventy-seventh Division recalled, his training camp contained thousands of foreigners who could speak "little or no English when they arrived." Using eager volunteers, including some schoolteachers in the regiment, classes "accomplished remarkable results" for "shy but eager Italians, Greeks and Russian Jews."[21]

Training Americans for combat took place both in the United States and behind the fighting front in France. The guiding principle set down by General John Pershing, commander of the AEF, called for American soldiers who were ready for more than a stint of trench warfare. Pershing anticipated offensive operations in which the American Army would defeat Germany on the battlefield. Thus, his soldiers needed to prepare themselves to be skilled riflemen and practitioners of bayonet fighting ready to rise from their defensive positions to move forward aggressively. Upon arriving in France, American divisions were to continue their training at camps there, and their component units were to enter the line in quiet sectors with experienced French units. American officers attended an elaborate system of schools for specialized training in France.

Pershing's plans soon collided with reality. The diary of an enlisted man in the Forty-second Division, Albert Ettinger, gives a sense of the hasty military preparation many received. As a product of the training at Camp Mills, New York, Ettinger had experienced the drill field, but, like most members of the Forty-second Division, he arrived in Europe never having fired a rifle.[22]

American combat training encouraged a naïve aggressiveness. French instructors reviewing the combat preparations of early American forces voiced a cautionary note. The Americans were attacking in waves with insufficient intervals separating the individual soldiers. Such tactics risked devastating numbers of casualties. In fact, when the AEF's First Division fought on the Marne in the summer of 1918, it left rows of corpses on the battlefield, the bodies close together in regular lines. Their brave attack had taken place in closely aligned formations against German machine-gun fire, precisely what more experienced French and British units now avoided.

American troops crossed the Atlantic in increasing numbers by the spring and summer of 1918. The need to move men quickly through training and then to send them abroad took precedence over actual instruction. The problem Alfred Ettinger described remained pressing: Two divisions in France in the summer of 1918 contained regiments in which more than four out of ten men had never fired a rifle.

NOTES

1. Richard Bessel, *Germany after the First World War* (Oxford: Clarendon Press, 1993), 5.

2. Dennis Showalter, *Tannenberg: Clash of Empires* (Hamden, Conn.: Archon Books, 1991), 123.

3. Ibid., 124–25.

4. J.M. de Beaufort, *Behind the German Veil: A Record of a Journalistic War Pilgrimage* (New York: Dodd, Mead and Company, 1917), 68–69.

5. Leonard V. Smith, *Between Mutiny and Obedience: The Case of the French Fifth Infantry Division during World War I* (Princeton: Princeton University Press, 1994), 26.

6. Alistair Horne, *The Price of Glory: Verdun, 1916* (New York: Harper and Row, 1962), 11; Paul de la Gorce, *The French Army: A Military-Political History*, trans. Kenneth Douglas (New York: George Braziller, 1963), 103.

7. Smith, *Mutiny*, 30.

8. La Gorce, *The French Army*, 101.

9. Quoted in Smith, *Mutiny*, 29.

10. Marc Bloch, *Memoirs of War, 1914–1915*, translated and with an introduction by Carole Fink (Ithaca, N.Y.: Cornell University Press, 1980), 48, 54; Smith, *Mutiny*, 78–79.

11. Jeffrey Verhey, *The Spirit of 1914: Militarism, Myth and Mobilization in Germany* (Cambridge, Eng.: Cambridge University Press, 2000), 97–99.

12. A.F. Wedd, trans. and ed., *German Students' War Letters* (New York: E.P. Dutton, [1929]), 17–18.

13. Herbert Sulzbach, *With the German Guns: Four Years on the Western Front, 1914–1918*, trans. Richard Thonger (London: Leo Cooper, 1973), 23–26.

14. Alan Seeger, *Letters and Diary* (New York: Charles Scribner's Sons, 1917), 1–11.

15. Ian Beckett, "The Nation in Arms, 1914–1918," in *A Nation in Arms: A Social Study of the British Army in the First World War*, ed. Ian F.W. Beckett and Keith Simpson (Manchester, Eng.: Manchester University Press), 2.

16. Ian Beckett, "The Territorial Force," in ibid., 129.

17. Russell F. Weigley, *History of the United States Army* (New York: Macmillan, 1967), 357–58.

18. William Langer, *Gas and Flame in World War I* (New York: Alfred A. Knopf, 1965), x–xix.

19. Edward M. Coffman, *The War to End All Wars: The American Military Experience in World War I* (New York: Oxford University Press, 1968), 29; also Weigley, *United States Army*, 356–58.

20. Quoted in James H. Hallas, *The Doughboy War: The American Expeditionary Force in World War I* (Boulder, Colo.: Lynne Rienner Publishers, 2000), 19.

21. Coffman, *War to End All Wars*, 64; quoted in Hallas, *Doughboy War*, 22.

22. Albert M. Ettinger and A. Churchill Ettinger, *A Doughboy with the Fighting Sixty-ninth: A Remembrance of World War I* (Shippensburg, Pa.: White Mane Publishing Company, 1992), 7.

2

Equipment and Rations

All the countries involved in combat on the western front strained to provide arms, equipment, and food for their fighting men. The expanded armies demanded extraordinary quantities of weapons. Moreover, the technical surprises of the war, including the stalemate on the battlefront, meant a search for new, more effective weapons. The American army of 127,000 men in April 1917 required thousands of modern artillery pieces, tens of thousands of machine guns and other automatic weapons, not to mention more than 2 million rifles over the next year and a half. Tents, shovels, and uniforms were needed as well on an unprecedented scale. Obtaining rations for millions of men, month after month, was an obligation no government dared ignore.

But, in the common struggle to match and eventually to overwhelm the enemy, Germany's men in uniform had a severe disadvantage. With their country hindered by isolation and limited resources, the Germans found themselves barely making do, especially in food for the military.

RIFLES

The most common weapon to be found on the western front was the infantryman's rifle. Each army entered the war with a bolt-action weapon equipped to hold several cartridges. The standard British rifle was the Short Magazine Lee Enfield (SMLE). To load it, the rifleman pulled the bolt backward and inserted two five-round clips of cartridges from above, pressing them down into the weapon's boxlike magazine. The magazine (a receptacle for ammunition) was located under the barrel in front of the rifle's trigger. A spring in the magazine pushed the first cartridge upward toward the barrel as the bolt was closed. After loosing a round, the marksman needed only a short pull backward on the bolt to eject the previous round and to pull the next one into firing position. This efficient mechanism permitted a rapid rate of aimed fire for which the pre-1914 professional British soldier had been trained.

The German soldier on the western front was equipped with the five-round Mauser Gewehr 98 (G98) rifle. The standard American rifle at the time the United States entered the war was the five-round 1903 Springfield. Both had box-magazines like the Enfield. The French equivalent was the 8-mm Lebel designed in 1886, modified in 1893, and thus designated the Lebel Model 86/93. It was longer and heavier than the standard British, German, and American weapons, and used a tubular magazine holding eight cartridges and located below the rifle's barrel. Difficult to load quickly, it was the least effective of the rifles used by any of the belligerents on the western front.

The Mauser, Lebel, and Springfield all operated on the same principle as the British weapon. After firing a shot, the rifleman pulled the bolt backward to eject the spent cartridge, then moved the bolt forward. This pushed a new round into the firing chamber, and cocked the weapon to fire once again. In all the belligerent countries, units in training and those on home guard duty had a low priority and often found themselves with older weapons.

The strains of producing large numbers of rifles fell with particular force on Germany and, later, the United States. An important solution for the German army was to depart from making the weapon from standardized parts. Marked with a star, the new "Stern Gewehr" indicated that it had been made from parts produced by different subcontractors. Whereas the original rifle was considered reliable, its parts could not be safely transferred to another weapon. The United States was unable to produce enough Springfields to equip its huge new army of 1917 and 1918, and only early arrivals in France got them. The solution was to use a modified version of the British Enfield (the "US Enfield") available in large numbers in American and Canadian factories where British arms orders had already been placed. The minority of troops who got Springfields thought themselves lucky. "It was a great weapon," one Marine lieutenant recalled. "Not only was it accurate, but it rarely jammed," and "it seemed to be able to absorb the dirt—and we were always living in dirt—and still work."[1]

MACHINE GUNS

The machine gun played an unexpectedly vital role in trench warfare. Prior to 1914, the weapon was considered to be the equivalent of a piece

German machine gun in use in the trenches. © Bettmann/
CORBIS.

of light artillery, and many military leaders found it only marginally useful. At the start of the war, the future belligerents on the western front normally had only two machine guns for each battalion, although the Germans were in the process of increasing this to six per battalion. Unlike earlier, multishot weapons like the Gatling gun, the weapon invented by Hiram Maxim in the 1880s did not require a cranking apparatus to fire a stream of bullets at the enemy. Instead, it operated automatically when the gunner pulled the trigger or pressed a button to commence firing.

In combination with barbed wire obstacles, machine guns made it possible for a small number of soldiers to halt enemy offensives by inflicting massive casualties. Various estimates claimed that the firepower of one machine gun was the equivalent of thirty, or perhaps as many as sixty, individual riflemen. Placing the gun in a stationary position, the machine gun's crew could calculate in advance the area the weapon was able to cover. Even in the midst of a surprise attack, a trained machine gun crew could put the weapon into action within four seconds and deliver devastating fire. The machine gun itself presented only a tiny target for enemy counterfire.

British, French, and American troops all encountered the standard German machine gun, the MG 08. The German army employed some 72,000 of these deadly weapons on both the eastern and western front. The water-cooled MG 08 was fed by bullets held in a fabric belt and could fire around 450 rounds per minute. Weighing about seventy pounds, it had the disadvantage of being mounted on a heavy sledge, but lighter mounts were developed as the war proceeded. The British equivalent was the equally heavy Vickers .303.

Offensives on the western front impelled the belligerents to develop a lighter machine gun that could be carried forward by advancing troops. For Britain, the result was the air-cooled Lewis gun; weighing only twenty-seven pounds, it was highly portable. This handy weapon dispensed with the bulky equipment needed by a water-cooled gun, and it used ammunition drums with 47 or 97 rounds instead of a heavy cloth belt. The Lewis gun replaced the Vickers .303 as the weapon carried by infantry battalions, the Vickers being transferred into special Machine Gun Corps companies. The Germans and French followed suit. The German light machine gun, the MG 08/15, weighed thirty-nine pounds. As its name indicated, it was a modified version of the army's standard machine gun: This lighter gun retained the original MG 08's water-cooled system and belt-fed ammunition.

The French had the least success in meeting the need for a light weapon with the firepower of a machine gun. Their 8-mm Model 1915 or Chauchat with its 20-round drum was notorious for jamming in the midst of battle, and the air-cooled weapon's light weight—barely twenty pounds—was little compensation for soldiers put in peril by its unreliability. Firing at a relatively slow rate of 250 rounds per minute only served to make it more unpopular, especially with American troops who were burdened with the weapon.

ARTILLERY

In 1914, artillery ranged from light field weapons designed to accompany advancing troops to heavy guns that had to be operated from fixed positions. Artillerymen in every army had two basic types of cannon at their disposal, "howitzers" and "guns." Howitzers, with relatively short barrels, fired shells into the air at a sharp angle—"high trajectory"—allowing them to strike even an entrenched enemy from above. Guns, with longer barrels than howitzers, fired shells directly at the enemy—"flat trajectory"—at a high velocity. Howitzers were limited, however, by their shorter range. Many cannon, especially those with larger calibers, came in both howitzer and gun models.

At first, artillerymen employed two varieties of shells. The high-explosive type contained a large charge intended to explode when the shell landed. Shrapnel shells contained anti-personnel devices like metal balls. They were designed to explode in flight over enemy troops. In 1914, most artillerymen still considered shrapnel rather than high explosive shells the more useful in battle. A third type, shells carrying poison gas, appeared later in the conflict.

German artillery in action. Courtesy of the National Archives.

By 1914, the major belligerents on the western front had all developed artillery pieces based on the French 75-mm gun. That weapon, soon to be the most famous cannon in the world, was loaded from the rear and had a recoil that was absorbed by a hydraulic system. Such features permitted the gun to remain fixed on the ground, aimed in a given direction, and capable of firing at the unprecedented rate of twenty or more rounds per minute.

But some armies were better equipped for trench warfare than others. The French had planned for a mobile war in which their light 75-mm guns would move up with advancing infantry. These weapons proved invaluable in the first weeks of the war, firing more rapidly and striking from a greater distance than their German counterparts. But the French had neglected to build up a stock of heavier weapons. The Germans were best prepared for an artillery war in which both sides fired on the other's trenches. Their 77-mm gun approximated the characteristics of the French 75-mm. But they had taken pains in the decade before the war to build up their army's store of heavy guns (155-mm) as well as medium artillery pieces (the 105-mm howitzer). Thus, when the conflict bogged down, the Germans had a significant advantage. French infantrymen assaulting German defenses in the first years of the war found that their lightweight artillery offered them little support. Only in 1916 did the French begin to match the weight of German weapons.

The British army in 1914 was better prepared in its artillery for trench warfare than the French. The British Expeditionary Force that fought in the first months of the war had an equivalent to the French 75-mm in its eighteen-pound (3.3-inch) gun. It also had a supply of 4.5-inch howitzers that matched the German 105-mm. The British possessed some heavier cannon like the sixty-pound (120-mm) gun as well, but here they still had to catch up with the better equipped Germans.

A basic problem for artillerymen was the shell shortage that afflicted all armies, particularly the British and French, by the winter of 1914–15. Remedying the situation by increased production created its own difficulties. Shrapnel shells were relatively easy and safe to produce quickly, and they were effective against soldiers exposed on bare ground. But trench warfare showed that pre-1914 expectations for artillery fire were mistaken. Armies needed massive quantities of high-explosive ammunition able to demolish enemy fortifications. Such shells required a higher level of skill to produce, given the danger they posed for armaments workers. The failure to solve the problem of quality control crippled operations. For example, the large number of "dud" shells British munitions factories produced weakened the crucial barrage that preceded the Battle of the Somme in July 1916.

Desperate to break through the enemy's lines, the various belligerents sought the biggest artillery pieces available. They built guns modeled on those carried by the era's battleships and borrowed those employed in coast artillery units. Such weapons weighed hundreds of tons and could only be moved on railroad cars. Some had to be operated by experienced naval gunners. Starting at the Battle of Verdun in 1916, both the Germans and the French employed such railway guns. The Americans brought a number of coast artillery cannon from the United States along with army crews trained to fire such heavy weapons. Using the American weapons and other giant guns supplied by the French, coast artillerymen in the AEF struck at the German rear during the Meuse-Argonne offensive in 1918.

On the whole, the American army found itself so deficient in heavy weapons that most of its artillery had to come from the French and British. The AEF relied upon supplies of French 75-mm guns for lightweight field pieces. French 155-mm howitzers provided the bulk of the heavy firepower the Americans enjoyed. Most American artillerymen received their training from experienced French instructors.

Effective artillery operations required an elaborate system of support. Forward artillery observers and aerial spotters combined their efforts with those of an extensive entourage on the ground. One British artillery officer described his weapon as "a dignified old autocrat" with "a suite of servants and attendants." His artillery battery with four howitzers required a staff of at least six officers and 120 enlisted men to serve the cannon. Still more men were needed for the four heavy tractors and fifteen three-ton trucks that moved the battery from place to place.[2]

After the first phase of the war, artillerymen on both sides operated from rear areas. Infantrymen in all armies expressed their hostility and jealousy toward gunners who seemed well away from the front. This apparent measure of safety was an illusion. Sophisticated techniques for locating and firing on enemy artillery emplacements ("counter-battery fire") made the gunners' lot a dangerous one.

MORTARS

The need to dislodge troops dug into trench fortifications gave mortars an important role in the war on the western front. Firing a shell high into the air, the mortar, like the much larger and heavier howitzer, made it possible to strike an entrenched enemy from overhead. The British Stokes mortar was little more than a lightweight tube with a spike at its base. A shell, containing a charge to propel it, was dropped down the tube, struck the spike, then flew toward the enemy. Its shells were color-coded with a green one set to go 300 yards and a red one 450, and a trained crew could fire a shell every three seconds. One German soldier, who had doubtless experienced enemy artillery and machine-gun fire, recorded his feeling that the trench mortar was the worst weapon he faced. "They fire noiselessly and a single one often kills as many as 30 men. One stands in the trench, and at any moment a thing like that may burst."[3]

Mortars also came in far larger forms. In trench operations, the standard German 170-mm mortar (*Minenwerfer*) contained more than 100 pounds of explosives and shards of metal. Shot high into the air, it was visible tumbling toward the enemy's lines.

HAND GRENADES

The realities of trench warfare made the hand grenade a useful infantryman's tool. The British army had found no need for such a weapon in the mobile warfare that characterized colonial conflicts of the late nineteenth century. With no grenades available, British soldiers had to improvise in 1914 and early 1915, creating small explosive bombs from common trench items like tin cans. The Germans, by contrast, entered the war with an effective grenade as standard army equipment.

By the first anniversary of the war's beginning, the British troops were supplied with the effective Mills bomb. Containing a small quantity of explosives in a metal case, such a hand grenade could be thrown over barbed wire barriers into the enemy's fortifications. Once released, it was timed to explode in a matter of seconds. Grenades could also be fired from rifles equipped with a special launching apparatus. One British soldier wrote home in May 1916 about the effectiveness of the device. "The Hun is very active and sends over coveys of rifle grenades at most inconvenient places and hours. . . . I hate their furking rifle grenades. They are more dangerous than shells and they have any number of them."[4]

As a portable, handheld bomb, the grenade more than other weapons endangered the soldier using it. It also imperiled those around him. Grenades were known to detonate instantly in the hand of the thrower, and a dropped grenade could injure scores of men in the immediate vicinity. Sometimes, the circumstances of battle made it impossible to release a grenade. A German soldier described combat with French troops in which one of his comrades "pulled the stopper out of the fuse, raised his bomb, and was just going to throw it" when the scene shifted. "At that very moment some German comrades came between him and his objective. He could not throw the bomb without hitting them; so he kept it in his hand, and in a few seconds it exploded, blowing him to pieces."[5]

THE FLAMETHROWER AND THE BAYONET

Both the flamethrower and the bayonet evoked special fear in potential victims. These weapons killed at close range, face to face in the case of the bayonet. The terror of being burned to death made the flamethrower a horror to the imagination. The Germans had developed a practical flamethrower in the years before the war and put it onto the battlefield in 1915, and soon all the other western front belligerents adopted the device. The German army became particularly adept in flamethrower attacks, assigning two-man flamethrower teams to pave the way for ground assault units. The weapon required that one man hold the pipe from which flame erupted while a second team member carried the reservoir containing the incendiary liquid and its gas propellant. The flamethrower attack was followed at once by an infantry advance.

The fire of a flamethrower frightened even those troops using it. To counteract this, the German General Staff sent instructions for assault troops specifying that "they have nothing to fear from the flames and smoke" because the tap on the flamethrower would be turned off before they moved into the enemy's trenches. Thus, "they can advance immediately after the cessation of the spray without danger, as small bursts of flame on the ground . . . will burn out at once, and a little fire on the ground is at once extinguished when trodden upon."[6]

All armies had rifles equipped to hold bayonets below the barrel. The target of a bayonet attack had to defend himself against the frightening prospect of a cold steel blade penetrating his body. The French Lebel rifle carried an especially long metal blade. Menacing in appearance, it was prone to break in actual combat. The broad-bladed German "butcher bayonet" featuring saw-teeth along part of one edge may have been designed specifically for its effect on the morale of those who faced it. Troops advancing with bayonets fixed presented a menacing picture to those on the other side of the battle line.

British and American military training emphasized bayonet attacks, as much to instill an aggressive attitude in troops as to prepare them for actual combat. Killing with the bayonet required close contact with the enemy, which occurred principally in surprise attacks and night assaults. British soldiers remembered what it felt like when bayoneting an enemy soldier: It was like driving a knife into butter. Because the victim's flesh and muscle tightened around the entry point, soldiers learned a three-step process: thrust with the bayonet, then twist the rifle to loosen it, then extract the blade.[7]

UNIFORMS AND HELMETS

With the exception of the French army, still dressed in the bright blue and red uniforms of the previous century, the combatants of World War I moved onto the battlefield in uniforms designed to conceal them from the enemy. After the slaughter of 1914, the French too accepted the fact that visibility to the enemy was less likely to terrify the foe than to offer him a wealth of attractive targets.

By contrast, from the first the German soldier wore a field gray (*feldgrau*) uniform with its camouflage aspects increased by a slight dull green tint. Calf-length boots, a seventy-pound knapsack, and an ammunition belt rounded out his burden. The characteristic spiked helmet was covered with a camouflage shield. In trench warfare, a soldier's head was the most exposed part of his body, and spiked helmets made of leather and other soft headpieces proved too dangerous to wear. The familiar German metal helmet with its extensions on three sides to protect the ears and neck appeared at Verdun in 1916 and soon went into general use. The French adopted the less protective "Adrian" helmet and the British and then the Americans a simple flat model. The flat helmet mainly protected the top of the head. In general, helmets served best against flying shrapnel. As many combatants found out, a bullet traveling at high speed could penetrate a helmet with deadly results.

RATIONS

All the armies on the western front tried to provide their soldiers with regular meals even at the cost of limiting the food available on the home front. In addition, soldiers carried a basic or "iron" ration of foods like hardtack (a hard, crackerlike bread) and preserved meat. These items would not spoil, required no cooking, and remained available to be used in emergencies. Normally, a soldier had to await orders from a superior before opening this emergency ration. For troops engaged in battle, the emergency ration was commonly the only food available.

Troops in the front lines received first priority for the food available to the army. Commanders everywhere fed men in supply and other units behind the fighting lines a daily diet 200 to 700 calories less than what was consumed by each man in the trenches. The British army's combat troops subsisted on a daily ration featuring more than a pound of meat as well as a pound and a quarter of bread. Bacon and jam were also components of the ration throughout the war.[8] A common complaint, registered in army cartoons, was the flavor of jam: Invariably it was plum and apple, a variety British troops came to despise. Meals often consisted of an unappetizing canned stew of meat and vegetables called Maconochie, the name of the manufacturer.

The Germans began the war with a comparable daily diet for the fighting man: almost two pounds of bread, just under a pound of meat, and a generous allotment of potatoes. German soldiers received wine or beer at the discretion of their commanding officer. Unlike the troops across the battle line, German soldiers felt the strain on their country's food supply, especially in a declining meat ration. Starting in June 1916, the troops had to adjust to one meatless day per week, and in April 1917, the bread ration was also reduced. The meat ration continued to shrink as the war proceeded. In the conflict's final year, a soldier who was not actually in combat got meat only every third day.[9] Dead horses, which had been left to rot on the battlefield or covered with lime in 1914, were now quickly carved up to supplement official rations.

When the general officer commanding a British sector unit agreed, the soldiers also received a daily rum ration. In the hours before the attack on the Somme on July 1, one commander famously denied his men the rum ration saying that they should be prepared to meet their Maker cold sober. French troops got alcohol on a regular basis. They received a daily ration (*le pinard*) of plain red wine along with a ration of brandy.

Initially, all troops in the front lines ate cold food. As the war went into its second year, armies attempted to provide a hot evening meal for troops in the trenches. One of the basic tasks of some infantrymen was carrying the food forward from field kitchens ("*Gulaschkanonen*" in German soldiers' slang, "soup guns" in American parlance). The intention of providing hot food could not always be carried out. Most meals arrived only hours after being cooked and in a lukewarm or still worse state.

The failure to provide good, or at least hot food became an issue in

British field bakery workers. © Bettmann/CORBIS.

the discontented French army of 1917. In a list of grievances from a soldier in one of the mutinous regiments in June, complaints about the food, "which is shameful," stood fourth on the list preceded by demands for peace, adequate leave, and an end to "butchery." Another soldier complained specifically about the failure to provide his unit with hot food for forty-five days in an active sector of the front where the kitchens were far in the rear.[10] Improving the food was one of the first measures taken by General Philippe Pétain to restore order and morale in the French army in the wake of the mutinies of spring 1917.

As representatives of the wealthiest society in the world, American soldiers ate predictably well—a daily diet of almost 5,000 calories. Troops in the trenches received a main meal consisting invariably of bread and butter, stew ("slum"), coffee with sugar, white bread, and jam. Many men put corn syrup ("Karo") on bread as dessert. Both officers and, more important, enlisted men commented that the quantity of the food, at least when troops were in a stationary position, was more than sufficient. Mainstays of the American diet in combat or on the march were cold canned corned beef ("corned willie") and canned salmon ("gold fish") with crackers. During the Meuse-Argonne offensive in the fall of 1918, bottlenecks in the supply system sometimes left frontline troops with nothing more than these emergency rations. Unlike the other combatants, American forces got no alcohol ration.[11]

The fighting ability of the German army showed a fatal decline as the quality of food deteriorated. The troops who attacked the British lines in late March 1918 in a desperate effort to win the war had become used to a thin morning "coffee" made from turnips. They also received a mea-

American troops eating in frontline trench. Courtesy of the National Archives.

ger lunch in the form of a transparent soup made from turnips or dried vegetables. It contained no meat but might perhaps be thickened with a few fragments of potatoes. Dinner meant bread and "tea" made from turnips. At this stage in the war, the bread was still palatable, but little else was. German soldiers overrunning British positions found an extraordinary abundance of food including items like chocolate and corned beef that they had not seen in years. Hungry troops slipped away from their officers' supervision in order to loot British supply dumps.

NOTES

1. Quoted in Henry Berry, *Make the Kaiser Dance* (Garden City, N.Y.: Doubleday and Company, 1978), 92.

2. Trevor Wilson, *The Myriad Faces of War: Britain and the Great War, 1914–1918* (Cambridge, Eng.: Polity Press, 1986), 468.

3. Quoted in Stephen Bull, *Stormtrooper: Elite German Assault Soldiers* (London: Publishing News, 1999), 13.

4. Quoted in Peter H. Liddle, *The Soldier's War, 1914–1918* (London: Blandford Press, 1988), 59.

5. Quoted in Bull, *Stormtrooper*, 20.

6. Quoted in ibid., 25.

7. Denis Winter, *Death's Men: Soldiers of the Great War* (London: Penguin Books, 1978), 110. On American bayonet training, see James H. Hallas, *Doughboy War: The American Expeditionary Force in World War I* (Boulder, Colo.: Lynne Rienner, 2000), 53–54.

8. Philip J. Haythornthwaite, *The World War One Source Book* (London: Arms and Armour Press, 1992), 380–81.

9. Ibid.

10. Leonard V. Smith, *Between Mutiny and Obedience: The Case of the French Fifth Infantry Division during World War I* (Princeton: Princeton University Press, 1994), 188, 226.

11. Hallas, *Doughboy War*, 183–84, 209.

3

Trench Life

ORIGINS OF TRENCH WARFARE

The trenches had their origins in the surprising turn the war took during its first few months. They were the products of failure: the unsuccessful French assault on Lorraine, the unsuccessful German drive southward to the Marne, the unsuccessful race northward by Anglo-French and German forces to outflank the enemy between Paris and the North Sea. Each of these efforts left large numbers of troops entrenched and facing their foes in what came to be a war of position.

The opposing lines stretched for over 450 miles from the Belgian coast to the Swiss border. In some areas, there were no trenches. In the extreme northern zone, the damp soil made it impossible to dig, and barricades provided soldiers with protection. In the Vosges, the mountain range at the southern part of the front, Germans faced Frenchmen in a series of village and rural strong points. But for most of the western front, soldiers dug into the earth, and as time went by, all armies built extensive trench lines.

The French faced an enemy on their own soil and committed themselves to driving him out as soon as possible. They constructed a line from which to launch attacks in the near future. As a result, French trenches were far less elaborate than those of the other belligerents. The British system was neater and more developed.

Unlike other armies, the German army had studied the lessons of the Boer War (1899–1902) and the Russo-Japanese War (1904–1905) about the value of field fortifications. Elaborate trench systems were a part of German maneuvers since 1906. Determined to hang on to the substantial portion of territory they held in Belgium and northeastern France, they also faced the burden of fighting on the eastern front against Russia. The Germans set up their first trench system by mid-September 1914, protecting the flanks of the city of Rheims. Their decision to stand on the defensive on the western front for much of the war led them to build the most extensive, even the most comfortable system. Over much of the fighting line, the Germans were able to choose the location of their defenses, avoiding difficult terrain such as areas prone to flooding in wet weather.

ARRIVAL AT THE FRONT

To serve on the western front meant entering a world most civilians could not imagine. A coal miner from the Ruhr or a farmhand from rural Scotland was probably less shocked by its hardships than someone from an urban, middle-class background. But nothing in prewar life, even for most professional soldiers, prepared them for the particular character of trench life on the western front.

Europe's means of long-range transportation at the start of the twentieth century was the railroad. From the start of the war, the move to the front began with a train journey. Crowded into cattle cars—a sign on the standard French railroad car stated that it was suitable for eight horses or forty men—soldiers of all the belligerents rode to the front, often at a snail's pace. Ammunition trains had priority, and the journey toward the fighting was likely to be an extended one with numerous delays. The discouraging sight of trains filled with wounded moving in the opposite direction was a common one. For British soldiers, and then for some Americans, the first leg of the journey was by Channel steamer to a port like Boulogne. They often encountered wounded British soldiers awaiting evacuation on the docks where they arrived.

Where rail transportation ceased, usually within ten miles of the front, the soldier's feet took over. The initial fighting soon destroyed a wide belt of territory in northwestern Belgium and northeastern France. Soldiers marching to the front passed through villages or cities that had been the scene of fierce fighting during the mobile combat of 1914. A British enlisted man on his way to the front in Belgium in May 1915 encountered such a scene in the outskirts of Ypres: "Just over the canal bridge a timber wagon and two shattered horses came into view and we walked through the blood of these noble animals as we passed them on the road. We were now in the town proper—everywhere nothing but ruins could be seen—not a house but was either shattered by shells or gutted with fire."[1]

Coming closer to the front, soldiers entered a zone of territory exposed to artillery fire from the enemy. Long before reaching a trench, a soldier could feel the dangerous potential of modern weapons. The young German soldier Ernst Jünger recalled reaching a village behind the lines when a series of shells struck at breakfast time. "A feeling of unreality oppressed me," he recalled, "as I stared at a figure streaming with blood whose limbs hung loose and who unceasingly gave a hoarse cry for help, as though death had him already by the throat."[2]

Soldiers normally entered the front lines at night via approach roads and communication trenches. Moving in the dark, along narrow and crowded sunken passageways, soldiers from all armies passed into this special world. One Englishman recalled what it felt like:

It was a two-mile trudge in the narrow ditches to the front line. No war correspondent has ever described such a march; it is not included in the official "horrors of war" but this is the kind of thing, more than battle or blood which harasses the spirit of the infantryman and composes his life. . . . He is only conscious of the dead weight of his load, and the braces of his pack biting into his shoulders, of his thirst and the sweat of his body, and the longing to lie down and sleep. When we halt men fall into a doze as they stand and curse pitifully when they are urged on from behind.[3]

STRUCTURE OF THE TRENCH SYSTEM

All trench systems consisted of several parallel lines of fortifications. A forward trench line was adjacent to "no man's land," the unoccupied ground separating the two sides, and had the greatest vulnerability to enemy attack. Here the enemy might enter and fire down the trench's entire length or an artillery shell might spread deadly metal fragments. To avoid such dangers, armies constructed "traverses," trenches built in zigzag patterns. Anyone moving down such a trench line had to make sharp turns into the next section.

Facing outward from the first trench, a soldier looked over several stretches of barbed wire protecting his position. One section, three feet high, was likely placed directly ahead in the outskirts of no man's land. Additional barbed wire entanglements were normally placed another fifty yards or so into no man's land. Eventually, barbed wire lines fifty yards thick were established, and sometimes a single or "international" barbed wire system, maintained by both sides, separated the combatants.

All defensive systems had at least one additional trench line where troops could remain to support the front position. Here the various trench occupants constructed dugouts carved out of the forward wall of the trench. These offered additional shelter and some protection against shellfire. Officers' dugouts were often fairly spacious and, on the German

British soldiers in the trenches. © Hulton-Deutsch Collection/CORBIS.

side, even elaborate, whereas the French and the British dugouts were more like enlarged caves. The dugouts enlisted men constructed in the portions of the trench they occupied were more likely to be shallow diggings into the trench wall. In some cases rival trench lines ran through a single village, and sometimes a trench running through an individual house was occupied at one end by the troops of one belligerent, and occupied at the other by the soldiers of their enemy.

The German system featured deep shelters able to resist enemy artillery fire. Dugouts at the Battle of the Somme in 1916 were thirty feet below the ground. Digging in to stay, the Germans also put wooden walkways on the trench floor. Machine-gun posts constructed of concrete, iron, and wood supported the German trench lines. The German second line was often on the reverse slope of the hill on which they had placed their front position, thus making it even harder for the enemy to attack with artillery. By the middle of 1917, German positions in Flanders consisted of a mixture of trenches and supporting positions nine layers deep.

The French preferred a system in which mutually supporting strong points, connected by barbed wire, formed the front lines. A strong set of barbed wire belts was to stretch across the entire front, and behind the front lines the bulk of French troops were concentrated in a second, reserve line. Such a policy was designed to reduce casualties in the front lines.

Few of the trenches of 1914 and 1915 survived unchanged until the end of the war. Rain and flooding made trench walls collapse. This ne-

An American dentist treats a soldier at the front. Courtesy of the Hoover Institution Archives.

cessitated constant repair and rebuilding. Moreover, although the shape of the western front remained static, trench lines were sometimes occupied permanently by the enemy. They then altered the trenches to their specifications.

THE TRENCH ROUTINE

The soldier in the trenches became enmeshed in an exhausting routine, one that reversed the normal patterns of daily living. Fighting on the eastern front, the Austrian concert violinist Fritz Kreisler wrote how the trenches brought men down to a more primitive level of existence than one could have imagined. Much of the work of the war—maintaining the trenches, repairing the barbed wire barriers that separate your trenches from those of the enemy, bringing up supplies—had to be done at night.

A "stand-to" (or combat assembly) at dawn and at dusk, when enemy attacks were considered most likely, gave some form to the soldier's day. But otherwise, unless he was on sentry duty or assigned to a work detail, he slept as best he could during the daylight hours—then moved on to his nighttime activities. Arriving in Champagne in 1914, Jünger found a workday that began before dawn; the need to guard the trench and to continue constructing it gave each man only two hours' sleep at night. An enemy attack would deprive soldiers of any sleep.

THE PROXIMITY OF THE DEAD

The dead men from past battles were everywhere one turned. Bodies hanging on the barbed wire entanglements of no man's land provided a grisly reminder of failed assaults. Decomposed corpses lying on the ground between the lines, in locations that made them too dangerous to remove, added to the grisly atmosphere. During an advance into no man's land in 1915, Ernst Jünger recalled: "My attention was caught by a sickly smell and a bundle hanging on the wire. . . . I found myself in front of a huddled-up corpse, a Frenchman. The putrid flesh, like the flesh of fishes, gleamed greenish-white through the rents in the uniform."[4]

The dead were buried near trenches or even interred in trench walls. As the soil shifted, a soldier might encounter a partially decomposed foot or hand sticking out from the side a trench. An American corporal of the Twenty-seventh Division recalled "an obstruction sticking out from the trench wall" that could not at first be identified in the dark. At daybreak, it was discovered to be "the foot and ankle of a French soldier who had been buried there by a shell" in a sector the French had evacuated more than a year before.[5]

TRENCHES AND THE WAR IN THE AIR

From the earliest stages of the war, soldiers encountered airplanes observing them from above. Their diaries recorded the sense of vulnerability that came from enemy flights over the trench lines. In the first years of the war, planes aided in directing artillery fire. Starting in 1916, soldiers on both sides of the battle line faced the threat of low flying enemy planes conducting strafing attacks.

Troops confined in their trenches could watch aerial duels taking place above them. German artillery Lieutenant Herbert Sulzbach recorded such an event in his diary. Sitting under cover with five of his comrades, he was soon able to "watch a number of dog-fights in the air and admire the way our new triplanes are operating. Nimble, lively, highly manoeuvreable and incredibly fast, they climb almost vertically to take on one enemy plane after the other. . . . The dog-fights go on in the afternoon; our squadron have knocked down five enemy planes in the course of today in our sector alone."[6]

SNIPERS, MORTARS, AND ARTILLERY FIRE

Each day soldiers on the western front faced the danger posed by enemy snipers. From the time the trench line took shape, individual riflemen sought targets among members of the enemy careless enough to expose themselves. As the war went on, sniping became the work of specially trained marksmen. Exposing the upper portion of the body, even for a split second, invited a fatal shot from a sniper in the enemy trench line or in no man's land. Ernst Jünger saw one of his men die that way in November 1915. The German soldier "climbed on to a ledge in the top of the trench to shovel earth over the top. He was scarce up when a shot . . . got him in the skull and laid him dead on the floor of the trench."[7] In certain instances, several enemy snipers fired on an exposed individual within a matter of seconds, and even senior officers on inspection tours died at the hands of these enemy marksmen. When snipers worked in teams—one as the spotter, one as the actual rifleman—their shots were especially accurate.

Snipers sometimes put their rifles in fixed positions, held by clamps, in order to cover an area that was certain to be frequented by the enemy: the entrance to a latrine, an exposed point in the trench line. This permitted them to fire even when there was no visible target in sight. Merely letting off a round at random from a fixed position gave a good chance of striking the enemy. At Aubers, a German rifle was set up to fire every two minutes at the opposing British forces.

Although soldiers could exercise caution to protect themselves from enemy rifle fire, there was no effective defense against random artillery or mortar shells. Artillery shells that struck a trench or exploded overhead to send fragments of shrapnel downward could take an awful toll. One English sergeant recalled the shock of an artillery attack that broke the quiet of the morning in Flanders in May 1915:

Suddenly a tremendous explosion, a deathly stillness as if all were paralyzed, then fearful screams and groans and death gasps. . . . A high explosive German shell had fallen right into a wide part of the trench where many men had been. The sight of the wounded shedding their blood from gaping wounds and their agonized cries [followed]. . . . [T]his one shell bursting right in the trench accounted for *a total of 25 men*. The trench after the dead and wounded were removed presented a ghastly sight—it was red with blood like a room papered in crimson while equipment lay everywhere.[8]

Firing a shell into the air at a sharp angle, a mortarman could place a round directly into the enemy line. Although the noise made by firing the piece gave some warning, no one could be sure of escaping when such shells struck the trench where they were located. The only certainty was that one's own mortars would retaliate.

THE ARTILLERY BOMBARDMENT

Individual artillery and mortar rounds posed a sudden danger, but soldiers also faced prolonged shelling from masses of enemy heavy guns. Such an experience took a heavy psychological toll, and soldiers from both sides of the battle line described their feelings in surprisingly similar terms. Henri de Lécluse, a captain in the French army, experienced a twelve-hour bombardment in the Vosges during the fall of 1915. He considered it his worst experience of the entire war, "an abominable day" that would haunt him for the rest of his life.

German shells, including some containing tear gas, pounded us without interruption. Many were large caliber, at least 105mm. They fell right on top of us, sometimes they landed near us, in front or behind us. We were huddled next to the wall, silent, resigned to death, our faces hardened by anguish. Surrounded by the cries for help, the cries of pain from the wounded and by the groans of those mortally hit, we were being showered by fragments of stones and chunks of dirt thrown up by each projectile and blinded by the burning and suffocating smoke.[9]

LEAVING THE LINE

Facing this multitude of strains, no group of men could remain in the trenches indefinitely. All armies developed a system of rotation. While assigned to the front, parts of an infantry battalion spent several days in the first trench, but then left their position to others and took up a post in the reserve line. After an entire unit had been at the front for a given period, it was withdrawn to a zone several miles behind. The length of time in the trenches varied from one army to another. When not involved in a major battle, a soldier might expect to spend four to eight days in the front line and the support trench followed by four days in a rear area.

DIRT AND MUD

Living in a ditch carved out of the ground meant that, even in the best of weather, a soldier was certain to become filthy. The onset of rain—and snow in colder weather—added to everyone's physical discomfort. The frequent rains of northwestern Europe turned trenches into muddy bogs. Laying wooden duckboards on the bottom of the trench provided only a partial solution, since men often slipped off them as they moved about.

Mud in the trenches or out in the open made movement for men and draft animals difficult. Heavy clothing, instead of easing the burdens of trench warfare, added to it. A coat weighing seven pounds could be transformed into a burden of more than thirty pounds when it was soaked with water and coated with mud. Standing in a waterlogged trench for days at a time put soldiers at risk for trench foot. A disease that resembled frostbite, it caused the feet to become numb and to turn red or blue. If it developed into gangrene, a sufferer might lose his toes or even his entire foot.

Exhausted or wounded soldiers sometimes drowned in the mud, something that happened to sixteen members of a British division on the Somme in November 1916. A French soldier described "communication trenches [that] are no more than cess-pools filled with a mixture of water and urine." In such an environment, trenches were "nothing more than a strip of water" and the soldiers themselves are transformed into "statues of clay, with mud even in one's very mouth."[10] Jünger recalled fighting in Flanders in 1918 when "knowing that a wound would drown one for certainty in a mud-hole. A suffusion of blood on the surface of a shell-hole here and there showed that many a man had vanished thus."[11]

LICE AND RATS

To live in an unsterile, outdoor environment brought an inevitable infestation of lice: "chats" and "greybacks" to the British, "cooties" to the Americans. The tiny insects lodged in men's clothing, especially in the seams, and despite sometimes elaborate efforts to remove them, they maintained a constant presence. Their bites caused unbearable itching as well as sores and scabs. Only pulling troops back from the trenches, letting the men bathe their bodies while their clothes were either washed or replaced, provided even temporary relief.

Even more horrible in the minds of those who served in the squalor of the trenches was the horde of rats to be found everywhere. Fattening on the corpses of the dead, they sometimes grew to the size of cats. As they grew accustomed to the presence of live humans, any fears of contact with people faded away. Soldiers sleeping in the trenches often found themselves awakened by a rat crawling over their bodies—or even nibbling at their flesh.

LATRINES

Basic biological needs added to the squalor of trench life. No trench line was complete without some primitive form of toilet. In the British

American soldiers killing lice in their clothing. Courtesy of the National Archives.

army, it was common to build a military toilet (or latrine) in an offshoot of a trench. Elaborately designed latrines existed on paper, but more often the reality was a small area off the main trench with receptacles like old food cans to hold feces. Special units had the task of removing the collected body wastes each night, and spreading chloride of lime as a disinfectant. For many soldiers who survived the western front, one of the most vivid memories was the smell of chloride of lime, a constant of trench life.

NO MAN'S LAND AND TRENCH RAIDING

The area between the opposing trench lines was appropriately named "no man's land," because it was too dangerous for any unit to be placed there. This space separating the belligerents was usually several hundred yards in width. In some circumstances, it might be as large as a thousand yards or, given the dictates of terrain, the trench lines might only be separated by a distance of five to ten yards. Snipers operated from no man's land, and the area was a bone of contention for both sides seeking to exercise at least temporary control.

Although gigantic battles were rare but spectacular occurrences, small-scale combat for those in the trenches took place without letup. In the territory between the two trench lines, groups of soldiers met and fought

Germans bathe near the front. Courtesy of the Hoover Institution Archives.

on a daily basis. Both sides sought to dominate no man's land, because the ability to patrol up to the edge of enemy territory provided valuable information about his defenses as well as his intentions for the future. The clash of patrols, usually fewer than a dozen men in each, meant a constant clamor of gunfire at night—and a constant stream of fatalities and wounded.

Beyond the tangible benefits of aggressive patrolling, there was also the psychological impetus to send troops forward in this way. For senior British commanders such as generals in charge of divisions, aggressive patrolling promoted a fighting spirit in their frontline units. Precisely because large-scale encounters were relatively infrequent, instigating such miniature battles was seen as useful.

In addition to skirmishes that took place in no man's land, trench raids brought violent episodes into the life of a soldier at the front. In a trench raid, troops from one side penetrated the enemy's defenses and seized a portion of his trench line for at least a few minutes. These raids offered an opportunity to kill numbers of the enemy and to capture prisoners for interrogation. Initiated by the British, the practice caught on with the Germans and eventually the Americans. The French by contrast preferred to avoid such efforts as a waste of manpower.

Trench raids often involved groups of volunteers. The complex character of a trench raid dictated careful planning and even several dry runs against defenses built to simulate those of the enemy. A raid might begin with an artillery barrage aimed at isolating a portion of the enemy line from his reserve trenches, thus preventing the targeted area from being reinforced. Engineer units cut away barbed wire and other defensive impediments to permit the trench raiders through. Finally, the raiding force itself, with faces blackened and carrying special weapons such as clubs and hand grenades designed for close contact with the enemy, moved forward at the appropriate moment.

A classic example of the trench raid came in the fall of 1917 when German units struck at the first Americans to occupy a portion of the fighting front. In skilled fashion, the Germans used a brief barrage to cut off the troops from the First Division's 16th Infantry Regiment, located east of Verdun. Boxed in by the fire of ninety-six German guns, the novice American soldiers faced an assault by the experienced troops of the 7th Bavarian Landwehr Regiment. German combat troops moved rapidly across no man's land, entered the Doughboys' positions, and left within a few minutes.

Three dead American soldiers and eleven more carried off as prisoners of war attested to the way this smoothly coordinated maneuver had taken place. The Germans had acquired prisoners for interrogation, but equally important, they had made a potent effort to gain a psychological advantage over the newly arrived American troops.[12]

LIMITATIONS ON COMBAT VIOLENCE: LIVE AND LET LIVE

Given the dangers of trench life and the aggressive posture of senior commanders, the fighting should have generated heavy casualties even in the long intervals between great battles. Similarly, all portions of the fighting front ought to have produced an ongoing chamber of horrors. That this did not happen has led historians like Tony Ashworth and Leonard Smith to focus on the limitations that combat soldiers themselves placed upon fighting the enemy.[13]

From the first months of the war, informal, unspoken, but nevertheless effective agreements between opposing units led to a limitation on bloodshed. Such arrangements depended on a multitude of factors, and no unit entering the fighting line could be assured that it would enjoy such a limitation. Confronting an elite enemy unit, confronting an enemy unit under a particularly aggressive commander, or confronting an enemy unit subject to close scrutiny from higher authority, could bar such a partial truce from occurring.

Nonetheless, soldiers on both sides of no man's land found both the reason and the opportunity to make such a quiet pact with the enemy.

To shell the foe's communication trenches and nearby road system, especially in the early evening, disrupted the delivery of food to his units. It was certain to provoke a retaliatory barrage to disrupt the other side's supplies. It was an easy matter to refrain from such fire. Fire against enemy positions in the hours after dawn imperiled soldiers who were visiting the latrine; to avoid interrupting the personal needs of the enemy meant he might show you the same consideration. Trench mortar and grenade attacks were certain to draw a similar response; thus, there was an incentive for soldiers not to begin such escalations of violence in the first place. Likewise, artillery units behind the front who fired too aggressively against enemy positions faced the probability of a return barrage.

At times, harsh conditions of climate and terrain dictated that one side turn its eyes away from a vulnerable enemy. When trench lines collapsed under the strain of rain and mud, soldiers on both sides of no man's land were known to abandon them—perhaps just to sit out in the open, perhaps to repair the damage in sight of the enemy.

Completely halting hostilities was less frequent than a tacit agreement to fire only limited numbers of rounds (of rifle fire or mortar shells or artillery) at agreed upon times. The brief artillery barrage after lunch or dinner was a frequent occurrence on the western front. Sergeant William Triplet of the American Thirty-fifth Division recalled how his company commander described their position in the line in Alsace in the spring of 1918. The sector was a quiet one, but both sides felt they should at least act the part of warriors. "So at 1200 every day the Germans throw four shells into Thann [the local town] and the French toss four shells into some German town on the Rhine. Everyone knows the schedule, so nobody gets hurt often."[14]

Educated Germans normally learned French and English. Numerous Germans from more modest backgrounds had worked, often as restaurant waiters, in Great Britain. The close proximity of the opposing trench lines meant that one could call out to the enemy, carry on conversations across the battle line—or even exchange bursts of song with him on festive occasions like Christmas.

LIMITATIONS ON VIOLENCE: TRUCES

The strongest limitation on violence was the outright truce in which members of both sides decided to meet in friendly fashion. The most famous truce took place on Christmas 1914. After shouted greetings between the two sides, men left their trenches to meet in the middle of no man's land. Observers recorded remarkable scenes of burial details working side by side, joint funeral services, and impromptu football

French troops dine in the field. Courtesy of the Hoover Institution Archives.

games. At one point, the Germans allowed British soldiers to borrow the famously superior German entrenching tools.

But such truces had occurred earlier in the war. Despite the alarm of upper-level commanders, they continued to take place as the conflict continued. Often beginning with a shouted conversation between the two trench lines, such truces involved men from both sides meeting in no man's land or even visiting the other side's fortification. Swapping items of clothing and foodstuffs, exchanging home addresses, and even engaging in soccer games were aspects of these apparently anomalous encounters.

The existence of quiet sectors owed much to these tacit agreements to diminish the violence of the war. The arrival of new and more aggressive—or more aggressively led—units on one side always had the potential of disrupting such a pattern. Some units of the British army such as the 1st and 2nd Battalions of the Welch Fusiliers were famous for their aggressive posture toward the enemy. But when units that had agreed to live and let live were replaced, they frequently gave their places to similarly minded forces. Because units entered a new sector of the western front only after an orientation in which they gradually took over from those holding the line, there was ample opportunity for the newcomers to discover—and to accept—the way things were done there.

NOTES

1. Quoted in Malcolm Brown, *Tommy Goes to War* (London: J.M. Dent, 1978), 61.

2. Ernst Jünger, *The Storm of Steel: From the Diary of a German Storm-troop Officer on the Western Front* (New York: H. Fertig, 1975), 2–3.

3. Quoted in John Ellis, *Eye-Deep in Hell: Trench Warfare in World War I* (New York: Pantheon Books, 1976), 33.

4. Jünger, *Storm of Steel*, 21.

5. James H. Hallas, *The Doughboy War: The American Expeditionary Force in World War I* (Boulder, Colo.: Lynne Rienner Publishers, 2000), 63–64.

6. Herbert Sulzbach, *With the German Guns: Four Years on the Western Front, 1914–1918*, trans. Richard Thonger (London: Leo Cooper, 1973), 159.

7. Jünger, *Storm of Steel*, 48.

8. Quoted in Brown, *Tommy*, 73.

9. Henri de Lécluse, *Comrades in Arms: The World War I Memoir of Captain Henri de Lécluse, Comte de Trévoëdal*, edited by Roy E. Sandstrom; translated by Jacques F. Dubois (Kent, Ohio: Kent State Press, 1998), 83–84.

10. Ellis, *Eye-Deep in Hell*, 45, 47.

11. Jünger, *Storm of Steel*, 216.

12. Hallas, *Doughboy War*, 67–70; also Byron Farwell, *Over There: The United States in the Great War, 1917–1918* (New York: W.W. Norton, 1999), 11–13.

13. Tony Ashworth, *Trench Warfare, 1914–1918: The Live and Let Live System* (London: Macmillan, 1980); Leonard Smith, *Between Mutiny and Obedience: The Case of the French Fifth Infantry Division during World War I* (Princeton: Princeton University Press, 1994).

14. William S. Triplet. *A Youth in the Meuse-Argonne: A Memoir, 1917–1918*, ed. Robert H. Ferrell (Columbia, Mo.: University of Missouri Press, 2000), 83.

4

The Experience of Battle

The initial fighting on the western front saw huge armies maneuvering against each other as German forces swept through Belgium and northern France. By the close of the year, the front had stabilized. Germany and its opponents faced each other across a line of trenches stretching from the English Channel to Switzerland. For soldiers on the western front, the experience of battle over the greater length of the conflict came as one side or the other attacked to break the trench stalemate and to bring the war to a decisive conclusion. In 1915, 1916, 1917, and 1918, major battles came each year and lasted for weeks or even months.

Some factors shaping a coming battle were within human control. Senior commanders could decide how many heavy guns would support the attack, although sufficient cannon and trained crews were not available until long after the war had begun. They could decide the form of the attack—by waves of carefully aligned infantrymen or by scattered groups clinging to ground cover. The location for an assault was also a matter of conscious planning: in the lowlands of Flanders, the chalk fields of Picardy, the highlands above the Aisne River in Champagne, the approaches to the fortified city of Verdun. The decision to respond to an emergency rested in the hands of the generals. They might take the fateful step of sending half-trained soldiers into the heat of battle.

Other factors were beyond leaders' decision-making. One was the mud that came in Flanders each year with the spring and late summer rains. The onset of fog—so important in the German offensive in March 1918— was also a force of nature. So too were the direction of the wind and its impact on employing gas to support a major ground assault. The influenza epidemic that swept across the fighting armies in the summer and fall of 1918 was likewise an act of nature. Commanders could respond to such physical forces—Field Marshal Sir Douglas Haig could have suspended the 1917 offensive at Passchendaele in deference to the muddy terrain—but they could not control them.

WORD OF THE ATTACK

Rumors spread like wildfire in military units. All soldiers learned to expect major battles with the approach of spring, and indications of an impending attack were easy enough to spot. Even civilians learned the signs. Pastor A. van Walleghem, the local priest at Ypres and an astute observer of events, recorded in his diary in the summer of 1917 that a great action was imminent. He noted how the British were building new railroads and how their ammunition depots were expanding. Even the local farmers saw what was coming and prepared to move their cattle from the danger zone.[1]

Large-scale attacks often came after troops had been removed from the line for a longer stretch than usual. This break in an accustomed routine might be accompanied by an improvement in the food. Clerks and orderlies around brigade and battalion headquarters saw a greater flow of telegraph messages coming in from higher command levels. Staff officers—in the British army highly visible because of the red tabs they wore—were increasingly seen as they arrived to transmit oral instructions from the general officers planning an operation.

Prior to a major assault, British soldiers found themselves drawn up in front of the colonel commanding their battalion. He would assure them of the operation's success, and remind them of their unit's tradition of courage under fire. Thereupon, a subordinate commander presented the harsher message that desertion in the face of the enemy and other dereliction of duty would evoke the severest penalties. Sometimes he read off lists of men recently executed, along with a recitation of their crimes.

THOUGHTS BEFORE BATTLE

Witnessing the preparation for a major offensive gave soldiers on both sides the chance to reflect on the dangers they had to face. Soldiers preparing to move across no man's land invariably had time waiting in areas adjacent to the front. Those on the other side of the line knew they too had only a limited time before facing death. In such circumstances, men confronted fears, hopes, and expectations. Many educated and ar-

Von Hindenburg and young German soldiers. Courtesy of the Hoover Institution Archives.

ticulate combatants recorded their ponderings in letters home and in diaries.

Lieutenant Lionel Sotheby had felt sufficiently concerned about his chances of survival to mail a will to his family attorney before leaving France at the close of 1914. In a final letter to his father in September 1915, before the Battle of Loos, the twenty-year-old Englishman presented a hopeful message mixed with realistic expectations. "Tomorrow morning we go over the parapet and I am in the front line," he began. "We are all cheerful & full of hope though no one knows what is before him." In a revealing passage, he noted, "I have not the uneasy tremors which one experiences during the night before one's first attack, partly because I suppose the novelty has worn off, & partly because of a greater & stronger determination to come through." And finally, "The general spirit of everyone is good & it bodes well for us."[2]

A young, doomed German soldier, about to assault the French position at Les Eparges in April 1915, presented a common message, that of gratitude to his family. "You know how I thank you all three for all your goodness to me . . . for all the sunshine and happiness in my life. If I am to die, I shall do so joyfully, gratefully and happily!"[3] An American lieutenant about to go into action in the Argonne in 1918—in an assault he also did not survive—likewise took the occasion to thank his parents for the fine upbringing they had provided him. Whatever happened to him, he was sure they would meet "on the shining sands of the other side."[4]

Many soldiers gave voice to a combination of patriotism and religious conviction. This was the case in a young German's letter to his parents in which he predicted his imminent death in attacking a French position at the start of June 1916. "[Do] not grieve," he pleaded, because he was proudly dying for "a new, a greater and a better Fatherland." He felt himself safe "in the Hands of God" and merely wished his parents to know that he begged their forgiveness for "old days [in which] I vexed and pained you."[5]

One message anxious relatives often received presented poignant advice on how to bear up if the writer happened to die. One British soldier told his father that his letter would be sent only if the young man died: "You I know, my dear Dad, will bear the shock as bravely as you have always borne the strain of my being out here.... The beyond has no terrors for me. I am quite content to die for the cause for which I have given up nearly three years of my life and I only hope that I will meet death with as brave a front as I have seen other men do before."[6] A German soldier, writing the day before he was fatally wounded at Verdun in February 1916, asked his parents, brothers, and sisters to "cherish me in your loving, faithful hearts." He tried to console them for their impending loss by asking them to consider that, with his moderately gifted nature, he "should probably never have achieved complete happiness and contentment." And so he was at peace when "I extinguish the lamp of my existence on the eve of this terrible battle."[7]

Private thoughts could turn to a morbid calculation of one's chance for survival. "All through that night I never slept a wink of sleep. My stomach would insist on rising to my throat to choke me each time I thought of some lurid possibility," one British soldier recalled. "Maybe one in three against being killed. One chance in four of being wounded which means a respite and one in four of being taken prisoner—as good as escaping scotfree."[8] A French sergeant about to go into action at Verdun pondered the intact state of his body and implicitly considered what might happen to it: "What a hideous thing; to say to oneself, at this moment. I am myself; my blood circulates and pulses in my arteries; I have my eyes, all my skin is intact, I do not bleed!"[9]

The hope one's memory might survive dominated the thoughts of some soldiers. A British private awaiting the German assault in March 1918 recalled making a pact with a friend that "whichever one was lost, the other would do his utmost to look for, or to find out what happened to, the other." On the other side of the battlefront, a young German enlisted man, unable to sleep, thought of important parts of life he had never known. "I was not engaged to get married, I hadn't even a sweetheart. I was only twenty and hadn't even been with a woman. I wanted to survive to have that experience."[10]

GOING INTO ACTION: MEN ON THE BATTLEFIELD

From the start of 1915, most major battles on the western front exhibited a set of elements that shaped the experience of combatants. These included the devastating force of the machine gun, the pulverizing effect of prolonged heavy artillery bombardment, and the difficulties posed by fighting in mud and rain. Frequently, the battlefield was the scene of gas attacks, and sometimes tunnel explosions and tank assaults were part of the bloody efforts to end the stalemate. On rare occasions, troops were able to break through the enemy's lines and unhinge his defenses.

Units often found themselves engaged in bitter combat for weeks at a time. At Verdun, for example, Lieutenant Henri Desagneaux's company was under fire for more than two weeks without being relieved. As he put it, "For sixteen days we have neither washed nor slept. Life has been spent amongst dead and dying, hardships of every sort and incessant anguish."[11]

THE BATTLEFIELD EXPERIENCE

The Machine Gun

Facing the destructive force of machine-gun fire was a novel experience for European soldiers. The carnage produced by massed rifles, with an effective range of 300 or 400 yards, had been evident since the battlefield slaughters of the American Civil War and the Franco-Prussian War. European military planners had also begun to calculate the effects of lethal modern artillery. But the machine gun's power came as a surprise. This ferociously potent military tool gave a few men or even a single individual the power to spray hundreds of bullets at an advancing enemy. But so far it had never shown its effectiveness on a European battlefield. The first hints of what it could do, especially in the Russo-Japanese War of 1904–1905, had not registered in the minds of most military professionals.

Mass infantry attacks, even following an elaborate artillery preparation, foundered as surviving machine-gun crews in the enemy lines opened fire. Even a few machine guns met advancing troops with a deadly hail of bullets. This potential for mass slaughter by machine-gun fire became evident during large-scale attacks in 1915. Advancing armies aided by artillery bombardments struck at what they hoped would be a shaken adversary. In bloody spring offensives at Neuve Chapelle and then at Ypres, first the British and then the German army began to learn

Wreckage of a French national monument from the era of Joan of Arc. Courtesy of the Hoover Institution Archives.

how the machine gun dominated the battlefield. The French offensives in Artois and Champagne likewise came to grief. One French officer recalled the slaughter in Artois in which 300 men of his regiment went into a hopeless attack. "At the first whistling of bullets, the officer had cried 'Line up!' and all went to their death as in a parade."[12]

Britain experienced the full impact of mechanized firepower at the Battle of Loos in September 1915. The war was now more than a year old. The Germans were forcing Britain's ally Russia into a humiliating retreat on the eastern front, and the British high command considered it imperative to strike somewhere in the west. British commanders hoped to use poison gas on a large scale to unhinge the German line. The initial advance went well in some sectors, but, as the fighting swirled around the small French mining town, machine guns took a deadly toll on both sides.

On September 25, the British advanced beyond Loos and onto the ridge to the east. Thereupon, the Germans launched a series of spirited counterattacks. A Scottish infantryman described how British machine-gun fire from the ridge "mowed the Huns down" during their initial counterattack and, when they returned, "we mowed them down again." In a third assault, the British "held on with machine guns and to see the Germans piling up was sickening. They came in mass formation and must have left hundreds piled up dead and wounded."[13]

The next morning 10,000 men from two novice British divisions marched in parade-ground fashion across a mile of open country into a solid network of German fortifications and machine-gun nests. They too suffered the predictable massacre: 8,000 dead and wounded. A German account catches the bloody moment, describing how "the machine gunners [had never had] such straightforward work to do nor done it so effectively. They traversed to and fro along the enemy's ranks unceasingly. . . . As the entire field of fire was covered with the enemy's infantry the effect was devastating and they could be seen falling literally in hundreds."[14]

The full power of the machine gun to spill blood on the battlefield appeared at the Battle of the Somme in July 1916. The British high command expected to crush German resistance by a massive, weeklong artillery bombardment. The British soldiers were all volunteers, most of them in units of the "New Army." These were the recently formed divisions filled with men who had answered Kitchener's call to enlist. They had instructions to move across the battlefield in tight alignment. Senior commanders did not wish to lose battlefield control of this large force of hastily trained men. Each British infantryman carried sixty-six pounds of equipment in the attack. Each had been told to expect an easy advance the first day; the British forces were to occupy the enemy's shattered front line, then move several miles beyond it.

German defenses were dug deeply enough to permit most of their soldiers to survive the enemy's artillery barrage. British cannon fire suffered from a lack of high-explosive artillery shells, and the artillerymen on the British side, novices like their comrades in the infantry, directed much of their fire inaccurately. When the whistles blew at 7:30 in the morning of July 1, 1916, to call the British infantry out of their trenches to advance, at least 200 German machine guns and their crews were ready to meet the enemy. The result was a gruesome and matchless horror, even by the standards of World War I.

Within a single day—mainly within the first hour—the British lost nearly 60,000 men, of whom 20,000 were fatalities. Aided by German artillery, German machine gunners cut down the slowly advancing, highly visible infantrymen as if the scene were a gigantic shooting range. The day's losses were the worst for any army in World War I; they were the worst losses for the British army in its entire history.

The difference between standing on the defensive and attacking in the teeth of entrenched machine gunners was evident in comparing losses on the two sides. The Germans suffered only one casualty for every seven they inflicted on their British opponents. In the confrontation between the British Eighth Division and the German 180th Regiment, eighteen British were killed or wounded for every German casualty.[15]

The view from the German side made it clear how such gruesome

A casualty of war: dead German machine gunner. Courtesy of the National Archives.

figures emerged. "We were very surprised to see them walking, we had never seen that before," one German recalled. British officers were an easy target to identify: They took a position in front of their units, carried walking sticks, and wore a fashionably tailored uniform different from that of the men under them. German fire was predictably devastating: "When we started firing we just had to load and reload. They went down in the hundreds. You didn't have to aim, we just fired into them."[16]

An individual British soldier told the same story from the field in front of those guns. This sergeant in the 26th Northumberland Fusiliers had a typically brief and grim experience once he had left the shelter of his trench. "I could see, away to my left and right, long lines of men. . . . By the time I'd gone another ten yards there seemed to be only a few men left around me; by the time I'd gone twenty yards, I seemed to be on my own." Before he could move much further, a bullet struck him as well.[17]

American troops advancing into the Argonne Forest in the fall of 1918 faced the same horror of massed machine-gun fire. Americans were mowed down by carefully hidden machine guns that fired when the doughboys approached. Firing low, the German gunners wounded men in the legs and finished them off as they fell or lay exposed on the ground. Only when American forces were able to reach the gun crews and to shoot or bayonet them could the advance continue. In the aftermath of the combat, American dead littered the ground.

General John Pershing, the commander of the AEF, drove his division commanders forward, and the men on the fighting line faced one deadly line of German machine gunners after another. An enlisted man of the 305th Infantry regiment described an attack on a ridge his comrades had dubbed "Machine Gun Hill" or "Suicide Hill" in the Bois de la Naza. His unit's advance immediately faced intense German opposition. "We were at once under direct machine gun fire, the worst yet, and it seemed as if the air was so full of bullets that a man could not move without being hit. A man standing upright would have been riddled from head to foot." The horrifying experience was intensified by the invisible nature of the enemy, and, in short order, the American's company had been reduced from a company to a group the size of a squad.[18]

Even a retreating enemy could delay his pursuers with a few machine-gun crews, and much of the war saw victorious forces unable to take advantage of their foe's withdrawal. In March 1918, German troops sweeping forward against General Hubert Gough's shattered Fifth Army in Picardy found British machine guns to be a potent obstacle. Trooper C.H. Somerset of the 9th Machine Gun Squadron recalled such a moment. There were "brave German infantry, walking calmly and with poise into our murderous machine-gun fire . . . we had nothing but admiration for them. . . . [A]s fast as we knocked them down, another wave would appear." His rearguard action went on for ten days before he himself was wounded and forced out of action.[19]

Heavy Artillery

The scope and intensity of artillery fire in World War I went beyond anything fighting men had ever experienced. The factories of the various belligerents turned out cannon of greater caliber than ever before. The Germans had a relative abundance of heavy weapons and ammunition from the war's start. Britain and France found themselves at a disadvantage represented by the "shell crisis" of early 1915. At the Second Battle of Ypres in April 1915, British artillerymen faced severe restrictions of the number of shells they could fire in a single day. Nonetheless, by the following year, massive amounts of artillery shells became available to belligerents on both sides of the battle line.

By 1916, medium and heavy artillery pieces, along with the machine gun, had become the dominant weapons on the western front. The great artillery barrages that preceded major attacks could be heard as far away as London. At the Somme, artillery fire not only prepared the field for the British assault, it accompanied the fighting itself. At Verdun, most of the fighting took place between dueling artillery units as

A shell hole on the French sector of the western
front. Courtesy of the Hoover Institution Archives.

infantry huddled under the firestorm. After the early part of the war,
despite the carnage produced by machine guns, most battlefield casualties came from artillery fire. And such casualties were shocking even
to veterans of earlier wars. As historian Alistair Horne put it: "In the
First War the crude iron of the shells . . . shattered into huge ragged
chunks that sometimes two men would be unable to lift. The effect on
the soft human carapace of impact with these whirling fragments may
be imagined."[20]

In any major attack, artillery fire served several purposes for both the
attacking force and the defenders. Long-range cannon struck at supply
depots and road centers behind the enemy's lines. Shorter-range weapons hit the areas leading to the trenches; thus their shells struck at reinforcements moving up to an active area of fighting.

But artillery could serve different purposes for each of the two sides.
The attacking force used cannon to bombard the enemy's trench fortifications, stunning the troops opposite and cutting their barbed wire

defenses. Such bombardments were often set to move forward at predictable intervals in a "rolling barrage." This, at least in theory, permitted troops to advance behind a constant curtain of artillery protection. For the defending side, a comparable measure was to fire at no man's land in order to decimate the advancing enemy before he could cross over.

Combat on the Somme combined intense infantry encounters with deadly fire from artillery batteries. Sergeant Gottfried Kreibohm of Germany's Third Guard Division recalled several days in the second week of the massive battle. Moving into a defensive position in High Wood, his unit fell under artillery fire that was "absolutely frantic." His trench was hit repeatedly as some of his comrades were "buried alive while others were blown into the air." On another occasion, heavy-caliber shells struck all over his sector of the front: "Geysers of earth a hundred feet high shot from the ground.... The ground rumbled and heaved with each explosion." Hearing a shell coming directly at him, he covered his head, then looked up to find a dud that had landed less than two yards away from him. The entire bombardment was "the most fearful ten hours I had ever experienced in my life."[21]

The Battle of Verdun, which lasted from February 1916 to the close of the year, stands as the longest battle in history. It also holds the distinction of being the greatest artillery duel of the entire war. General Erich von Falkenhayn presented his soldiers and subordinate commanders like Crown Prince Rupprecht of Bavaria, the leader of the Sixth Army, with the task of attacking Verdun. Located in a French-held salient, Verdun could be assaulted from several sides. Meanwhile, French public opinion saw it as one of the great historical fortresses along the frontier, a fortress that could not be permitted to fall into enemy hands. Falkenhayn in fact envisioned destroying the French army by compelling French commanders to feed their troops into a bloody battle to hold Verdun.

Fighting in the cramped approaches to the city, both the Germans and the French concentrated their forces so densely that the enemy's artillery had a multitude of helpless targets. Units occupied then left the trenches time and again without ever encountering a visible enemy; meanwhile the exchange of artillery bombardments decimated one unit after another. German artillery prevailed at first. As French artillery power came to match its German counterpart, the suffering on both sides of the battle line reached a grisly par. In June a German infantryman put it with brutal force. "The torture of having to lie powerless and defenceless in the midst of an artillery battle," he said, was "something for which there is nothing comparable on earth."[22]

That same month a newly arrived French infantry officer, Henri Desagneaux, was sent to the front lines to lead a company trying to hold the trench line. The unit soon found themselves in a ditch that had been repeatedly shelled and that contained the body parts of its previous oc-

American visitors to a wrecked French village. Courtesy of the Hoover Institution Archives.

cupants, "legs and arms protruding out of the ground." This "battle of extermination" for Desagneaux was "Man against the Cannon." Bombardments lasted for twenty-four hours at a time. The men could relieve themselves only by using a can or shovel and throwing their body wastes over the top of the shell hole in which they found a scant bit of shelter.[23]

Combat in Mud and Rain

Trench life in rain and mud tormented soldiers during much of the war. The climate in northwestern Europe guaranteed that living outdoors exposed a soldier to these harsh elements during much of the year. Merely holding ground in such conditions wore men down. But in operations like the Third Battle of Ypres in the late summer and fall of 1917, soldiers were expected to fight massive actions while hindered, and sometimes crippled, by the elements.

Shortly after the start of the British attack in late July 1917, August rains of rare force and duration turned the battlefield into quagmire. The rains returned in even greater intensity in October and November. The entire Ypres salient was below sea level, a swamp that had been drained over the centuries and transformed into fertile farmland. The artillery bombardments from both sides wrecked the carefully maintained drainage systems. Attacking British troops now tried to assault the enemy

Victims of battle. © Hulton-Deutsch Collection/CORBIS.

over fields of mud. Forces moving up to support the attack as well as supply columns carrying food and ammunition bogged down hopelessly. Men unfortunate enough to be wounded in such circumstances drowned—and sometimes disappeared—in the mud. Some unwounded but exhausted combatants drowned in puddles of clear water.

The slowly advancing British troops found themselves confronting Germans in trenches supported by miniature concrete fortresses. Carefully sited and containing multiple machine guns, these concrete structures protected their occupants from the rain and gave them a base from which to mow down the attackers. One British officer described such an attack. The troops were aided for a time by their own artillery barrage, "[b]ut there was no chance of the infantry getting across. I watched them gradually trying to work their way forward, struggling like blazes through this frightful bog to get at the Germans." No such effort could succeed in those circumstances, because "they were up to their knees in mud" and getting halfway across the distance to the enemy lines, "it was virtually impossible for them to move either forward or back." German machine guns easily disposed of the trapped infantrymen.[24]

British troops stumbling into the mud sometimes sank up to their armpits. That was the experience of rifleman G.E. Winterbourne. He was fortunate enough to be found by two of his comrades from the next wave of attackers, who managed to pull him out. But Winterbourne himself encountered another soldier who had been entrapped in the mud for five days before he could be rescued.[25]

Sometimes rescue was impossible. Major C.A. Bill of the Royal Warwickshire Regiment recorded how British troops had found a British soldier trapped in mud so thick that four of them could not pull him out. Forced to move on with their attack, they returned two days later. By then, the soldier had sunk from his knees to the top of his neck "and he was raving mad."[26] A sergeant of the Rifle Brigade recorded watching helplessly while a fellow soldier gradually sank below the mud to his death. "He kept begging us to shoot him," the sergeant recalled, but no one could bring himself to do it. "We stayed with him, watching him go down in the mud."[27]

Even greater than the exertion of attacking in the mud was the work of trying to carry the weight of a wounded man to safety. Stretcher-bearers struggled to move in this impossible environment. Instead of two men carrying a stretcher, as many as six had to bear the burden. Moving a few hundred yards in these conditions could take hours.

Mining and Tunnel Operations

In 1914, German commanders had whenever possible retreated to high ground. Thus, their forces had the advantage of overlooking their opponents' lines. But deadly danger accompanied the benefits of such entrenchments. German soldiers on elevated sectors of the western front faced the frightening possibility that the enemy was digging mines directly under their positions. When these cavities were filled with explosives and detonated, they killed, maimed, and stunned the soldiers above. And such massive explosions, such as the one the British set off at Messines south of Ypres in 1917, came at the start of vigorous, aboveground assaults.

But no Allied soldier tunneling under German positions could breathe easily, because the enemy employed deadly countermeasures. The Germans dug their own mine tunnels to intercept the British ones, and the competing digs were sometimes only a few feet apart. The success of an operation and the safety of the miners often depended on a matter of timing: which side could place its explosives and detonate its mine first. Nonetheless, the British still managed to conduct the most successful mining operations. At Messines, British soldiers who had been miners in civilian life were one source of tunnelers. At times civilian miners, in uniform but not trained for any other military task, worked alongside them underground.

Starting in 1916, British engineers dug twenty-one tunnels in preparation for an assault on the Messines-Wytschaete Ridge. When the attack took place on June 7, 1917, observers witnessed a spectacular sight, and there followed a rare, bloodless success for the Allies on the western front. Observers described how "[t]he earth seemed to open and rise to the sky." With the entire ridge engulfed in flame, "[t]he whole world seemed to go up into the air." Dazed and terrified Germans dragged

American officers with their tank. Courtesy of the Hoover Institution Archives.

themselves out of their trenches and staggered down the hill to surrender without resistance to the advancing British infantry.[28]

The Tank Assault

For German troops, the last years of the war brought a new, scary battlefield enemy; they watched with terror and dismay as the armored vehicle known by its code name "the tank" lumbered and jerked across the battlefield. Germany could not stretch its resources to allow its own army to invest heavily in such a tool, although a few German tanks did take part in the spring offensive of 1918. British, French, and American tanks lumbered across Flanders and northeastern France to confront an enemy who could not match them—but who had to stop the new threat.

The tanks of World War I lacked the speed or striking power of those that appeared two decades later. Nor did the generals of this earlier era have a clear view about how to employ them. Nonetheless, a weapon that could not be halted by machine guns, trenches, and barbed wire made a deep psychological impression on the foe. One German soldier who encountered them at Cambrai in November 1917 stated bluntly, "One stared and stared as if one had lost the power of one's limbs." They seemed like slow but unstoppable monsters. "Someone in the trenches said 'The devil is coming,' and the word was passed along the line like wildfire."[29]

Within the armored beast itself, the crews suffered from a different kind of anguish. The four men operating the tank and the four others directing its guns could barely fit into the cramped interior. The noise of the engine made conversation impossible; the tank commander passed orders to his crew with hand signals. Intense heat and the smells of a straining engine created even more discomfort. And no member of a tank crew could forget that he was only inches away from forty gallons of highly flammable motor fuel and a store of high-explosive cannon shells.

The strains of armored warfare appear in vivid form in an official study by the British army shortly after the successful assault on the German lines at Amiens on August 8, 1918. The "exhaustion of the crews" was not merely fatigue, but physical and psychological illness. "The pulses of one crew were taken immediately after they got out of their tank; the beats averaged 130 to the minute or just twice as fast as they should have been." Evidence of the psychological pressure on tank crews was clear: "Two men of one crew temporarily lost their reason and had to be restrained by force, and one tank commander became delirious." Nor was it only the crew that was stricken. "In some cases, where infantry were carried in the tank, they fainted within three-quarters of an hour of the start."[30]

A tank was unreliable and difficult to maneuver despite the monstrous appearance it presented to the Germans. The weapon aroused hopes for breaking down enemy barbed wire at a low cost in casualties, but often the tanks broke down before reaching their own infantry's line of departure. At Passchendaele, tanks accompanied the first infantry attack, but most soon sank into the mud. Even in the Allied summer offensive in 1918, when tanks were used en masse, they continued to be mechanically unreliable. As the biggest targets on the battlefield, they also drew the heaviest enemy fire. It was ferociously effective.

Poison Gas Attacks

Men suffered injury and death from gas attacks as well. Used to harass troops on an everyday basis, gas attacks could also come in massive form as a part of a major offensive. Gas might approach via the prevailing wind, or it might arrive encased in an artillery shell. Soldiers occupying a trench were temporarily disabled by lachrymatory gases that caused eyes to tear. Other gases like chlorine and phosgene killed their victims by disabling the tissues of the respiratory system. Mustard gas caused the skin to burn and blister, produced temporary blindness, and, if breathed in, could be fatal. One of the particular horrors of mustard gas was its propensity to remain on the surface of the ground for long periods of time. Phosgene had a different long-term effect: It could cause sudden death in an unsuspecting victim two days after he had come into contact with the substance.

From the first extensive use of gas—by the Germans at Ypres in the spring of 1915—soldiers were trained in precautionary measures. Primitive methods like placing a pad soaked in urine over one's face gave way to elaborate masks and hoods containing respirators. These prevented gas from entering the respiratory tract, but they could not prevent mustard gas from blistering the skin. And gas masks caused difficulties of their own. Straps itched and burned, and the rubber tube placed in the soldier's mouth not only caused the jaw to ache but made him drool like an infant. Any exertion like running forced the wearer to gasp for oxygen.

Overwhelming the Enemy's Defenses

At rare moments in the course of war, soldiers had a sense of escaping the limits of static warfare. Moving rapidly on an open battlefield was the image of war men remembered and hoped to see again. In the end, most such hopes faded.

For German troops on the Somme in the spring of 1918, however, the impression was a vivid one. The offensive began on the morning of March 21. The end of the fighting on the Russian front permitted the Germans to concentrate in France and Belgium. In places on the western front, they outnumbered the British more than two to one. The skilled use of gas shells and a short, precisely planned artillery bombardment stunned General Hubert Gough's Fifth Army. The barrage disrupted British command posts, and the supply and communication network supporting the British front lines also suffered severe damage. Then, aided by dense fog, specially trained German assault divisions crossed no man's land. They had instructions to bypass British strong points and to strike as deeply into the enemy rear as possible. Other, less mobile forces followed to clean up the surviving British defenses.

Thrown off balance by the sudden German assault, many of Gough's units crumbled, and 21,000 British troops laid down their weapons to become German captives. The remnant of Gough's army retreated westward, and German forces pushed forward in a fashion not seen on the western front since 1914. In a single day the Germans advanced as much as four and a half miles and seized almost 100 square miles of territory.

One German sergeant expressed the feeling of freedom and exhilaration the day's success had brought. "The whole front was in motion, all going one way. . . . We heard no shooting. . . . We kept asking where the English were but no one knew. We believed that we had at last broken right through the English front and that the moment we had awaited all through the war had arrived. Now we could finish it off. It was a thrilling moment."[31]

German success continued for more than a week as their armies advanced forty miles westward to the outskirts of Amiens. The fall of that city threatened the entire British position on the western front. In the end, the Allies restored their lines, German advances bogged down, and the stage was set for the final Anglo-French-American offensive of the summer and fall of 1918.

Abject Fear

The combatants of World War I encountered stresses for which no experience in civilian life prepared them. In such circumstances, the normal restraints society places upon its adult members disappeared.

Prior to the German assault on the British lines in March 1918, German artillery pounded the enemy with almost 6,500 cannon. It was the greatest concentration of artillery pieces ever gathered on a single battlefront. Over a million shells struck the British lines during a bombardment that lasted five hours. Men huddled in fear under the onslaught. As one British private recalled, "The first to be affected were the young ones who'd just come out. They would go to one of the older ones— older in service that is—and maybe even cuddle up to him and start crying."[32]

At Montdidier, a young American private of the First Division, traumatized by a shell that killed two of his fellow soldiers nearby, likewise lost control under an artillery barrage. His lieutenant described how the soldier "commenced to shake badly" and then "lay flat on his stomach in the mud and water on the bottom of the trench and wept and wept."[33]

Raw American troops moving into the Argonne Forest in the fall of 1918 confronted a trench where 200 of the dead had been gathered. As a result of rigor mortis, the limbs of the dead soldiers had twisted and turned in hideous fashion. The replacements stopped dead in their tracks, then crowded to the opposite side of the road to distance themselves from the scene before them. A private of the Twenty-sixth Division also in the Argonne recalled how he lost control of his bodily functions: "Most of us were scared stiff, to the point that some of the boys had diarrhea. . . . Soon we could all smell this stool odor from each other. There was nothing in this experience to be ashamed of, because it happened to all of us, and it didn't make any difference whether you were an officer or an enlisted man, but we were all reluctant to talk about it."[34]

NOTES

1. Lyn Macdonald, *They Called It Passchendaele: The Story of the Third Battle of Ypres and of the Men Who Fought in It* (London: Michael Joseph, 1978), 83–84.

2. *Lionel Sotheby's Great War: Diaries and Letters from the Western Front*, edited and with an introduction by Donald C. Richter (Athens: Ohio University Press, 1997), 133.

3. Quoted in A.F. Wedd, trans. and ed., *German Students' War Letters* (New York: E.P. Dutton, [1929]), 70.

4. Quoted in Robert Ferrell, *Woodrow Wilson and World War I, 1917–1921* (New York: Harper and Row, 1985), 81–82.

5. Quoted in Wedd, *German Students' War Letters*, 195.

6. Quoted in Denis Winter, *Death's Men: Soldiers of the Great War* (London: Penguin Books, 1978), 172.

7. Quoted in Wedd, *German Students' War Letters*, 242–43.

8. Quoted in Winter, *Death's Men*, 173.

9. Quoted in John Ellis, *Eye-Deep in Hell: Trench Warfare in World War I* (New York: Pantheon Books, 1976), 97.

10. Quoted in Martin Middlebrook, *The Kaiser's Battle: 21 March 1918: The First Day of the Spring Offensive* (London: Allen Lane, 1978), 144–45.

11. Henri Desagneaux, *A French Soldier's War Diary, 1914–1918*, ed. Jean Desagneaux, trans. Godfrey J. Adams (Morley, Yorkshire, Eng.: Elmfield Press, 1975), 30.

12. Quoted in Alistair Horne, *The Price of Glory: Verdun, 1916* (New York: Harper and Row, 1962), 25.

13. Quoted in Trevor Wilson, *The Myriad Faces of War: Britain and the Great War, 1914–1918* (Cambridge, Eng.: Polity Press, 1986), 261.

14. Quoted in Ellis, *Eye-Deep in Hell*, 93.

15. Martin Middlebrook, *The First Day on the Somme: 1 July 1916* (New York: Norton, 1972), 245.

16. Quoted in Ellis, *Eye-Deep in Hell*, 94.

17. Quoted in John Keegan, *The Face of Battle* (New York: Viking Press, 1976), 245.

18. Quoted in Frank Freidel, *Over There: The Story of America's First Great Overseas Crusade*, rev. ed. (Philadelphia: Temple University Press, 1990), 170–71.

19. Quoted in Middlebrook, *Kaiser's Battle*, 349.

20. Horne, *Verdun*, 65.

21. Quoted in Lyn Macdonald, *1914–1918: Voices and Images of the Great War* (London: Michael Joseph, 1988), 161–62.

22. Quoted in Horne, *Verdun*, 178.

23. Desagneaux, *French Soldier's War Diary*, 22–26.

24. Quoted in Macdonald, *Passchendaele*, 143.

25. Ibid., 138–39.

26. Quoted in Wilson, *Myriad Faces*, 473.

27. Quoted in Macdonald, *Passchendaele*, 200.

28. Ibid., 41–45.

29. Quoted in Malcolm Brown, *Tommy Goes to War* (London: J.M. Dent, 1978), 260.

30. Quoted in John Terraine, *To Win a War: 1918, The Year of Victory* (London: Sidgwick and Jackson, 1978), 116–17.

31. Quoted in Middlebrook, *Kaiser's Battle*, 221–22.

32. Quoted in ibid., 161.

33. Quoted in James H. Hallas, *The Doughboy War: The American Expeditionary Force in World War I* (Boulder, Colo.: Lynne Rienner Publishers, 2000), 79.

34. Quoted in ibid., 274–75.

5

The Sea and Air War

Most military men involved in the western front served in their nation's army. Even traditional naval powers like Great Britain saw the size of their land forces dwarf the numbers in other branches of the armed forces. Nonetheless, significant numbers served in navies, which had been established before the war but now expanded to meet new needs. Still more joined the recently formed air units. In Britain, while the army consisted of 3.5 million at the close of the war, 415,000 men served in the navy at that time and about 300,000 in the air force.[1]

The men in the navy and air force fought a different war from that of their brothers-in-arms in the trenches. The average British soldier had a one in two chance of being killed or wounded during extended service on the western front. On the other hand, sailors in all navies faced enemy fire only infrequently. Despite the crowded conditions on board naval vessels, most sailors had eating and sleeping arrangements beyond the wildest expectations of their army counterparts. All members of air units could expect to sleep in a bed at night and to be supplied with regular meals. The large ground crews needed to support an air squadron's fliers confronted danger mainly when the enemy bombed their airfields.

But the navy and air force faced their own hardships. Sailors, particularly in the British navy, found themselves in remote bases and difficult seafaring conditions for long periods. All sailors serving in seagoing vessels faced the possibility of going down with their ship in the open ocean. In such a situation, chances of survival for even a small portion of the crew were minuscule. Service in a submarine was perilous beyond any-

thing the average soldier encountered. Fliers faced enemy fire frequently—sometimes several times a day—and at close quarters. The
possibility they would survive if their plane was shot out of the sky was
slim.

THE SURFACE NAVY

Most sailors served on surface vessels during the first part of the war.
Naval planners had planned for a great oceanic battle between the British
Grand Fleet and the German High Seas Fleet soon after the start of the
war. The winner, it was thought, would then dominate the sea lanes.
But the great fleet encounter leaders anticipated prior to 1914 did not
materialize. British admirals worried that new weapons like mines and
submarines might cripple a British fleet that acted too aggressively.
German naval leaders were just as cautious. With their smaller collection
of capital ships like battleships and battle cruisers, they hesitated to take
on the superior British forces.

Fleet units, including the great capital ships, maneuvered and sometimes skirmished in the North Sea. But the average sailor's most common
experience was tedium and boredom. British sailors sometimes got into
street brawls with civilians when they were taunted about the fleet's
inability to bring the Germans to bay. In April 1915, Richard Stumpf, a
German seaman aboard a battleship in the High Seas Fleet wrote in his
diary that "I no longer care if we get to fight or not. . . . One can get used
to anything but it is extremely difficult to be kept waiting all the time
in the knowledge that our tremendous power is being wasted."[2]

Occasional naval encounters broke the tedium. But with both fleet
leaders feeling cautious, the sight of one battleship squaring off against
another was rare. Instead, ships of unequal size and armament frequently met in battle with the smaller vessel and its less powerful cannon
at a deadly disadvantage. A British officer described an encounter his
destroyer flotilla had with a German cruiser in the second month of the
war. Before British torpedoes turned the tide, men of the smaller Royal
Navy ships faced a hale of deadly fire. The Germans' shooting "had our
range to a yard and her salvos came whistling about our heads in grand
fashion." Well-aimed German shells blew British gun crews to bits and
toppled the masts in several destroyers. One shot struck a destroyer captain's cabin, exploded in the officers' quarters, and went on to bring the
ship's engines to a dead stop.[3]

Men were under fire for only a few hours at most. The Battle of Jutland
in the spring of 1916 was the long awaited clash between the great fleets
built largely in the prewar years. Even here, no sailor at sea faced the
kind of sustained bombardment the British inflicted on German soldiers
a few weeks later prior to the Battle of Somme. And most sailors never

saw the battle in which they were engaged. Ships often bombarded each other at great distances. Some men on deck—and especially those serving as observers at the top of masts—could see the enemy clearly. But about half the crew on a large vessel performed technically sophisticated tasks; most of the rest tended the engines. Few in the first group and none in the second had any indication of what was happening in the course of combat unless their ship suffered grievous damage from shellfire, torpedoes, or mines. British engine room sailors at Jutland recalled performing their well-practiced tasks automatically as if they were engaged in a drill or normal maneuvers.

If a ship went under, especially at night or in the midst of a heated battle, most of the crew was doomed. There was little chance a sailor's sister ship or an enemy vessel would rescue him. The danger was too great, and the intact vessel had other duties to perform. And so sailors died in the sea. Men were sucked into the propellers of passing ships or killed by shells hitting the water nearby. Others choked to death on the oil deposited on the sea, froze in the perpetually cold waters, or simply drowned. A wounded sailor might receive adequate medical care, but, unlike a soldier evacuated to the rear, he remained in danger so long as his ship was under attack.

Death and injury in a sea battle had uniquely grisly features. Men were confined in a small space, and the effects of an exploding shell could be horrendous. A German officer under fire in the North Sea in January 1915 left a record of the carnage. "All loose or insecure fittings are transformed into moving instruments of destruction." Blood flowed everywhere while doors "bend outward like tin plates and through it all, the bodies of men are whirled about like dead leaves in a winter blast to be battered to death against the iron walls—men were swept from the deck like flies from a tablecloth."[4]

The greatest danger a seaman faced was a direct hit from the enemy that ignited his vessel's ammunition magazines. Such a calamity blew the ship and its crew out of the water. At Jutland in 1916 three British battle cruisers sank in this fashion. In the late afternoon of May 31, two German shells penetrated the forward magazine and destroyed *Indefatigable*. Two men out of the thousand in her crew were rescued. A few minutes later, *Queen Mary* exploded in two stages when a German salvo ignited the forward magazine and a second struck the magazine at the vessel's rear. Twenty men survived out of a crew of 1,300.

A third episode of instant mass death occurred two hours later. A gunnery observation officer in the *Invincible*'s mast remembered the horrible scene when that battle cruiser went down with 1,026 men. "Then I saw the roof of [a turret on the starboard side] hit by a heavy shell and blown off like bit of scrap metal. Almost immediately there was a huge explosion as Q and P magazines blew up, destroying and cutting in half the ship."[5] For a time the two segments of *Invincible* stood erect in eerie fashion on the ocean bottom, part of each visible above the waves. Then each toppled over and sank to the bottom. Six men survived to be pulled out of the water by other British vessels.

Battleships were the largest vessels afloat, and they had sufficient armor to survive even the heaviest shelling. But men in various portions of the ship like the gun turrets were vulnerable to enemy fire. At Jutland, *Malaya* was struck in one of the starboard gun batteries with an ensuing fire that incinerated the men serving the cannon. The result, as one young midshipman recalled, "was the smell of burnt human flesh, which remained in the ship for weeks, making everybody have a sickly nauseous feeling the whole time."[6] Damage below decks subjected engine room workers to a ghastly fate. Escaping steam cooked men's bodies; damaged machinery continued to turn and mangled crew members. Being trapped below decks as water entered a ship's lower compartments meant death from drowning in a dark, isolated void. Smoke and noxious gases spread readily, sometimes through a ship's own ventilation system.

A crewman aboard any warship knew that a torpedo from a submarine or a floating mine could blow a hole in his ship's hull that was impossible to repair. Such sudden attacks occurred frequently enough to give admirals nightmares and to create constant fear among ordinary sailors. In late October 1914, the British battleship *Audacious* struck a mine in the waters off northern Ireland, and the most frantic efforts of the Royal Navy failed to keep the vessel from sinking. Luckily for the crew, other vessels were nearby to conduct a rescue operation. By contrast, the German battleship *Pommern*, en route home after the Battle of Jutland in 1916, fell victim to a British submarine. A single torpedo split the vessel in two, and it sank with more than 800 members of its crew.

THE SUBMARINE WAR

The major naval powers began to incorporate submarines into their fleets in the decade before the outbreak of World War I. In the pre-1914 era, naval leaders could only speculate about the new weapon's potential, because submarines had not yet been used in combat. Most believed that the underwater boats would serve best as scouting vessels to support capital ships. But from the war's earliest days, submarines began to attack merchant shipping.

The typical World War I U-boat was about 200 feet long and carried five to ten torpedoes. Such a vessel carried a crew of about thirty. Two diesel engines propelled the submarine on the surface, and the diesels recharged the two electric motors that powered the submarine during underwater operations. Because the electric motors could operate for only brief periods, submarines were unable to stay underwater for long.

The vessels cruised on the surface and often conducted their attacks there as well. One or two deck guns, fired when the U-boat had surfaced, permitted it to sink other vessels without using up its limited supply of torpedoes.

The crews of submarines consisted almost exclusively of volunteers. As the German navy curtailed its surface operations after the Battle of Jutland, ambitious and restless officers and men sought assignments in the underwater arm of the service. In the British navy as well, many energetic young officers, especially naval cadets who had just received their commissions as sublieutenants (or ensigns), sought duty in submarines. Only in the final months of the war did the German navy assign men to underwater duty.

Service aboard a submarine was both uncomfortable and dangerous. A bath and a change of clothes were impossible luxuries, and every member of the crew had to make do with cramped quarters. A submarine's air was so foul that men had to use bottled oxygen, and breathing fresh air after surfacing produced the same sensation as downing a shot of whiskey. The toilets worked only at shallow depths; when the sub went deeper, the crewmen were forced to relieve themselves in empty canisters in various parts of the vessel. Whereas the odds strongly favored a sailor's likelihood of survival if he served on a surface craft, submarine crews had a four in ten chance of dying in combat.

On the other hand, virtually all crew members were skilled technicians, and the need for every man to rely upon the actions of every other made for a unique team spirit. The tensions between officers and enlisted men so common on surface vessels, especially in the German navy, were generally absent.

Whether attacking on the surface or from underwater, the U-boat sailor, even more than his counterpart aboard a surface ship, was cut off from a sense of the battle in which he was engaged. Only the captain operating his periscope underwater or the few crew members with him on the conning tower during a surface action had a view of what was happening. But when a U-boat itself came under attack, everyone could feel the danger. Assaulted by destroyers or subchasers, U-boats faced terrifying depth-charge attacks. Shaped like a trash can, a depth charge could blow in the sides of a U-boat if it exploded nearby. If the U-boat had more space separating it from the detonation, a depth charge still had the punch necessary to knock out a submarine's key equipment.

Being trapped in a submerged U-boat meant certain death for all members of the crew. A German submarine officer who escaped a sinking craft and fell captive turned his thoughts to his shipmates: "I couldn't forget my crew, my friends going down out there, drowned like rats in a trap, with some perhaps left to die of slow suffocation . . . lying in the

American sailor in the war against the submarine.
Courtesy of the National Archives.

darkness, hopeless, waiting for the air to thicken and finally smother them."[7]

The U-boat crews faced other dangers. Submarines were hard to identify even by their own countrymen. Thus, a submariner stood a good chance of being hit by "friendly fire." Enemy warships and even merchant vessels could respond to a U-boat sighting by trying to ram the attacker. A German U-boat attempting to pass through the mine and submarine net barriers the Allies set up, first across the English Channel and later in the war across the North Sea, might be trapped and destroyed by these stationary perils. British Q-ships, vessels disguised as merchant ships but heavily armed, attracted submarines to surface nearby, then threw off their civilian trappings and opened fire.

A submarine that descended too far risked being crushed by the sea pressure. Water that leaked into the interior at these extreme depths could produce poisonous chlorine gas if it reached the ship's batteries. One German U-boat experienced that special horror off the coast of Ireland in the spring of 1916. Its captain noted, "I don't think there is anything that will strike such fear in a submarine man as the thought of being trapped in the iron hull while choking gas seeps from the batteries bit by bit. No death could be more agonizing."[8]

DISCOMFORT, TEDIUM, AND MUTINY

Even on the largest ships, enlisted men found themselves in cramped quarters. They commonly ate and slept in the same small compartments, slinging and taking down hammocks depending on the time of day. German ships were particularly cramped, because the area below decks was divided into separate, watertight compartments. These aided vessels in surviving when damaged below the waterline, but the added safety came at the cost of the crew's discomfort.

For months on end, enlisted men in all navies carried out monotonous chores such as loading coal into their vessels, chipping paint, and standing watches. All the while, the nearest enemy was hundreds of miles away. At the huge, isolated British naval base at Scapa Flow off northern Scotland, only officers had frequent opportunities to go ashore to one of the barren nearby islands. The British fleet units guarding the waters between Scotland and Norway, the "Northern Patrol," became famous for the hardships their crews faced in these rough and frigid waters. Such conditions led to the danger of military discipline breaking down in small and large ways.

The British fleet met the problem with an active sports program and an elaborate system of entertainment. There were boxing matches, hikes, concert parties, and movies, and several ships were converted into floating amusement centers with stages on which professional entertainers could perform. Some sports activities and concert performances even brought officers and enlisted men together in a common activity. Combined with adequate rations and the intangible force of British naval tradition—which claimed a 300-year legacy of dominating the waters around Europe—these measures promoted order and discipline as well as fighting spirit. Officers got the same rations as enlisted men, an important symbol of common purpose and common sacrifice.

The German High Seas fleet suffered by comparison. A program to keep the sailors occupied with sports entered the picture only in the last year of the war. Meanwhile, tedium combined with increasingly poor rations to create widespread bitterness. The privileges of the officers, living in close proximity to the enlisted men of the crews, made the difficult situation into an explosive one. Unlike the British navy, the Germans increased shipboard tensions by providing officers with separate kitchens that produced luxurious meals.

Enlisted men, well aware of what the officers had to eat, made do with

The King of Saxony visits a German naval vessel. Courtesy of the Hoover Institution Archives.

a wretched diet. By early 1917, the common sailors' main meal often consisted of thin soup with fragments of sausage, potatoes, peas, turnips, and various unknown ingredients. They dubbed the nauseating compound "chopped barbed wire." Stumpf expressed the resentment of many when he noted sarcastically that a rich diet of "rolls with their coffee" and "cutlets at noon" was being bestowed on those "who spend all their time filing their nails and combing their hair."[9] Seamen assigned the heavy work of stoking the engines with coal were entitled to special rations of fat or sausage. Even these essential crewmen found their rations cut back, and hot weather pushed their bodies to the point of collapse.

In the spring and summer of 1917, discontent over the food available in the crews' quarters provoked cases of open indiscipline on many German vessels. By the closing weeks of the war, the collapse affecting the German army showed itself in the navy as well. The supreme naval commanders planned a final sortie against the Allies to force a great fleet battle in the North Sea. There was no hope of success, but, to the eyes of the admirals, such a suicide run offered a way to salvage the navy's honor and to pave the way for building a new navy sometime in the future. The crews who were scheduled to sacrifice their lives saw things differently. Starting on October 29, the sailors mutinied.

LIFE AS AN AIRMAN

The air war began with small and fragile planes piloted by a small number of men who had only recently learned to fly. Planes quickly proved their value in reconnaissance missions, as well as in directing artillery fire. Pilots also began strafing attacks against enemy ground forces. By 1916, large air armadas fought for control of the skies over battlefields like the one at Verdun, and the Germans set the example—soon followed by the other belligerents—of attacking cities behind enemy lines with bombing planes. By the close of the war, air forces employed thousands of large, technically sophisticated planes. The numbers of airmen had grown beyond any expectation. Britain's Royal Flying Corps (RFC) and the parallel Royal Naval Air Service (RNAS) had only 2,000 officers and men between them in August 1914. The two groups were amalgamated into a single force, the Royal Air Force, in April 1918. By the Armistice, Britain's air strength boasted 14,000 trained pilots supported by more than 250,000 uniformed men and women on the ground.[10]

The life of the airman differed from that of the typical infantry soldier. Airmen rarely encountered the filth of the trenches with its combination of mud, rats, lice, rain, and rotting corpses. An American naval flier, Irving Sheely, noted "as from what I've seen of the men that came back from the front, they lead the life of a dog."[11] Bogart Rogers, an American flying with the British Royal Flying Corps (RFC), wrote home that "there's not much danger of our beds being suddenly covered up by five feet of mud. Those men up in the line must have nerves of steel. I'd go crazy as a March hare if I had to be up there one whole day."[12]

Combat often took place in a predictable fashion: Two patrols per day, one in the morning, one in the afternoon or in the early evening. This allowed forms of leisure far removed from the atmosphere of war. Rogers played tennis, soccer, and bridge during his time off, sometimes varying his recreation by hunting for rabbits. For British fliers, football games occupied many afternoons, and rowdy parties in the mess—sometimes resulting in broken limbs as well as bad hangovers—were an accepted means of letting off steam. Irving Sheely spent six stress-free weeks in mid-1918 at a course in high altitude daylight bombing. Stationed in Clermont-Ferrand in central France, he wrote home that it was "just like a vacation" with three hours of work a day, pretty French girls, good food along with peace and quiet.[13]

Fliers and the ground crews supporting them slept in tents, barracks, or requisitioned civilian houses. They sometimes moved at short intervals, but airmen had no occasion to march like the infantry. Trucks and sometimes their own planes took them where their orders directed. In *Sagittarius Rising*, his memoir of his days in the Royal Flying Corps, Cecil

Lewis noted: "We had a bed, a bath and mess with good food and peace until the next patrol.... [W]e were never under bodily fatigue, never filthy, never verminous or exposed to the long, disgusting drudgery of trench warfare."[14]

Lieutenant Jean Villars of the French air service recalled pilots called to duty from the "hors-d'oeuvre of lunch" and taking off while "our comrades, napkins on their arms, salute our departure."[15] When he saw a column of shaken infantrymen moving up to the front, he reflected, with some discomfort, on the luxuries the men in his unit enjoyed. "We are ashamed of our clean uniforms and our dry huts, of our nights of rest. And we almost want to abandon the profession we love, follow them ... pitiful and magnificent who are going to fight the hardest and most glorious of combats."[16]

Fliers were usually far younger than the members of ground units. The physical demands of flying combined with heavy casualties to keep the average age of a squadron member less than twenty-five. As Villars put it, "Except for the chief [squadron leader] who is thirty or so, there is none among us more than twenty-five years of age. Not one of us is married, and each operates with the freedom and cheerfulness of youth which nothing can restrain."[17] Captain Wilfred "Wilf" Green, appointed the commander of Bogart Roger's flight in June 1918, was nineteen.

The life and customs of the officers' mess showed men recovering from a trial in the air. All faced the likelihood of another deadly encounter with the enemy. French pilots returning from a mission often took time for an extensive group conversation detailing their recent adventures and escapes. "The pilots talk, talk" with anyone who will listen, according to Villars, speaking "with their comrades, with the mechanics, with strangers, idlers, off-duty infantrymen, or artillerymen, gathered to listen." After two hours of strain and discomfort, "they relax in broken chatter, nervous and incoherent."[18] British fliers seemed to prefer a period of quiet to wind down from such an intense experience. In their off-duty moments, a variety of rough games and "ragging" served to release—or at least to block—tension. The cliché of the drunken flyer—inebriated during his evenings off and even more so during his off-duty trips to Paris—was one of the vivid images to come out of the war.

AERIAL COMBAT

In contrast to the constant activity and strain of trench warfare, fliers had limited hours facing the enemy. The rain that tormented the ground troops meant a rest for aviators, because, in times of bad weather, flying was impossible. Villars recalled his feelings at such moments: "The freedom to do nothing, a cigarette, hot coffee, the novel put aside for three weeks, guiltless laziness rocked by the noise of the rain on the tar paper of the roof."[19] French aviators spoke of "temps mauvais pour l'aviation; excellent pour les aviateurs" (bad flying weather, but fine weather for the pilots).

The relative normality of the flier's living conditions could not mask the presence of deadly danger. From training onward a World War I aviator found himself living a bizarre life with "its mixture of short flying hours and lengthy stretches of relaxation: its mixture of gentlemanly routines and rakish individualism with death constant, utterly unpredictable, stunningly quick."[20] One British pilot, writing during the summer of 1917, recalled his feelings:

No one can imagine the [mental] strain of two hours over the line. First one has to keep one's place in the formation. . . . There is nothing more nerve wracking than getting really badly archied [attacked with antiaircraft fire] for a long time. Then there's every machine in the sky to be suspicious of. As a matter of fact, with all this wretched aerial activity we get a dogfight now nearly every time we go up—too often for my liking. It is extraordinary how warlike one feels before one gets to the line. Then suddenly it conks out when you cross it.[21]

Flying brought immense physical strains: from the noise, the cold, the vibration, the oxygen deprivation, and from the increase in blood pressure brought on by an existence at high altitudes. Returning to the ground from a high-altitude flight could bring on painful, even fatal attacks of the bends or body spasms.

The dangers of low-level flying can be seen in one RFC pilot's description of the damage ground fire had done during two reconnaissance flights in the spring of 1915. "[P]icked up fifty bullet holes thro' my plane . . . one chipped the propeller, one a strut, one through my exhaust pipe, one thro' my tail skid and one into my leg. It fell out when I took my sock off and I have sent it home as a souvenir."[22]

But the principal daily danger to an aviator was death from the enemy in the air. The limits of slow, flimsy, and poorly armed planes shaped the nature of aerial combat. Throughout the war, most combat planes were constructed of wood, wire, and fabric. The machine guns they carried constituted their only defense except evasion when attacked by an aerial enemy. Those guns were legendary for their tendency to jam. Changes in temperature and the plane's vibration could make a weapon that fired perfectly on the ground into a useless metal stick during aerial combat. Machine guns whose rate of fire was timed to pass through the blades of a turning propeller were a source of special concern to pilots. Bogart Rogers had both of his aerial guns jam beyond repair, one after the other, during an encounter with a German plane in late September 1918.

The fear of flying in an inferior aircraft was part of a pilot's mind-set.

A German reconnaissance plane and pigeon messenger. Courtesy of the Hoover Institution Archives.

Technical improvements in air speed, maneuverability, ability to climb rapidly, and armament sometimes appeared on the battlefield within a matter of months. The enemy plane a pilot encountered might well be technically superior—with deadly implications. Villars expressed a common complaint about the obsolescent Farman and Voisin reconnaissance planes provided by the French air service. "How much longer will we have these crates?" he wrote in June 1916. "There is work to do over the lines. But it is sad to think that our ability and our nerve are used not to fight the enemy, but to fight against the poor tools which have been put into our hands."[23]

In order to do serious damage, pilots needed to bring their planes into close proximity to the enemy before firing. Aces such as Manfred von Richthofen and René Fonck claimed that their successes came from reaching a position within a few yards of their targets. The common tale of the fighter pilot returning to base with the blood of a defeated enemy on his windshield indicated how close these opponents came to each other. Over Verdun, the French aviator Albert Deuillin described a victory at close range over a German Fokker and added an indication of the hot blood that accompanied such combat: "The fellow was so riddled that vaporized blood sprayed on my hood, windshield, cap, and goggles. Naturally, the descent from 2600 meters was delicious to contemplate."[24]

Enemy antiaircraft fire ("archie") was a constant threat, and planes returning to base often showed the holes made by nearby aerial explosions and the shrapnel fragments they propelled outward. But pilots could evade ground fire by using natural elements like cloud cover, and unpredictable winds augmented his ability to evade ground fire. Hitting a small plane as high as sixteen thousand feet above the earth appeared an impossible task. By 1916, however, German observation units could calculate an enemy plane's altitude and the proper gun settings to hit it within seconds.

Some pilots considered machine-gun and rifle fire from the ground to be an even more hazardous accompaniment to their work. At Cambrai in 1917, British pilots assigned to ground strafing suffered 30 percent casualties each day. One pilot was shot to the ground three times within a single week. As direct attacks on enemy ground troops became a more important mission for all aviators, low-level strafing and bombing attacks added to the pilot's peril. The Germans alone took the intelligent measure of creating special units for strafing. They also made sure that these squadrons were protected from ground fire with armored engines and fuel tanks.

The speed of aerial combat, with the possibility of being fatally attacked in an instant, made friendly fire a deadly reality. The American ace Eddie Rickenbacker nearly attacked French aircraft on two occasions, and he himself was the target of both French and American air assaults. Camouflage colors were different enough to provide a warning, but in the heat of combat, the temptation to shoot first and only then to verify another plane's nationality later could become irresistible. In the prolonged summer and fall battle of 1917 for Passchendaele in the region east of Ypres, leaders of the RFC felt compelled to caution British fliers that they would have to face a court-martial in the event of shooting down a French plane.

Two factors made flying especially frightening: the absence of any means of escaping from a crippled plane and the likelihood of fire. Whereas German pilots like Ernst Udet were able to use a parachute to escape a doomed "crate," their British and French opponents had no such option. The commanders of the RFC felt that parachutes would diminish fighting zeal on the part of their pilots. In any case, the cumbersome devices, which weighed forty pounds, were considered a hindrance for a pilot in the carrying out of his duties.

The absence of a parachute joined with the likelihood that enemy bullets or shells would set a pilot's plane on fire. The badly burned pilot—or his badly burned corpse—was a stock element in the memoirs of the war. Pilots sometimes carried pistols to end their own misery if trapped in a burning "ship." Combat veterans recalled seeing their comrades jumping out of a burning plane to drop to a quick death upon hitting the ground. After witnessing a crash followed by the outbreak of a fire, Bogart Rogers noted: "That's the thing everyone fears—fire. Crashing or getting shot down isn't so bad, but being penned in a machine perfectly conscious and yet unable to get out is ghastly. And catching fire in the air is even worse."[25] Some planes like the American-made DH-4 (the "Flying Coffin") acquired a grim reputation because of their tendency to catch on fire. With its poorly protected gas tanks and its mechanism for pumping fuel rapidly—even out of damaged fuel lines—this craft became particularly feared. One enemy incendiary bullet could drive it out of the sky.

A lesser but significant fear was the possibility of capture. By the nature of their work as artillery spotters, reconnaissance agents, and ground assault fighters, air crews were close to enemy lines or even over enemy territory. A single lucky shot from the ground could cripple an aircraft's motor. Villars put it clearly in observing the fate of two Germans from a downed observation plane. Looking at the pilot, a sergeant, and the officer who accompanied him as an observer, he speculated on his own future and that of his comrades:

[W]e cannot help feeling that a similar fate perhaps awaits us, imagining the possible day when, bareheaded, coatless, we might be driven off in the cars of aviators of the other side, be brought, downcast, before our captive plane, now useless, immobile and ridiculous; submitted to the curiosity of a hostile crowd jabbering in a strange language, then cut off, abandoned, lost, leave for the prison like a pauper's grave, toward boredom, cold, hunger, awaited packages, letters which do not arrive.[26]

Visible and calamitous losses magnified the fears most fliers felt. In the British air arm, and likely in the others as well, 80 percent of the casualties were incurred by newcomers flying their first twenty missions. The flying life in combat for a British pilot in the spring of 1917 was between seventeen and eighteen hours.[27] The veterans of the RFC on the western front deliberately avoided learning the names of young squadron mates whose presence among the oldsters was certain to be brief. Even the better-trained and more cautious French fliers faced comparable losses. The French ace René Fonck noted that a daring French pilot was likely to survive for three months of combat; flying with a greater view to one's own safety might double that period.

Most of the pilots on all sides lacked the abilities that permitted a René Fonck or Billy Bishop or Max Immelmann to become an ace. Neither their training nor their physical and mental attributes prepared them for such eminence. As Villars put it, most pilots, like himself, were "watch dogs." They interfered with the enemy's efforts to penetrate across the trench line, they screened their own reconnaissance planes, and they blocked enemy efforts to strafe friendly troops in their trenches.

The psychological strain of combat flying led to a limit on the time an aviator could be kept at the front. Ground troops were rotated into trenches and pulled out periodically, but they nonetheless served until they were killed or crippled. Enlisted soldiers went a year or more without home leave. By 1916, British aviators could expect to fly for six months followed by leave (or training duties) for three months to recuperate.

THE DANGER OF ACCIDENTS

Flying was one form of military activity in which accidents rivaled combat as a source of death and injury. Beginning with their training days, fliers saw their comrades die in huge numbers. Better training could reduce the toll: Germany suffered only about one training death for each combat fatality, and improved instruction cut British losses after late 1917. Nonetheless, out of some 14,000 British airmen fatalities during the entire war, more than half (8,000) died during their training in the British Isles. Everyone knew that a novice's flying skills could bring disaster. Bogart Rogers, while training to serve with the RFC, described two such calamities. One of his fellow cadets flew under another's plane, created a mid-air collision, and fell to the ground. His gas tank exploded on impact. On the same day, a second pilot in training pulled out of a dive too quickly, broke off both his wings, and fell to his death from a height of 4,000 feet.[28]

Once at the front, the accident continued to play a deadly role. The Frenchman Villars wrote a vivid account of a downed aircraft from his squadron of flimsy observation planes, the Mefeu-Farmans. The plane had rolled over upon landing. "The cockpit, made of a ridiculously light plywood, is completely crushed, the gun turret is twisted, the tail spars bent, the wings broken and their skeleton of white pine wood pushes out from the torn canvas." The toll of accidents sometimes approached—or even exceeded—that of combat. In April and May of 1917, accidents on the western front cost the French 107 fatalities and 142 injuries. In those same months, only 41 airmen lost their lives in combat (70 more were listed as missing); and combat produced 104 wounded.[29]

Some events were grisly because of the numbers involved. All twenty planes in a single squadron of French bombers crashed while attempting to land on a fog-bound field in Flanders in 1917. Other calamities were eerie because there was no apparent cause. Two days after arriving at the Naval Air Station at Dunkerque, Ensign Curtis Read of the United States Navy suffered an all too frequent fate. For no reason, his seaplane moved into a vertical dive, fell out of control, and crashed into the water.

Read died soon after being pulled out of the sea; his fellow aviator, Petty Officer "Eich" Eichelberger, was never found.

THE GERMAN AIRSHIPS

The crews of the German dirigibles that patrolled the North Sea and bombed targets in southern England experienced a special strain. The round-trip flight to England from bases near Hamburg like Nordholz, Tondern, and Ahlhorn put German airmen at risk for as long as thirty hours. The extreme heights at which the dirigibles flew made crew members vulnerable to extreme cold in all seasons, and bombing from those altitudes made it difficult to strike targets accurately. Moving around via the ship's narrow catwalks was a terrifying experience. But the worst terror was to be caught in a storm. Heavy weather threw dirigibles wildly off course; dirigibles disabled by storm sometimes carried their helpless crews to crash out at sea.

For security reasons, no crew member, including the captain, learned the destination of a bombing mission until the flight was underway. At first, dirigible fliers leaving for their unknown destinations enjoyed a degree of luck. England's lack of preparedness for air attack was evident in the first attacks of January 1915. The German dirigibles found the country's urban areas completely illuminated. "Our crews could distinguish the streets, the squares and the facades of the theatres," one airman recalled at that time. "They could almost read the letters of the illuminated signs." The British soon began to black out their cities, and combinations of searchlights and antiaircraft cannon gave German dirigible aviators an agonizingly long exposure to ground fire. Attacking Dover in June 1917, one dirigible commander recalled desperate moments. "Twenty searchlights have gripped us and seem to be trying to drag us down with their pallid rays. The ship is illumined as brightly as by day. . . . Bluish-white incendiary shells hiss up towards us; we can follow their trails quite clearly." For this German airman, "Heaven and earth are alive with forces that threaten our destruction."[30]

NOTES

1. Stephen Richards Graubard, "Military Demobilization in Great Britain following the First World War." *Journal of Modern History* 19, no. 4 (1947): 304, 309.

2. Richard Stumpf, *War, Mutiny and Revolution in the German Navy: The World War I Diary of Seaman Richard Stumpf*, edited and translated by Daniel Horn (New Brunswick, N.J.: Rutgers University Press, 1967), 82.

3. Peter H. Liddle, *The Sailor's War, 1914–1918* (Poole, Eng.: Blandford Press, 1985), 36.

4. Quoted in ibid., 59.

5. Quoted in Richard Hough, *The Great War at Sea, 1914–1918* (Oxford: Oxford University Press, 1983), 276.

6. Quoted in John Keegan, *The Price of Admiralty: The Evolution of Naval Warfare* (New York: Penguin, 1989), 168.

7. Quoted in Edwyn A. Gray, *The Killing Time: The German U-boats, 1914–1918* (New York: Charles Scribner's Sons, 1972), 151.

8. Quoted in ibid., 120.

9. Stumpf, *War, Mutiny*, 315.

10. John H. Morrow, Jr. *The Great War in the Air: Military Aviation from 1909 to 1921* (Washington, D.C.: Smithsonian Press, 1993), 329, 364; Chaz Bowyer, *History of the RAF* (New York: Crescent Books, 1977), 46.

11. Lawrence D. Sheely, ed., *Sailor of the Air: The 1917–1919 Letters and Diary of USN CMM/A Irving Edward Sheely* (Tuscaloosa: University of Alabama Press, 1993), 132.

12. John H. Morrow [Jr.] and Earl Rogers, eds., *A Yankee Ace in the RAF: The World War I Letters of Captain Bogart Rogers* (Lawrence: University Press of Kansas, 1996), 170.

13. Sheely, *Sailor of the Air*, 134–36.

14. Cecil Lewis, *Sagittarius Rising* (Harrisburg, Pa.: Stackpole Books, 1963), 137.

15. Jean Beraud Villars, *Notes of a Lost Pilot*, translated and edited by Stanley J. Pincetl and Ernest Marchand (Hamden, Conn.: Archon Books, 1975), 41.

16. Ibid., 126.

17. Ibid., 30.

18. Ibid., 190.

19. Ibid., 68.

20. Denis Winter, *The First of the Few: Fighter Pilots of the First World War* (London: Penguin Books, 1982), 40.

21. Quoted in ibid., 82.

22. Quoted in Peter H. Liddle, *The Airman's War, 1914–18* (Poole, Eng.: Blandford Press, 1987), 44.

23. Villars, *Notes of a Lost Pilot*, 49–50.

24. Quoted in Morrow, *Great War in the Air*, 134.

25. Morrow and Rogers, eds., *A Yankee Ace*, 93.

26. Villars, *Notes of a Lost Pilot*, 108.

27. Winter, *First of the Few*, 156.

28. Ibid., 36–37; Morrow and Rogers, eds., *A Yankee Ace*, 37–38.

29. Villars, *Notes of a Lost Pilot*, 62; Morrow, *Great War in the Air*, 199.

30. Rolf Marben, comp., *Zeppelin Adventures*, trans. Claud W. Sykes (London: John Hamilton, [1932]), 35, 115–16.

6

Casualties and Medical Care

The carnage of World War I produced casualties in unprecedented numbers. The war also provided new challenges to the medical profession. The weaponry of the war was so potent that, when it did not kill outright, it wounded men's bodies with violent force. Beyond that, the terrain in which much of the fighting took place—fields cultivated over centuries with animal droppings—helped create infectious wounds foreign to recent medical experience. Doctors on both sides of the fighting lines came to grips with the problem of reconstructing or, if need be replacing, the aftereffects of combat such as torn faces and crippled limbs. Finally, the shock to men's minds was often as calamitous as a physical injury, and medical science moved to treat this problem as well.

Doctors had to adjust to unprecedented numbers of patients in the wake of the great battles on the western front. All too often they themselves were under enemy fire. Sometimes they faced death at dressing stations near to the front, where they were in the same danger combat soldiers faced. Sometimes they were imperiled in rear area medical centers that, deliberately or fortuitously, became the targets of enemy air or long-range artillery attack.

THE NUMBERS OF WOUNDED

The number of men wounded during the war can only be estimated, and sources vary—sometimes wildly. Standard figures for Germany give a total of approximately 4.3 million military men who were wounded

American medical facility in ruined French church. Courtesy of the National Archives.

and survived their wounds. The German army typically lost 2.4 percent of its field army strength each month due to wounds. Almost 75 percent of that number returned to some kind of further service. The official British figure counts approximately 2.3 million wounded. In both instances, but especially for Germany, some of those counted received their wounds in areas other than the western front.[1]

French and American figures point in a different direction. For one thing, both countries saw their fighting men wounded primarily on the western front. Another characteristic is the smaller set of numbers than for Britain or Germany. French figures vary wildly. Official estimates place that country on the same level of the other major belligerents: a postwar French parliamentary study came up with a figure of nearly 3 million with many of those wounded on more than one occasion. But several authorities give the startling low figure of approximately 400,000 wounded; this estimate indicates that many wounded French soldiers did not survive and were counted among the 1.4 million dead.[2]

The French experience at Verdun suggests what occurred in a poorly organized and overwhelmed medical system. Thirty-two officers were wounded during a surge of fighting in April 1916; nineteen died of their wounds as gas gangrene set in. Overall, the French forces at Verdun suffered 23,000 fatalities among men who had been hospitalized in the first four months of the battle. An American ambulance driver described the chaotic scene at a major hospital four miles south of Verdun: "Pasty-faced, tired attendants unloaded mud, cloth, bandages and blood that turned out to be human beings; an overwrought doctor-in-chief screamed contradictory orders at everybody, and flared into cries of hysterical rage."[3]

American losses were conditioned by the relatively brief period of time in which American soldiers participated in the fighting. Nonetheless, approximately 190,000 men in the AEF were wounded.[4]

THE EXPERIENCE OF BEING WOUNDED

A wounded soldier often remembered the suddenness of the sensation and the sense of helplessness. A British private at the Battle of the Somme recalled getting ready to jump over the front line "when I was hit in the shoulder with a bullet which penetrated my spine causing temporary paralysis." Vomiting blood, he fell into the trench with his body swept by nausea. "Afraid of losing consciousness I dug my nails in the earth . . . as I realized that in my position I could be trampled on and regarded as dead."[5] Fighting in the Argonne Forest in the fall of 1918, Colonel William Donovan of the American Forty-second Infantry Division recalled a "smash, I felt as if somebody had hit me on the back of the leg with a spiked club." He later learned he had been shot in the right knee.[6]

H. Hale, a British artillery corporal, recalled what it was like being the victim of a mustard gas attack that had lasted for several hours. "After about six hours, the masks were no good. . . . By morning everyone was round the shell holes vomiting." It took two men to guide each of the injured back for treatment, and, as his comrades began to panic while unable to breathe, Hale kept telling himself "Hold tight and take no notice." His stomach cramped from repeated vomiting, and by the time a wagon had carried his group to the rear, "we were blind, we couldn't see anything." When treated at the 4th Canadian General Hospital, he found "the worst part was when they opened your eyes to put droplets in them—it was just like boiling water dropping in!"[7]

In the fall of 1918, an American officer survived an artillery attack on a small building where he was standing. He recalled a terrific blast that blotted out everything, a sense of being stunned, and "a feeling one would experience after a violent fall to the ground." Pains in his face and left hand told him he had been struck there, and when he touched his face with his right hand, "my fingers came in contact with a mass of warm sticky matter, which I knew at once was blood and lacerated flesh." He saw pieces of bodies scattered around including "a severed foot" standing upright. For a moment he thought mistakenly it was his own.[8] Equally vivid were the recollections of a British victim of an earlier artillery attack, Lieutenant John Bagot Glubb. On a road near Arras in 1917, he felt himself lifted by a "tremendous explosion almost on top of me" which then set him down. Running in "a kind of dazed panic," he felt "the floodgates in my neck seemed to burst, and the blood poured out in torrents." While sitting in the dressing station, he noted "I could feel something lying loosely in my left cheek, as though I had a chicken bone in my mouth. It was in reality half my jaw, which had been broken off, teeth and all, and was floating about in my mouth."[9]

WOUNDS AND HEAVY WEAPONRY

The intense concentration of heavy weaponry on the battlefields of World War I presented surgeons with cases they had never seen before. Soldiers wounded by machine-gun fire rarely had a single injury; rather they were likely riddled with bullets. The extensive use of artillery, both before and during attacks, meant soldiers were brought to aid stations with metal fragments that had done grievous damage to their bodies. Large chunks of metal could decapitate a man or sever one half of his torso from the other. But even slivers of metal moving at great speed could penetrate the body with traumatic effect. The American surgeon Harvey Cushing noticed that an artillery shell exploding near the sand bags ostensibly protecting troops could propel grains of sand outward with a velocity that penetrated a man's eyelids and threatened his sight.

Another American doctor, William L. Peple, treated one soldier who had been wounded by a high-explosive shell. The man eventually lived although he had more than ten wounds from his right thigh down through his leg. As Peple recalled, "The shaft of the thigh was shattered just above the knee. Gas gangrene had developed. . . . A big piece of metal had torn through the left ankle joint and lay buried in the tissues of the leg." The soldier had also lost the sight in his left eye due to another shell fragment that had struck him in the temple.[10] A French military doctor, working at a casualty clearing station, described the mutilated bodies he encountered: "[T]hey reminded us of disabled ships letting in water at every seam."[11]

Artillery caused most of the wounds suffered by soldiers on the western front. Bullet wounds followed, with injuries from gas attacks making up a relatively small number. Despite the emphasis on using the bayonet during military training, military doctors recorded only a tiny number of bayonet wounds. Troops seldom closed with the enemy in a way that permitted extensive combat with the bayonet. And men penetrated by a bayonet probably died quickly without receiving medical care.

Harvey Cushing saw the damage to human bodies and the future prospects of their owners in a visit to a British amputee ward in March

1918. Here he encountered a former stable worker who had lost both legs at the knee and a brass polisher who had to return home without his right arm. A twenty-year-old ploughboy from the Orkney Islands had to face a future without one of his legs; so too did a Yorkshire house painter. The ward also contained an apprentice butcher whom the war had left with a single arm.[12]

INFECTED WOUNDS

By the late nineteenth century, doctors customarily performed operations using aseptic techniques, which blocked the danger of infection, and antiseptic techniques, which killed bacteria that had not penetrated deeply into the body. Even infected wounds were susceptible to antiseptic drugs applied to tissues close to the body's surface, and antisepsis had worked in the Franco-Prussian and Boer wars. As Europe approached World War I, standard practice for physicians called for standing aside and permitting wounds in portions of the body like the head, chest, lungs, and abdomen to heal largely on their own. In a future war, doctors expected to dress wounds, to amputate shattered limbs, and to set fractures.

The most experienced military physicians on the western front in 1914, British doctors who had served in the Boer War, were acquainted with injuries that struck vital organs and killed. They had also met wounds that penetrated the body without deadly harm. Belgium and France presented another possibility: wounds contaminated by dirt from fields that had been manured for centuries. Physicians were unprepared for the deadly infections that accompanied even the smallest wound, especially when men were hit by shell fragments. High explosives produced wounds in which shards of metal, shreds of soiled clothing, and mud invaded the body.

Antiseptics were useless against infections that thrived deep in the body's tissues or found their way into the bloodstream. In 1914, physicians on all sides encountered untold numbers of patients struck by an infection they labeled "gas gangrene." Bacteria that required no oxygen developed inside wounds that had been treated and closed. A swelling emerging within a few days indicated an infection that no tool available to the doctors of the day could treat. Medical science seemingly marched backward. All wounds became infected, and serious ones, like compound fractures of the femur, killed eight out of every ten men who bore them. Mortality figures climbed back to the level of the American Civil War.

As early as October 1914, a German surgeon described how even small shell fragments could lead to immense damage as they rapidly penetrated a body. Larger chunks of metal did even greater violence to bones and flesh. The worst consequence, however, was infection. "Healing these irregular, jagged wounds is complicated by the fact they are frequently dirty, and . . . most are penetration-wounds, which means that a large area of the wound is deprived of blood and hence subject to gangrene." Such a gangrenous wound meant "substantial wound discharge, infection, bleeding, and putrefaction."[13] A young German military physician described his first clinical encounters with this deadly phenomenon. "Quite often the temperature of a soldier with an innocent-looking wound rose rapidly, and then I found the dreaded gas-gangrene had set in."[14]

Only new techniques could cope with such a threat. Doctors learned to cut away damaged tissues (the process called debridement) and, against conventional medical practice, left the wound open. In that state it had to be bathed constantly in a special cleansing fluid designed by Alexis Carrel, a physician, and Henry Dakin, a chemist. After debridement, rubber tubes were placed in all parts of the wound, which was flushed with Dakin-Carrel fluid every few hours. In conditions closer to the front, such a technique was not feasible. Instead, dressings were soaked in the fluid, applied to the wound, then removed and replaced every four hours. Provided it could be applied in time, the treatment proved effective. But it also meant that even minor wounds required doctors to slice away large amounts of flesh or even amputate. Similarly, doctors learned the necessity of treating all wounds with tetanus antitoxin.

The difficulties of applying Dakin-Carrel fluid to wounded American soldiers being shipped home by a long sea voyage encouraged American doctors to develop a different technique to combat infection. After removing diseased tissue, doctors covered the wound with one or more layers of vaseline gauze, then surrounded the dressing with a plaster of Paris cast.

But gas gangrene left tragically maimed men in its wake. In September 1917, one of Harvey Cushing's colleagues amputated both legs of a young soldier only to find that "fulminating gas-bacillus infection" had developed. The following day "a double thigh amputation, high up" took place offering the young victim a hope of keeping his life.[15]

FACIAL INJURIES

The nature of trench warfare put some parts of the body at special risk. Anyone peering over the top of a trench was likely to draw the attention of one or more enemy snipers. The helmets adopted by 1916 only protected the skull, while leaving the face exposed. A bullet passing through the face—especially if it spun after being deflected en route to its target—could damage most of the soft tissue of that part of the body. Severe disfigurement and blindness were the likely outcomes.

Patients with wounds to the face presented both standard and novel problems. Like all wounded, these men required treatment for shock. It could kill someone immediately or at any time throughout his journey back to a hospital. The infections that threatened all wounds, especially gas gangrene, needed to be countered by keeping the wound open and washed, and by aggressively and rapidly removing diseased tissue. But special lessons also emerged. For example, unless the patient with a facial wound was made to travel sitting forward he would likely choke and die of asphyxiation.

All four of the major countries that fought on the western front made an effort to deal with such casualties, if only to return as many of them as possible to combat. British soldiers received a sophisticated form of treatment at the hands of special teams. Surgeons, dentists, anesthetists, and—most novel of all—sculptors and artists combined their skills to treat men with smashed faces or sometimes no faces at all. By the time of the Battle of the Somme in 1916, British facilities for treating facial wounds were able to deal with a sudden influx of 2,000 cases. In the closing years of the war, American and Canadian physicians trained at the British hospital at Sidcup, Kent, the center for the treatment of such wounds.

The leading reconstructive surgeon and the director at Sidcup was former ear, nose, and throat specialist Harold Gillies. Inspired first by German textbooks recounting treatment techniques and then by a visit to Hippolyte Morestin, the era's leading French plastic surgeon, Gillies determined to establish a center in Britain where facial injuries could be repaired. German military surgeons acquired a reputation for doing only enough to send men back to the front. Their French counterparts had no striking rehabilitative successes to which to point. In this framework, Gillies became a renowned and sympathetic figure within British society.

Colorful if exaggerated stories circulated in London about young officers with unmarked faces whom people met at social occasions. Ensuing conversations with these apparently unwounded men allegedly revealed that they had been Gillies' patients. Reality was far less romantic. The course of treatment stretched for months or even years, because Gillies preferred to repair injuries in deliberate stages. One soldier injured toward the close of the war was still being offered surgery four years later.

The psychological impact of disfigurement affected both the wounded and those around them. Sculptor Derwent Wood worked as an orderly in a hospital. That experience impelled him to create facial masks for the hopelessly maimed and disfigured. Working from prewar photographs of a wounded man, he molded, painted, and fitted a mask that would last for several years and permit him to go out in public once again.

Hospital authorities forbade those with facial wounds to have mirrors, but some men discovered enough of their disfigurement to go into hopeless depressions. A number found a way to kill themselves. Doctors, nurses, orderlies, and all others involved in treating these men had to learn to look at their patients without revealing the horror severe facial wounds evoked. As one orderly put it, he had never thought how normal it was to look someone directly in the face and how difficult it was to do so when the face before him was hideous. To have a face from which children would flee, he noted, "must be a heavy cross for some souls to bear."[16] A number of men whose gargoyle-like faces prevented them from appearing comfortably in public devoted their lives to caring for similarly wounded men at military hospitals.

POISON GAS

In April 1915, German forces used a chlorine gas attack against the Allied defenses at Ypres. Terrified Algerian troops in the French army first felt the impact of this novel weapon. The gas assault had the frightening feature of shutting off a man's breath and affecting him even as he fled the battlefield. From the spring of 1915 onward, both sides began to employ this weapon, and medical personnel had the standard task of treating the victims of poison gas attacks. In reality, there was often little a doctor or nurse could do either to prevent death or to ease the soldier's passage from life. Serious lesions on the lungs and other parts of the respiratory system meant that a gassed soldier's system would inevitably fill with fluid.

Ironically, more than a month before the gas attack at Ypres, three Germans had died and fifty were injured by the weapon. Carrying gas cylinders, 200 pounds each, to the front lines had been a noisy affair that attracted Allied shellfire on several occasions. One bombardment smashed some cylinders, and made the Germans the western front's first gas casualties. It also showed the perilous nature of this weapon.

Witnesses recalled watching terrified casualties from the first gas attacks—their disorientation compounded by the blindness that often accompanied such injuries—drowning in their own fluids. In May 1915, a sergeant in the Northumberland Fusiliers passed a dressing station with a dozen gassed men. He described how "their colour was black, green & blue, tongues hanging out & eyes staring . . . some were coughing up green froth from their lungs."[17] A German lieutenant suffered a severe gas wound at the Battle of Loos in September 1915 when he fell into a shell hole filled with chlorine. He described his injury as a feeling of soap bubbles in his chest, and, despite extensive treatment, had to be discharged. He could no longer breathe deeply enough to remain on active duty.

The growing use of more deadly phosgene gas in 1916 overshadowed chlorine, and 1917 saw the introduction of mustard gas. Both sides sought ways to protect soldiers exposed to such attacks. Gas masks were useful in defending against attacks of chlorine and phosgene. But surprise assaults might find soldiers unready to put them on, and gas attacks with artillery shells spread gas with deadly speed.

The quality of gas masks differed, putting the Germans at a disadvantage. German masks protected their wearers for only four hours, and facing prolonged Allied gas bombardments in the second half of the war put German troops in serious peril. In the summer and fall of 1917, German units faced harrowing British gas attacks by the powerful Livens projector. This device was a type of mortar that could put massive amounts of gas on a position across the battle line without warning. Officers of Germany's Fifty-fourth Division, which had been assaulted with the Livens projector, calculated that they would incur 100 to 200 casualties from each such attack, of whom 10 percent would be fatally injured.[18]

As the war proceeded, treatment for gas wounds of all types improved. The number of gas casualties remained low compared to those produced by artillery fire and machine guns. Fresh air, rapid removal from the strains of the battle zone, and good nursing care aided recovery. Medical personnel learned to bathe gas victims as soon as possible and to spray their eyes, noses, and throats with bicarbonate of soda. Other treatments included the use of oxygen bottles to aid in breathing.

Spasms of coughing and retching induced by some gases put a strain on the heart, and doctors resorted to the hoary technique of bleeding patients to reduce the volume of the blood and the consequent strain of pumping it. Olive or castor oil helped protect the digestive systems of soldiers who had swallowed food or water contaminated by gas. More than 70,000 Americans had to be hospitalized following gas attacks, but only 1,221 of these died while under treatment. An additional 200 probably died on the battlefield.[19]

The total number of gas casualties on the western front remains impossible to calculate. Different armies began to list those killed and injured by gas at different points in the war; the French did not do so until the start of 1918. The chaos of the battlefield bred uncertainty of causes of death, and many men's bodies were never recovered. One authority gives an apparently impressive total of half a million. This figure, however, amounts to only 3 or 3.5 percent of a total of 15 million casualties on the western front throughout the war.[20]

PSYCHOLOGICAL TRAUMA

With the onset of trench warfare, the armies began to produce large numbers of men who, though unfit for combat, had no visible physical injury. Their disability took such forms as uncontrollable shaking, blindness, and deafness. To puzzled medical officers and angry combat commanders, such a "shell shock" casualty fit the model of a malingerer rather than a conventional patient.

Patients suffering psychological disabilities resulting from exposure to combat challenged deeply held elements in European culture. The nineteenth century had promoted an image of the calm, brave, and stoic patriot-soldier willing to sacrifice his life for his country. Such psychological disabilities fit more closely the maladies associated with females.

One view that emerged during the war held that the disability came literally from a nearby shell explosion. Alternatively, doctors blamed the passage of machine-gun bullets nearby for disrupting the functioning of a man's body. Rest, quiet, massage, and a bland diet were considered to be appropriate therapies. But many of the psychologically disabled turned out to be soldiers who had never been exposed to direct artillery or gunfire. Their malady came simply from the experience of trench life.

Another theory attributed psychological injury to a man's prewar disposition, not the strains of combat. It remained influential in the British army down to the end of the war despite the fact that many officers, representing the best families of the nation, appeared on the rolls of the stricken. In a postwar study, Lieutenant Colonel Lord Gort, a renowned infantry commander and future field marshal, proclaimed that elite units were immune from shell shock; such behavior "must be looked upon as a form of disgrace to the soldier." Even well-drilled troops in less distinguished formations, Gort insisted, could fend off the condition.[21]

The pre-1914 debate over the cause for psychological maladies had taken sharp form in Germany. There it was a practical issue, because it involved government-paid disability benefits for those injured in industrial accidents. At least some medical authorities had pointed to the trauma of having an accident to explain the psychological disabilities of the victims. Such a viewpoint had failed to persuade the government bureaucrats. Now, in wartime, most German doctors assumed that soldiers' psychological difficulties stemmed from character flaws.

In a conference held in Germany in 1916, the character flaw approach was formally adopted. It followed that a victim of shell shock had to be disciplined or subjected to painful medical therapies, and doctors in Britain, Germany, and France often applied painful electroshock treatments. One British medical officer made lines of shell-shocked patients watch while he applied electroshock (faradization) to the throat of a mute soldier. When the tormented patient finally screamed, he was told that he had been cured. The onlookers presumably took notice. In France, the forced use of electroshock (*torpillage*) produced a scandal when a soldier was court-martialed for refusing to submit to the treatment.

In Germany too, treatment centered around a punitive regime that transformed the hospital into a barracks. A soldier being treated for shell shock first confronted a sympathetic and benevolent psychiatrist who tried to convince him that the subsequent treatment was necessary. This therapy, pioneered by Dr. Fritz Kaufmann and eventually adopted widely in the German military system, relied on excruciating electrical shocks. Accompanying these were military-style commands and physical exercises designed to shake the patient from his paralysis, muteness, or other disability. All the while, the therapist urged the patient to throw off his disability as quickly as possible. The therapist also insisted that recovery would occur rapidly and even a single agonizing session would bring progress. In England, Dr. Lewis Yealland at the Queen Square Hospital in London used a comparably harsh disciplinary therapy.

A minority of German doctors attempted to use other concepts. Some turned to a regime of rest, quiet, and good food, but the results seemed disappointing, and the punitive method reigned supreme. Others attempted a form of "talk therapy" in which the patient was encouraged to remember his traumatic experiences, to ventilate his feelings about them, and thereby to regain the ability to return to duty.

By 1917, doctors in several of Britain's twenty special hospitals for shell shock treatment tried an alternative. They abandoned the use of pain and discipline for patients suffering from this allegedly deficient personality. Instead, they presumed that the patient was a normal individual who had undergone a traumatic experience. Thus, psychotherapy became the treatment of choice for some medical men. Many of them had had little interest or knowledge of psychological maladies before 1914, but they later took this form of treatment into their postwar practices.

A famous figure who used these methods was Dr. William Rivers, who practiced at the officers' hospital at Craiglockhart, Scotland. There he persuaded traumatized officers like Wilfred Owen to return to the front lines. His most famous patient, Siegfried Sassoon, had more the character of a rebel against the military system—he had published a letter calling for a negotiated peace—than a victim of shell shock. Sassoon had been an aggressive and successful officer in trench warfare. Army authorities sent him to Rivers to avoid the embarrassment of court-martialing this distinguished but outspoken officer. After therapeutic meetings with Rivers, Sassoon also returned to combat; unlike Owen, who was killed shortly before the Armistice, he survived his new period in the trenches and lived to old age.

American military doctors took a more sophisticated approach toward psychiatric casualties than most of their counterparts elsewhere. A study commission under Dr. Thomas Salmon had examined the issue of psychiatric disability even before the United States had entered the war. American physicians suggested that part of the remedy be to screen prospective recruits for psychological weakness before inducting them.

At field hospitals near the front, most American mental casualties received short-term treatment lasting from three to ten days. It featured good food, rest, and exercise, and the careful segregation of the mildly disturbed from those less likely to recover. Patients received constant reminders of the good performance of their units and the way in which their speedy return would aid their comrades. They also heard repeatedly how their permanent evacuation would amount to deserting their fellow soldiers. They were encouraged to watch as lines of German prisoners of war passed by en route to the rear.

In January 1918, the chief surgeon of the AEF also instructed his psychiatrists to "recommend the evacuation, with the least possible delay, of all persons likely to continue ineffective or to endanger the morale of the organization of which they are a part." Even so, the certainty that instances of combat stress could be treated successfully led army authorities to protect psychiatrists from being diverted to conventional medical duties. An order from the chief surgeon in September 1918 cited an instance when a trained psychiatrist had been assigned to dress minor wounds. This was intolerable when recent weeks had seen "nearly 4000 cases of slight war neurosis . . . evacuated to base hospitals that should never have left their divisions." It was essential to use psychiatrists to prevent such a loss of vitally needed manpower.[22]

During the Battle of Passchendaele, Bernard Gallagher, an American doctor attached to the British army, expressed a view of shell shock that would become conventional wisdom after World War I. Even the bravest and most devoted soldier had a breaking point beyond which he could not serve effectively. "Each individual," Gallagher wrote, "perhaps has a certain amount of 'reserve nerve power', more for some than for others. As this reserve is used up under great stress . . . some reach their limit sooner than others and develop 'shell shock'."[23]

Many of the hundreds shot for desertion in the British army—men found wandering distraught behind the lines—probably suffered from shell shock. Even veterans with records of combat heroism over the years received the death penalty in such circumstances. One professional soldier, on active duty almost without interruption since September 1914, was absent from his post during the Battle of Passchendaele in the fall of 1917. At his court-martial, he attempted in vain to defend himself by stating, "My nerves are completely broken down. I suffer pains in the head when in the line. Sometimes I don't know what I'm doing." He faced a firing squad on September 23.[24]

On the whole, military authorities in all the armies on the western front conflated psychiatric maladies with malingering or even cowardice. Such maladies seemed, at best, questionable reasons for removing a soldier from his duties. The military system's goal, including that of the system's medical officials, remained to keep men in the fighting line. If removed, the patient must be made to return to active service as rapidly as possible unless the mental disturbance constituted something even a layman could label evident lunacy. The need of all military systems to maintain discipline and to keep as many men as possible able to fight constrained the physicians who encountered "shell shock." Their task was to return the soldier to fighting trim through a short-term solution to his psychological pain.

THE CARE RECEIVED: THE MEDICAL SYSTEM

All of the belligerent countries developed systems for moving and treating battlefield casualties. The course of the war let military leaders estimate, with some accuracy, how many casualties a given action would produce. Prior to the successful British attack at the Messines Ridge in June 1917, for example, there were preparations to treat 30,000 wounded. In theory, the mechanisms were as efficient as combat circumstances permitted. Each of the belligerent armies stationed doctors and auxiliary personnel near the front lines in advanced aid stations. Medical orderlies guided the lightly wounded, and stretcher-bearers carried the more seriously hurt back to these field-dressing stations. There, the fatally wounded were put aside and the lightly wounded treated and returned to duty.

The second phase took place at the "casualty clearing stations" of the British army or the equivalent "advanced field hospital" of the American Expeditionary Force. Here doctors diagnosed the seriously wounded, gave them emergency treatment, and prepared them for shipment to more elaborate facilities. The casualty clearing stations were facilities in which damaged and infected limbs could be amputated.

The third phase meant shipment to a large and fully equipped hospital far from the fighting front. For a wounded British soldier, this could mean one of the several hospitals set up along the French coast or return to a military hospital in Britain. For a wounded German, it meant evacuation to a large rear area hospital like the one at Le Cateau or to a hospital back in Germany. American wounded at the Second Battle of the Marne in the summer of 1918 went to French hospitals, where the frequently deficient French medical system led to numerous complaints. By the time of the massive fall offensive in the Meuse-Argonne, American base hospitals had been set up in eastern France to treat the AEF's casualties.

American Red Cross volunteer aids the wounded. Courtesy of the National Archives.

The French system often failed. Medical services had been set up for a short, mobile conflict, and French facilities provoked complaints throughout the war. Two-man carts served to collect French wounded and to carry them from the front lines. Then, injured soldiers underwent a harsh process of sorting. This triage identified those who would die anyway, those who would recover but could never serve again, and those capable of returning to the battlefront. In a technique called "conservation of effectives," doctors received orders to focus virtually all their attention on the third group. From the start, mortality was high during the movement rearward, and an initial scandal broke out in 1914 when Georges Clemenceau's newspaper decried the practice of transporting the wounded in filthy cattle cars. The base hospitals were also notorious for their ineffective treatment of the wounded.

But all countries failed to provide a reassuring level of medical care. Many times, wounded soldiers were ignored or simply lost in the conditions of battle. The badly hurt could not always be moved from the battlefield without further injury, serious or perhaps fatal. Casualty clearing stations in supposedly safe areas were shelled, and the number of battle casualties could swamp all preparations to treat them either near the front or in rear area hospitals.

In the wintry first stage of the fighting at Verdun, French wounded

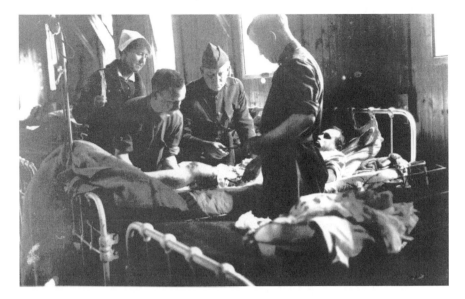

American medical team at base hospital in France. Courtesy of the National Archives.

by the thousands lay in the open outside overcrowded clearing stations. Under fierce German shelling, each ambulance took half a day to remove a handful of patients from the danger zone over frozen roads. As the battle went on, conditions continued to deteriorate. A wounded French soldier in the 1916 inferno was fortunate to receive any treatment in the first twenty-four hours after being hit. Troops trapped in underground fortifications in the summer fighting at Verdun sometimes faced a six-day delay before evacuation to the rear.

On July 1, 1916, the first day of the Battle of the Somme, British losses exceeded all predictions. Twelve thousand wounded men swamped the casualty clearing stations by evening, and the ambulance convoys continued to arrive throughout the night. The flood of wounded overwhelmed base hospitals near the Channel, and those facilities reserved their beds for the most critically wounded. All other casualties had to leave for England, even before the bandages they had gotten at field dressing stations could be removed. Hospital ships were packed to capacity, and the huge number of wounded poured into southern England. Again, the more seriously injured got priority for a hospital bed. Walking wounded—or at least those who could move somewhat—were sent all over northern England and Scotland.

Dr. Stephen Westman, a young surgeon in the German army, described the frustrations of treating newly wounded men in an advanced dressing station during the height of the Battle of the Somme. A physician aiding the injured in such circumstances could do little more than put temporary splints on fractured limbs and place temporary dressings on wounds. "This sounds comparatively simple, but to find a wound on a mud-covered and dirty soldier, especially at night and without any light, is not exactly easy." The doctor with his dirty hands had to grope for the wound and bandage it, all the while exposing his hands to blood that could not be washed off for hours or days.[25]

The expanded knowledge on how to prevent gas gangrene and other infections served little purpose when patients could not be treated promptly. And the surge of casualties during intense combat made that difficult throughout the war. In March 1918, in the face of the great German spring offensive, Dr. Harvey Cushing lamented that he was doing autopsies on men who had died shortly after arrival at his hospital suffering from forty-eight-hour infections. There had been no way to operate on them, and techniques developed in recent years could not be applied. In the summer of 1918 as the war neared its conclusion, Cushing continued to complain that soldiers with "stinking wounds" were arriving at base hospitals up to three days after being hurt.[26]

Other military needs—transporting ammunition to the front, for example—frequently clogged the transport systems set up to move the injured. Military trains, military barges, and trucks served to transport casualties away from the fighting, but they often proceeded at a snail's pace. A lucky British soldier might find himself carried rapidly by train to the large hospital at Boulogne and even home. If the hospital at Boulogne was filled, however, that same Tommy might spend days on a hospital train as it traveled on to find a place for him at Le Touquet, Rouen, or Le Havre. Reaching the latter meant a trip of 200 miles.

A shortage of ambulances hindered the evacuation of American wounded during the Meuse-Argonne campaign. Medical authorities had wrongly calculated that American casualties would have to travel no more than twenty miles. As it turned out, many injured doughboys needed emergency transportation to carry them much farther. French sightseeing buses had to be pressed into service to close the gap.

The experience of Lieutenant John Glubb in the spring of 1917 shows the agony a hitch in the system could create. He received an initial operation for his severe facial wound in a casualty clearing station near Arras and went quickly to England. En route, he discovered that his wound had become infected. He required sophisticated facial surgery, but there was no room at the English hospital specializing in facial repairs. He was sent, infection and all, to a regular London facility. For three months, he received "no medical attention," and only in November 1917 did he reach the hospital in Kent where Gillies was caring effectively for such casualties.[27]

The Allied blockade and the consequent pressures on the German economy created a special set of difficulties for German physicians. Effective treatment for gas casualties required a complete change of clothing and equipment, but this was often impossible. By 1918, doctors had only flimsy crepe paper bandages to cover wounds. In place of cotton wool, there was only a kind of cellulose paper, which one military physician recalled "in no time got soaked with blood and pus and just dissolved into a wet and stinking mass." Surgical gloves were no longer available, and even soap was in short supply. With only "sand-soap" (a mixture of three parts sand to one part soap) to scrub his hands before and after an operation, a surgeon had to risk his own health in treating a dirty and infected wound. When German forces overran British positions in the spring of 1918, doctors were astonished to find "crate upon crate of dressing material, bandages by the thousand, real cotton wool and masses of gauze."[28]

MILITARY DOCTORS

All the belligerents needed physicians desperately for the front, and governments pulled large numbers of doctors from civilian practices into the military. More than half the physicians in the British Isles (14,000 out of a total of 25,000) were mobilized. In Germany, the government made an even greater call for physicians' services: Almost 80 percent of Germany's 33,000 doctors were called into the military. The pace of medical practice in dealing with battlefield casualties went beyond most physicians' peacetime experience. Harvey Cushing, the pioneer neurosurgeon, noted in August 1917 that he now did eight operations daily rather than the single one that was his norm in civilian life.[29]

A young medical student like Stephen Westman, serving in the German army's infantry, was transformed into a junior surgeon in 1916. He was given additional training in large, rear-area hospitals where there were "real university classes in clinical medicine, surgery and many other subjects" and whose faculty included some of the country's most eminent specialists. But the pressing needs of the service moved him along quickly to treat the wounded in a hospital train and then in the front lines.[30]

Much of military medicine for a frontline physician consisted of routine activities to promote the health and combat efficiency of his unit. This meant checking for trench foot, assuring that latrines were well situated and covered regularly with lime, and holding a daily sick call ("sick parade" in British parlance). A physician had the authority to excuse a man from his duties. Consequently, the military hierarchy imbued medical officers with a sense of obligation to their unit, not the individual before them.

The army expected military doctors to guard vigorously against malingering. Most did so in a way that led the men in the ranks to see them as part of the disciplinary structure. One British physician declared that meeting the military doctor's first duty of maintaining "the discipline and morale of his unit" made it necessary "that the health of individuals may have to be sacrificed temporarily, even permanently." Another noted that he had to prove to himself that the man before him was still able to do his duty. Thus, as a military doctor, he was pushed by the military to adopt "an attitude of mind guaranteed to ruin the same physician in the shortest time possible in any other place on earth."[31]

Military medicine in moments of combat put a physician's life at risk. Medical officers assigned as battalion or regimental surgeons faced the same artillery barrages, gas bombardments, and aerial attacks as front-line soldiers. Even rear areas were dangerous. As early as 1915, German bombing raids killed and maimed British doctors and their volunteer American colleagues in base camps along the English Channel. By the final two years of the war, German bombing raids on the Ypres salient and rear-area concentrations like the base at Étaples regularly put the lives of medical personnel at risk. On May 30, 1918, German bombs struck No. 3 Canadian Stationary hospital at Doullens. An entire surgical team of two doctors and three senior nurses lost their lives.

Eighteen hundred German medical officers died during the course of the war; so too did nearly a thousand of their British counterparts.[32] Most of those fatalities resulted from doctors working in the front lines. Often wounds were too serious to permit a victim to be carried back to the trench line, and heroic physicians cared for soldiers in no man's land. The only British officers to win the Victoria Cross twice were two military doctors decorated for bravery in World War I. One of them had first received the honor in the Boer War; the other got his nation's highest decoration on two separate occasions between 1914 and 1918.

Captain Gideon Walker, medical officer of the Second Battalion, Scots Guards, personified the self-sacrificing military doctor. In the fighting at Passchendaele in October 1917, Walker accompanied the unit's stretcher bearers on to the battlefield drawing praise from a nearby machine gunner for being "in the thick of it." At the close of the following month, Walker perished in the fighting at Cambrai. To his friend Cushing, who found him "a brave lad," the British doctor's death in combat came as no surprise: "I've long expected it," the American physician recorded in his diary.[33]

Dr. James Dunn, Second Battalion, Royal Welch Fusiliers, performed in the same way. During an attack in the spring of 1917, a member of his battalion noted how Dunn "had been wandering about no-man's land attending to the wounded and doing what he could for them." Under intense fire, Dunn's display of bravery led this observer to wonder about his fate: "How he didn't get riddled was a mystery." Dunn was forced to leave his elite unit, after two and a half years' service, only after he was wounded in a gas attack.[34]

DISEASE

Doctors' ability to control infectious disease among soldiers stands as one the great medical successes of the war. In the American Civil War, 24 men became sick for every man wounded, and 2 men died of disease for every one killed by enemy action. The British in the Boer War fared only slightly better: 13 sick for every man wounded and just under 2 men killed by disease for every combat death. A typical soldier on the western front received fifteen immunizations. The British army on the western front saw only 1.3 men sick for each one wounded; ten times as many Britons in uniform died as a result of combat than perished from disease. Inoculations put diseases like cholera that had traditionally been the scourge of armies under control.[35]

Commanders on both sides of the battle line viewed sexually transmitted disease as a threat to the effectiveness of their units. General John Pershing, the commander of the AEF, took a punitive attitude toward both soldiers who contracted venereal disease and their unit commanders as well. He rejected a French suggestion that houses of licensed and inspected prostitutes be made officially available to American forces. Instead, the threat of harsh punishment for an infected American soldier combined with effective treatment centers close to the front held the numbers down. Only one American soldier in a thousand was infected in September 1918, and a survey done in the summer after the Armistice showed that 96 percent of diseased soldiers had contracted their ailments before entering military service.[36]

German military doctors had comparable success. The image of German troops being led astray by loose French and Belgian women was a potent one. Concerned delegates to the German Reichstag predicted hordes of diseased soldiers returning home. In reality, troops in rear areas of the western front suffered from venereal disease at no more than peacetime levels. Soldiers at the front contracted sexually transmitted disease less frequently than soldiers in peacetime.[37]

The great exception to medicine's successes against mass disease was the great influenza epidemic of 1918. Mild versions of the flu appeared earlier in the year, but the full force of the epidemic hit in the summer and fall. Striking military men and civilians alike, it killed approximately 21 million throughout the world in the course of the year. There was nothing in the medical books of the time to help identify the ailment, nor were there the sulfa drugs and antibiotics of the latter part of the century with which to treat it. Puzzled physicians encountered formerly strong and healthy individuals suddenly afflicted with high temperatures, headaches, difficulty in breathing, and minds pushed to the point of delirium. When the flu developed into pneumonia, death was likely to follow.

Doctors on both sides of the front tried with only limited success to control the epidemic. German military physicians reported instances of an entire army corps in which only half the soldiers were fit for duty. Aerial squadrons were grounded when the majority of the pilots and ground crewmen were hit by the disease. Influenza threatened physicians as well. Only rest and a measure of good luck offered the chance for recovery, and one German military doctor recalled how he passed through the danger period with "six aspirins and half a bottle of brandy."[38]

More than half a million Americans, civilians and military, died from influenza and its complications. In the American armed forces at home, the fall of 1918 saw so severe an epidemic that all draft calls and most training came to a halt. One out of every 4 military men in the United States caught the disease; the flu developed into pneumonia for 1 out of every 24; 1 out of every 67 men wearing a uniform died. Recent recruits from rural backgrounds appeared most susceptible. At Camp Sherman in Ohio where most of the soldiers were recent draftees, 4 of every 10 men fell ill in a two-week period starting in late September. More than 1,100 men, 3 percent of the post's population, lost their lives.[39]

American forces now fighting in large numbers in Europe tried to contend with the flu and the strain it put on the medical system. At one base hospital located near the Argonne Forest, many of those infected were so close to death upon arriving that the mortality rate for pneumonia cases escalated above 80 percent. The ravages of influenza appeared most strikingly in the ships carrying American troops across the Atlantic. Troop transports with infected men aboard became breeding grounds for the spread of the disease. When the liner *Leviathan* docked at Brest on October 7, it carried almost 200 dead and dying members of the 57th Pioneer Regiment. On both sides of the Atlantic, doctors and nurses complained of their inability to treat the disease effectively. The sight of strikingly healthy young men struck down and dying within two days appears in many accounts. So too do complaints about the lack of beds—and the lack of coffins.

THE CARE RECEIVED: REHABILITATION

Medical systems were able to cope with some of the most badly wounded, and severe injuries did not invariably bring death. Thus, tens of thousands of former soldiers, maimed during the conflict, faced a future without limbs or without eyesight. The belligerent powers had to develop programs to return physically wrecked human beings to normal—or at least civilian—life. The German system can serve to show how Britain, France, and the United States also tried to cope with this dilemma.

Blind soldiers and amputees had the most radical adjustments to make. But the blind made up only a small percentage of those who survived their wounds. Injuries to the head normally killed the victim, and Germany had fewer than 3,000 blind veterans by the war's close. There were many more amputees. Those who lost a limb most commonly experienced the amputation of one leg. Six out of every 100 wounded German soldiers, almost 45,000, suffered such a loss; another 3 percent, 21,000, suffered the loss of a single arm. The loss of two legs was far less common, and the loss of both arms exceedingly rare (only 2 out of 10,000 wounded).[40]

Specialists in orthopedic medicine, of whom there were few before the war, had an unprecedented demand for their services. When the development of artificial limbs became a national priority, a contest sponsored by the German Association of Engineers to develop an artificial arm drew eighty-two entries. By war's end, German orthopedists and engineers working together made thirty kinds of artificial arms and fifty kinds of artificial legs available to the maimed.

Rehabilitation involved learning to walk with crutches or to use the artificial limbs of the time. Such a change in lifestyle meant a continual confrontation with pain and fatigue. The German army attempted to boost the recovery of those who had lost arms by presenting them with a pamphlet of advice. Written by an individual who had only one arm from birth, it suggested such practical measures as wearing boots rather than shoes and using one's mouth and knees to aid in dressing.

NOTES

1. Robert Whalen, *Bitter Wounds: German Victims of the Great War, 1914–1939* (Ithaca, N.Y.: Cornell University Press, 1984), 39–40; Lyn Macdonald, *Roses of No Man's Land* (London: Michael Joseph, 1980), 303.

2. For the official parliamentary figures, see Leonard V. Smith, *Between Mutiny and Obedience: The Case of the French Fifth Infantry Division during World War I* (Princeton: Princeton University Press, 1994), 126, n. 7. The grim figures suggesting a high level of deaths for wounded men while under French medical care are found in Alistair Horne, *The Price of Glory: Verdun, 1916* (New York: Harper and Row, 1962), 66; also, Jean-Jacques Becker, *The Great War and the French People*, trans. Arnold Pomerans (Leamington Spa, Eng.: Berg, 1985), 330–32, and Macdonald, *Roses*, 132–33.

3. Quoted in Macdonald, *Roses*, 133.

4. Edward M. Coffman, *The War to End All Wars: The American Military Experience in World War I* (New York: Oxford University Press, 1968), 363.

5. Quoted in Malcolm Brown, *Tommy Goes to War* (London: J.M. Dent, 1978), 165–68.

6. Quoted in James H. Hallas, *The Doughboy War: The American Expeditionary Force in World War I* (Boulder, Colo.: Lynne Rienner Publishers, 2000), 280.

7. Quoted in Lyn Macdonald, *1914–1918: Voices and Images of the Great War* (London: Michael Joseph, 1988), 223.

8. Quoted in Hallas, *Doughboy War*, 153–54.

9. Quoted in Andrew Bamji, "Facial Surgery: The Patient's Experience," in *Facing Armageddon: The First World War Experienced*, ed. Hugh Cecil and Peter Liddle (London: Leo Cooper, 1996), 492–93.

10. Quoted in Hallas, *Doughboy War*, 167.

11. Quoted in Alistair Horne, *The Price of Glory: Verdun, 1916* (New York: Harper and Row, 1962), 65.

12. Harvey Cushing, *From a Surgeon's Journal, 1915–1918* (Boston: Little, Brown and Company, 1936), 313–14.

13. Quoted in Whalen, *Bitter Wounds*, 51.

14. Stephen Westman, M.D., F.R.C.S., *Surgeon with the Kaiser's Army* (London: William Kimber, 1968), 72–73.

15. Cushing, *Surgeon's Journal*, 202.

16. Quoted in Bamji, "Facial Surgery," in ed. Cecil and Liddle, *Facing Armageddon*, 496.

17. Quoted in Albert Palazzo, *Seeking Victory on the Western Front: The British Army and Chemical Warfare in World War I* (Lincoln, Nebr.: University of Nebraska Press, 2000), 42.

18. Ibid., 152.

19. Hallas, *Doughboy War*, 161.

20. L.F. Haber, *The Poisonous Cloud: Chemical Warfare in the First World War* (Oxford: Clarendon Press, 1986), 239–42.

21. Quoted in Hans Binneveld, *From Shell Shock to Combat Stress: A Comparative History of Military Psychiatry*, translated from the Dutch by John O'Kane (Amsterdam: Amsterdam University Press, 1997), 102.

22. Edward A. Strecker, "Military Psychiatry: World War I, 1917–1918," in *One Hundred Years of American Psychiatry*, ed. J.K. Hall et al. (New York: Columbia University Press, 1944), 389, 401.

23. Quoted in Macdonald, *Voices and Images*, 248–49.

24. Anthony Babington, *Shell-shock: A History of Changing Attitudes to War Neurosis* (London: Leo Cooper, 1997), 102.

25. Westman, *Surgeon*, 98–99.

26. Cushing, *Surgeon's Journal*, 313, 404.

27. Bamji, "Facial Surgery," in *Facing Armageddon*, ed. Cecil and Liddle, 493–94, 497.

28. Haber, *Poisonous Cloud*, 254; Westman, *Surgeon*, 159–60.

29. Noel Whiteside, "The British Population at War," in *Britain and the First World War*, ed. John Turner (London: Unwin Hyman, 1988), 88–90; Robert Weldon Whalen, *Bitter Wounds: German Victims of the Great War, 1914–1939* (Ithaca, N.Y.: Cornell University Press, 1984), 61; Cushing, *Surgeon's Journal*, 187.

30. Westman, *Surgeon*, 69–71, 81–85, 91–92.

31. Quoted in Keith Simpson, "Dr. James Dunn and Shell-shock," in *Facing Armageddon*, ed. Cecil and Liddle, 505.

32. Whalen, *Bitter Wounds*, 61; Ian Whitehead, "Not a Doctor's Work? The Role of the British Regimental Medical Officer in the Field," in *Facing Armageddon*, ed. Cecil and Liddle, 469.

33. Cushing, *Surgeon's Journal*, 224, 269.

34. Simpson, "Dr. James Dunn," in *Facing Armageddon*, ed. Cecil and Liddle, 502–6.

35. Geoffrey Noon, "The Treatment of Casualties in the Great War," in *British Fighting Methods in the Great War*, ed. Paddy Griffith (London: Frank Cass, 1996), 87–88.

36. Coffman, *War to End All Wars*, 80–81, 132–34.

37. Whalen, *Bitter Wounds*, 67.

38. Westman, *Surgeon*, 172–73.

39. Hallas, *Doughboy War*, 293; Coffman, *War to End All Wars*, 82.

40. Whalen, *Bitter Wounds*, 54–57.

7

Women and the Military

Females in all the belligerent countries entered the war bound by a range of peacetime social restrictions. Women of the middle class and upper class rarely worked, and their opportunities for higher education, especially professional study, were limited. Travel for young women took place only under the watchful eye of their parents or other responsible adults. But many of those women wanted to play a role in the war, and the intense and expanding nature of the conflict made it necessary for governments to listen to their wishes. Shortages of manpower opened the way, but so did the view that women could bring valued talents to the war effort.

Any consideration of women and the armed forces begins with the military nurse. She and her auxiliaries played the most predictable role, and the one all societies found most acceptable. Countries like Britain and France had brought female nurses into their military systems around the start of the century. They now recruited many more for wartime service. With the nurse's well-defined position as subordinate and helper to the physician, she did not overtly challenge what the era thought a woman's work should be. Nonetheless, these skilled and experienced women played a larger role in the lives of millions than ever before. The circumstances of war sometimes gave them responsibilities far beyond what they found available in peacetime. And nurses had the best chance of any women to approach the fighting line and to share the experiences of the combat soldier.

But other women saw service. Despite the neutrality of the United

States, almost 10,000 American women began assisting the war effort of Britain, France, and other members of the Allied coalition starting in 1914. British women flocked to their own nation's service in even greater numbers. Starting in 1917, more than 16,000 American women served abroad as part of the American Expeditionary Force or as members of various auxiliary organizations that worked with the military.

The first women to attach themselves to the military services were determined volunteers. From the first days of the war, women's organizations sprang up in Britain, France, and Germany to offer direct assistance to the fighting forces. Affluent women dominated the membership rolls of such organizations, because they could serve without pay. Working-class women were unable even to afford the cost of the uniforms these formations adopted.

Prominent individuals founded hospitals and put them at the disposal of military authorities. Groups like Britain's First Aid Nursing Yeomanry, for example, took on a variety of tasks. As the war went on, Allied governments accepted the services of civilian women from a variety of backgrounds to work near the fighting front: as clerks, cooks, ambulance drivers, canteen workers, and, in a particularly large number, telephone operators. In Britain and later the United States, women served—if only in a limited way—as actual members of the armed forces. France dealt more cautiously with the issue of women in military service and, at the close of the war, Germany was still preparing to take the step of placing women formally in the armed forces.

MILITARY NURSES AND THEIR AUXILIARIES

All the principal belligerents on the western front drew on large numbers of nurses to serve in military hospitals, sometimes well behind the front, sometimes in closer proximity to the fighting. Nurses had been an official part of the British army since the Boer War in Queen Alexandra's Imperial Military Nursing Service. As war approached, it had 300 experienced professionals on its rolls. In addition, nearly 3,000 nurses were enrolled with the Territorial Army, the British equivalent of the American National Guard. By the time of the Armistice, approximately 23,000 women served as nurses for the British military. Another 15,000 served as nurses' aides—the VADs—trained by organizations like the Red Cross to work alongside Britain's professional nurses treating military patients.[1] (The VADs took their name from the Volunteer Aid Detachments formed before the war to help care for wounded members of the Territorial Army.)

The United States formed the Army Nurse Corps (ANC) in 1901; the Navy Nurse Corps was organized seven years later. The ANC expanded from 400 nurses at the start of the war to more than 21,000 by its con-

World War I nurse. © Underwood & Underwood/CORBIS.

clusion. Thus, more than 21,000 American nurses were to serve in World War I, half of them with the military in Europe. The expansion in the Army Nurse Corps was paralleled by the growth of the Navy Nurse Corps, which went from 160 to 1,400 members.[2]

The French army began to use Red Cross volunteer nurses in Morocco in 1907, trained a small number of military nurses in the years following, and planned to call up 23,000 Red Cross nurses in the event of a future conflict. Eventually more than 63,000 served. Germany enlisted female nurses for the first time with the outbreak of the war in 1914, and, along with nursing assistants, their numbers eventually totaled 92,000.[3]

Intensive training courses increased the number of nurses. In France, thousands of women took hastily organized classes that concentrated on how to dress wounds. In Britain, enthusiastic and numerous amateurs—the VADs—who volunteered for service in military hospitals augmented the supply of professionally trained nurses. VADs attracted young women of affluent families like Vera Brittain, the most famous of them.

Training at the 1st London General Hospital, Vera Brittain found herself putting in nearly thirteen hours a day. This former Oxford University student from a sheltered upper middle-class family in northern England had never seen an adult male's naked body. She now found herself dealing with wards filled with mutilated soldiers. Brittain recalled that tasks from dressing horrible wounds to scrubbing bed linen "had for us in those early days a sacred glamour which redeemed it equally from tedium and disgust."[4] Like Brittain, VADs took on more and more of the responsibilities of nursing professionals as the war went on.

Women volunteered for a variety of reasons. Some were personal, as one French nurse put it clearly when she wrote that it was her first opportunity to seem important. "A young girl, in ordinary life, is nothing or next to nothing. For the first time I was going to be someone. . . . I would count in the world."[5] But the call of patriotism was strong in each of the belligerent countries. German nurses spoke vehemently of their desire to be "off to the field" to serve the fatherland: They echoed the enthusiasm of the young male volunteers who enlisted in the war's first weeks and found their baptism of fire at the First Battle of Ypres. As one woman put it, "[I]t was a day of honour for us all: the F2 was the first hospital train off to the front . . . into the line of fire."[6]

In their diaries and memoirs, German nurses suggested one of the attractions of serving near the front was to escape from the stultifying and oppressive routine of peacetime nursing. Especially during the strained circumstances of the war's last two years, German nurses asserted their confidence, criticizing and boycotting doctors they found incompetent. They stood firm until "even the surgeon had to capitulate before the nurses' caps."[7]

The special horrors of the western front became evident to nurses in the first weeks of fighting. A British military nurse cared for wounded from the Battle of the Marne who arrived in Le Mans. Many had wounds that already developed gangrene. "They were nearly all shrapnel-shell wounds—more ghastly than anything I have ever seen or smelt; the Mauser wounds of the Boer War were pinpricks compared with them."[8]

As the war went on, nursing developed a routine resembling combat service in the front lines. Much of the time was spent in regular housekeeping chores. But the onset of a major battle changed everything. First off, it brought more work than anyone could imagine. The arrival of "convoys" of wounded from the battlefield required a nurse in an evacuation hospital close to the front, or a base hospital in the rear, to work as long as two days without a break. "The rush," as American hospital personnel described such episodes, took place in medical systems on both sides of the front. And nurses everywhere experienced what one American nurse's aide remembered: "Hundreds upon hundreds of wounded poured in like a rushing torrent. . . . The crowded, twisted bodies, the screams and groans, made one think of the old engravings in Dante's *Inferno*."[9] An American nurse described caring for the newly wounded during the German spring offensive in 1918: "They came much too fast for us, and within fifteen minutes were standing twenty deep around the dressing-table. As the hours went by we ceased to think. We worked through the night until dawn."[10]

The rigid hospital hierarchy of civilian life and regular military service broke down in such circumstances. Nurses—and even nurses' aides—took on increased responsibility as doctors found themselves confined to surgical work. A French nurse in 1915 took the duties of an anesthetist for as many as twenty-one operations a day. An American nurse described what frantic hours in a doctor-nurse operating team at a casualty clearing station meant for the nurse: "no mere handling of instruments and sponges, but sewing and tying up and putting in drains while the doctor takes the next piece of shell out of another place."[11] The fierce fighting preceding the Armistice meant that the formal end of hostilities on the western front had little significance for nurses. They still found themselves busy caring for a horde of wounded soldiers from the final days of combat.

The influenza epidemic that swept through the military ranks in the closing months of the war created an additional burden for nurses. They were already straining to care for masses of the wounded, and now they were confronted with masses of disease victims. There was little to be done for those infected except to keep them warm and provide them with fluids. The incontinence of many patients meant nurses were kept busy changing beds and washing the stricken soldiers, many of whom could not be saved. "They called it influenza," one British VAD recalled, "but it seemed to us to be some frightful plague. . . . It was so near the end. They'd gone through all that frightful thing, and then they couldn't go home."[12]

Some nurses had the opportunity to serve in a casualty clearing station close to the actual fighting. Considered to be a "plum" assignment by American nurses, these rare openings attracted ten volunteers for every slot. Two hundred American nurses received decorations for bravery under fire from the American, British, and French authorities.

But many nurses found only drudgery in out-of-the-way places. Some American nurses were assigned to French facilities where American patients as well as French casualties were being treated. They found themselves in "lonely and remote villages where living conditions were primitive and social customs strange" where they "scrubbed floors in dirty and dilapidated French buildings or in rude wooden barracks, set up wards, made beds and nursed contagious patients."[13]

The relationship between a wounded soldier and a nurse was charged with emotion. Wartime propaganda paintings showed the sharp contrast between the warrior—now dependent and helpless—and the caring woman who hovered over him. The picture of the angelic nurse radiating concern for the wounded man was compelling but unrealistic. Nurses recorded more graphic impressions of filthy and maimed soldiers with malodorous battle dressings coming into the sheltered world of the military hospital. Encountering soldiers suffering from shell shock, nurses found themselves caring for men in extreme mental distress. Such men wept uncontrollably, and many could not control their bodily functions. "They were very pathetic, these shellshocked boys," one British nurse recalled, "and a lot of them were very sensitive about the fact they were incontinent. . . . I used to give them a bedpan in the locker beside them and keep it as quiet as possible. Poor fellows, they were so embarrassed—especially the better-class men."[14]

The emotional link between the caregiver and her charge sometimes reflected the difference in their ages as well as the soldier's helplessness. German nurses recalled caring for the wounded in the "infants' ward" where all the patients were only eighteen years old. These women shouldered the psychological burden of hearing dying youngsters calling for their mothers with a final breath.

Nurses sometimes shared the danger of the battle zone. By 1917, German, British, and French nurses served close to the front where they ran the risk of being struck by enemy artillery fire. British and French nurses in rear areas perished from enemy air attacks. British nurses ran substantial risks, because their duties often took them on sea voyages where submarines were a threat. A total of 195 British nurses perished during the conflict; 36 were the victims of enemy action.[15] Although no American nurses died of combat wounds, three were wounded by aerial bombs or shellfire. One of the duties of nurses that wartime propaganda omitted to mention was maintaining calm among panicking and helpless wounded men when a hospital came under enemy fire.

The perils of wartime extended beyond the danger of combat. Proximity to the sick and wounded combined with physical exhaustion to expose nurses to a variety of diseases. Treating septic wounds meant that the slightest cut in a caregiver's hand would infect her as well. American medical authorities in France set up 2 hospitals, out of a total of 133, to care specifically for nurses who had fallen seriously ill. Approximately 120 American nurses died overseas and some 180 more at home. Most of the Americans were felled by influenza or typhus.[16]

German nurses had special experiences that set them apart from nurses in the Allied countries. They frequently found themselves transferred from the western front to eastern Europe and the battle zone facing the Russians. There diseases like malaria and typhus took a deadly toll of noncombatants and soldiers alike. The growing shortages in a blockaded Germany made hospital work especially grim. As one nurse wrote in her diary, "We are supposed to care for up to 300 wounded here, but there are absolutely no supplies! In the morning helpful soldiers found us some mattress ticking. We began by tearing it up for bandages, since there was no material for dressings. Later we took down the curtains and made bandages of them. Our charges are starving, and all we can give them is dry army bread."[17]

Some nurses in all of the belligerent countries had extended, personal contact with enemy soldiers. When wounded German troops entered Allied hospitals, they occupied beds in separate wards from the other patients. Allied soldiers got similar treatment in German hospitals. But nurses found themselves assigned regularly to care for these men from across the battle line. The situation gave rise to wartime propaganda featuring imaginary and melodramatic events in the hospital. One story recounted how a German deliberately crushed a nurse's hand so that she could no longer minister to any of the hospital's inmates.

The reality was less colorful but more humane. Nurses put aside their patriotic feelings, treated enemy casualties with the full set of skills they possessed, and often developed a close personal relationship with the captured soldiers under their care. One American nurse recalled that a recovered German soldier, assigned duty as an orderly in her hospital, had a singular role in comforting the American soldiers who lay in pain under their joint care.

The restricted role women occupied limited the vital work nurses performed. American and British nurses had the ambiguous status of officers without formal military rank. The system worked smoothly in the British system, but American nurses found their status troublesome. They could give orders to enlisted men concerning the medical treatment of soldiers under their care. On the other hand, they could not command obedience regarding the conditions and cleanliness of the hospitals and others facilities where they worked. Angry confrontations between nurses and the ward sergeants who were formally responsible for medical surroundings occurred regularly. The former chief nurse at Boston's Peter Bent Brigham Hospital, serving in France as the chief nurse of a base hospital, lamented her limited authority: "I never should do army nursing from choice. . . . I feel much like the fly that has accepted the spider's invitation and finds he can't escape."[18]

American nurses could tap a number of special sources of support. Many of them served in hospital units recruited intact from civilian universities and medical centers. Thus, they worked daily with fellow nurses whom they had known, often for an extended period of time, in civilian life. Although the need for nurses in the AEF meant that some came directly from nursing school, most were highly experienced professionals with medical specialties and even a background as nursing supervisors.

Nurses constituted the majority of American women who served with the AEF or in auxiliaries attached to it. The image of a privileged society lady who matures by serving her country in wartime loomed large in American press accounts of women at war. But the American woman in her country's service was more likely the tireless professional in the nurse's cap and uniform. One recent study found that "the vast majority of AEF servicewomen were wage earners, white, literate, lower-middle-class, and often self-supporting.[19]

American soldiers in Europe also received treatment from some 300 reconstruction aides, while another 1,700 of these women worked in hospitals in the United States. Trained either as physical or occupational therapists, they offered assistance to wounded, sick, and mentally disturbed members of the armed forces. These skilled women provided services ranging from massage and instruction in using artificial arms and legs to teaching crocheting, weaving, and basic literacy.[20]

WOMEN IN UNIFORM

No country moved quickly to put women into formal military service. By 1917 manpower shortages pushed Britain into leading the way. Auxiliaries to the army, then the navy, and finally the air force came into existence during the last two years of hostilities. Women from the upper and middle classes were welcomed into the WRNS (the Wrens) to augment the navy and into the WRAF to free men in the air force for combat duties. The army equivalent, the WAAC, soon got a reputation as the one auxiliary that opened the door to women from the working class. By the war's close, more than 100,000 women were serving in these adjuncts to the army, navy, and air force.[21]

British women volunteered in numbers that far outstripped the places available. A typical aspirant for a slot in the WAAC submitted an application accompanied by personal recommendations and went before a medical board composed of female physicians. A recruit who had reached the age of eighteen was eligible for service in Britain; at the age of twenty, she could be sent abroad. She received about a month's military training before being sent to a rear area assignment in France. In Britain, some WAACs were permitted to live at home. WAACs were enrolled starting in March 1917, and the following month the first of them arrived for duty in France. Members of the WAAC filled assignments as clerks, cooks, and telephone operators for the most part, but some went on to such "unladylike" work as servicing army vehicles.

A woman in one of Britain's armed services was subject to military discipline, and she faced the dangers of war. The contract each signed upon enlistment threatened her with fines and imprisonment if she violated its terms. Members of these organizations were killed and badly wounded when the Germans bombed rear areas in France. But change went only so far. British military custom dictated that leaders of the women's services not hold a commission from the king, and all ranks were deliberately different from those of men in the military. Women filling the role of officers held the title "administrators." Women who performed the duties of noncommissioned officers got the title of "forewoman" or "assistant forewoman." Enlisted women were "workers."

Whereas administrators received a set payment each year, enlisted women under them received compensation depending upon the job they performed. Thus, a clerk received more than a woman working in a military kitchen, and a WAAC who could qualify as an automobile mechanic was paid more than twice what a cook, waitress, or laundress received. All served with the understanding that they were releasing a man to go up to the front lines.

The United States provided a more reluctant response. The army refused to enlist women, but Secretary of the Navy Josephus Daniels saw no reason why enlisted clerks (yeomen) in the navy's ranks had to be male. Because so few men had the requisite skills in taking dictation, women could fill a pressing need. In March 1917, on the eve of American participation in the war, the American navy began to enlist "yeomanettes," whose number eventually reached 11,000.[22] A bureaucratic dilemma arose because navy regulations barred women from serving at sea while those same regulations dictated that all yeomen had to be assigned to a ship. The navy's yeomanettes were assigned, at least on paper, to tugs that had sunk in the Potomac River.

With the onset of heavy fighting in the summer of 1918, the United States Marine Corps found itself short of trained men and followed the navy in calling for women to volunteer. In New York City alone, 2,000 volunteers appeared. In the end, the Marines enrolled about 300 women, selecting only a tiny percentage of those who applied. Marine recruiters eliminated most applicants with a ferocious test of their secretarial skills.[23] Although barred from serving on ships at sea, females in the Marine Corps and navy held ranks equal to men in the same military specialties, and in the navy some rose to become senior petty officers. At the close of the war, all became eligible for veterans' benefits.

Female service members had to pass a physical examination as well as a test of their office skills. Unlike male recruits, women received no basic training. Many of them reported to their office assignments the day after they were sworn into service. Similarly, the military had no living accommodations for women, and they had to use their own energies, helped by a military housing allowance, to find a roof over their heads. The typical woman sailor or Marine filled a clerical position in the United States, although some worked as messengers. One woman Marine had the important but disheartening job of writing letters of condolence on behalf of the Marine Corps Commandant to families that had lost a relative in the war.

The Germans proved almost totally recalcitrant about placing women in uniform. Only in the closing months of the war did they consider a

Women in the United States Marine Corps. Courtesy
of the National Archives.

female auxiliary to the Signal Corps. The conflict ended before the plan
could come into operation. The French government and military were
no more flexible.

CIVILIANS SERVING THE MILITARY

Civilian women involved themselves with the military forces from the
start of the war. French women set up canteens at railroad stations to
provide some comforts to the troops leaving for the front and the
wounded making their way to hospitals in the rear. Individual women,
often of prominent social background, set up hospitals and other organizations, then offered them to the armed forces. At Dunkirk, Britain's
Duchess of Sutherland set up a hospital within three months after the
start of hostilities. An organization of British physical therapists to aid
the recovery of the wounded, the Military Massage Corps, was founded
at the war's beginning. Its original complement of 50 masseuses grew to
2,000 by the Armistice. When the British armed forces refused the serv-

ices of female physicians, several went to the western front anyway to treat French and Belgian patients. Individual Americans set up canteens behind the lines and volunteered to drive ambulances. Some formed private organizations to look after refugees and to rehabilitate blinded French soldiers.

Women's organizations that offered the chance to wear a military-style uniform appealed to many in Britain. The first two years of the war produced, among others, the Women's Legion, the Women's Emergency Corps, and the Women's Volunteer Force. The Women's Volunteer Force, formed in September 1914, was intended to protect noncombatants in the event of a German invasion. The Women's Legion, founded by the Marchioness of Londonderry in July 1915, served a more practical purpose. Its Military Cookery and Motor Transport sections offered useful help to the armed forces, and these women quickly received tasks to perform.

At the same time, the sight of women in something resembling a uniform stirred furious opposition to this blurring of gender lines. Letters to British newspapers took these ladies to task for "making themselves and, what is more important, the King's uniform, ridiculous." They should, instead, "put on sunbonnets and print frocks and go and make hay or pick fruit or make jam, . . . the thousand and one things that women can do to help."[24]

The French women who served as war godmothers (*marraines de guerre*) provided a unique but more conventional form of support for the military. They became pen pals for soldiers at the front, especially those from French territory occupied by the Germans. In lieu of their real relatives, the godmothers offered French soldiers moral support through the mail. The godson (*filleul*) often had an invitation to visit his godmother on leave.

As early as 1915, the pinch of military losses raised the question of having French women provide direct assistance to the armed forces. By 1917, some spokesmen for public opinion, pointing to the British precedent, even called for women in uniform. Such a campaign had no impact on official policy.

Young women did find themselves invited to sign on as civilian employees of the army starting in 1916. The new strains on French military manpower inflicted by the fighting at Verdun opened such opportunities. But the typical woman in the service of the military remained firmly identified as a civilian. She swore no oath to the country; she could leave her position at any time. Placed in kitchens and clothing shops, her work differed little from a peacetime occupation. If she wanted to enter an army office to work as a secretary or clerk, she found such positions largely barred to her.

Only in 1917 did the situation change. The government needed to

American women feed soldiers at the front. Courtesy of the Hoover Institution Archives.

place women in remote locales and to keep their services even though it could not pay them competitive wages. Policy now required a woman willing to work for the military to sign a three-month contract. This forbade her from leaving her job. Even more of a departure was the government's willingness to let a small number of women, other than nurses, enter the combat zone. These were the drivers of the Woman's Transport Corps.

A woman who entered this organization—there were only 300 in all—served as a chauffeur for army officers, as a motorcycle messenger, and as a driver transporting wounded soldiers. She probably found herself welcomed by some battalions as a valuable addition to their staff, but elsewhere the reception was likely to be frigid. A sign of her ambiguous status was the official requirement, often evaded in practice, that she provide her own food and clothing. In reality, units at the front bent the rules to make the work of such women easier.

After the United States entered the war, numbers of civilian women made their way to the front. Recruited by such organizations as the Red Cross, American Telephone and Telegraph Company, and the YMCA, thousands served as canteen hostesses, clerks, translators, and most frequently as telephone operators (the "Hello Girls"). All these women wore uniforms. The telephone operators had formally been sworn into service.

"Hello Girls" along with workers who had merely signed contracts to work for the army were expected like soldiers to obey military authorities. Nonetheless, the uncertainty and hesitation of army authorities—in contrast to those of the American navy—kept them from being formal members of the American Expeditionary Force. Unlike their sisters in the navy, they received no veterans' benefits with the war's conclusion.

The role of canteen hostess brought only a small departure from a woman's role at home in peacetime. America's YMCA hostesses were intended to maintain the soldier's tie with the world he had left across the Atlantic. These women were expected to provide a comfortable resting place for soldiers, to give them refreshments and a friendly female partner with whom to talk. Implicitly, they were to keep soldiers away from sordid sexual encounters with French women and the accompanying threat of venereal disease. Their own social lives and free time were closely supervised, and almost all found themselves under a hierarchy of male officials.

No special skills were required for a canteen worker, who spent much of her time washing dishes and handing out donuts. The donut, easily made in large quantities, replaced labor-intensive treats like fudge and caramels that required more time and effort than overwhelmed canteen workers could muster. The young women, often educated and affluent, who made up the majority of these canteen workers, were grossly overqualified for the tasks they carried out.

In marked contrast, hundreds of clerks and telephone operators whom the United States Army brought to France in 1918 had crucial talents that the military needed. Many army officers had doubts about bringing American women across the Atlantic to help run a complex communications network. General John Pershing, the commander of the AEF, decided that the need was pressing, especially for telephone operators. The inefficient French system brought intolerable delay to the transmission of important military messages, and bilingual American operators, under the control of the AEF, offered a solution.

The first group of thirty-three operators arrived in March 1918. They had been recruited following a newspaper campaign by the American Telephone and Telegraph Company to which more than 7,000 had replied. Most of the operators had no experience with telephone equipment, and the company chose them on the basis of their language skills. They received a month's training in switchboard operations along with some military drilling and an introduction to the procedures of the United States Army Signal Corps. The original number soon swelled to a total of almost 500. Approximately half crossed the Atlantic to serve with the AEF.[25]

American "Hello Girls" in France. Courtesy of the National Archives.

Once in France, operators were dispatched to seventy-five locations. Military officers remarked upon the morale boost provided by hearing a friendly female with an American accent when they used the telephone. But the operators contributed in numerous ways to the Allied victory. When a small number of operators were required to serve near the front during the St. Mihiel offensive in September 1918, all 225 of the women on duty in France volunteered.[26] Throughout their service, the "Hello Girls" helped to transmit sensitive military messages efficiently. The military also relied upon their discretion. For example, some telephone operators had advance information about the date and time of the Armistice in November 1918. They also provided small services that lingered in their memories to become the stuff of family legends after the war. An operator remembered that General John Pershing had called her once to verify the time of the day.

The need to house and supervise female clerks and female telephone operators created a novel problem for the leaders of the AEF. They solved it by placing these women under the control of the YWCA. The officials of that organization set up residence halls for American women in France, and they provided chaperones and parietal rules that resembled those in a college sorority.

The most skilled women were not always welcomed by the armed forces. When women physicians in the United States asked to serve in the war, they received a flat rejection from the War Department. Supported by the women's suffrage movement in the United States, a group of women doctors formed their own hospital unit whose entire staff—from surgeons to technicians and ambulance drivers—was female. It received a warm reception from the French government.

NOTES

1. Anne Summers, *Angels and Citizens: British Women as Military Nurses, 1854–1914* (London: Routledge and Kegan Paul, 1988), 253; Trevor Wilson, *The Myriad Faces of War: Britain and the Great War, 1914–1918* (Cambridge, Eng.: Polity Press, 1986), 711.

2. Mary T. Sarnecky, Colonel, USA (Ret.), *A History of the U.S. Army Nurse Corps* (Philadelphia: University of Pennsylvania Press, 1999), 91–92, 122; Lettie Gavin, *American Women in World War I: They Also Served* (Niwot, Colo.: University Press of Colorado, 1997), 66–67, n. 1.

3. Margaret H. Darrow, *French Women and the First World War: War Stories of the Home Front* (Oxford: Berg, 2000), 137, 141; Regina Schulte, "The Sick Warrior's Sister: Nursing during the First World War," in *Gender Relations in German History: Power, Agency and Experience from the Sixteenth to the Twentieth Century*, ed. Lynn Abrams and Elizabeth Harvey (Durham, N.C.: Duke University Press, 1997), 123–24.

4. Vera Brittain, *Testament of Youth: An Autobiographical Study of the Years 1900–1925* (New York: Macmillan, 1933), 210.

5. Quoted in Darrow, *French Women*, 154–55.

6. Quoted in Schulte, "The Sick Warrior's Sister," in *Gender Relations*, ed. Abrams and Harvey, 127.

7. Quoted in ibid., 131.

8. Quoted in Lyn Macdonald, *Roses of No Man's Land* (London: Michael Joseph, 1980), 48.

9. Quoted in Susan Zeiger, *In Uncle Sam's Service: Women Workers with the American Expeditionary Force, 1917–1919* (Ithaca, N.Y.: Cornell University Press, 1999), 132.

10. Quoted in Macdonald, *Roses*, 254.

11. Quoted in Sarnecky, *Army Nurse Corps*, 98.

12. Quoted in Macdonald, *Roses*, 287.

13. Quoted in Dorothy Schneider and Carl J. Schneider, *Into the Breach: American Women Overseas in World War I* (New York: Viking, 1991), 111.

14. Quoted in Macdonald, *Roses*, 214–15.

15. Ian Hay, *One Hundred Years of Army Nursing* (London: Cassell, 1953), 152.

16. Gavin, *American Women*, 248–56; there are slightly different figures in Sarnecky, *Army Nurse Corps*, 122.

17. Quoted in Schulte, "Sick Warrior's Sister," in *Gender Relations*, ed. Abrams and Harvey, 130.

18. Quoted in Schneider and Schneider, *Into the Breach*, 109.

19. Zeiger, *In Uncle Sam's Service*, 2.

20. Gavin, *American Women*, 110–14.

21. Wilson, *Myriad Faces*, 712.

22. Gavin, *American Women*, 2.

23. Ibid., 26–27.

24. Quoted in Jenny Gould, "Women's Military Services in First World War Britain," in *Behind the Lines: Gender and the Two World Wars*, ed. Margaret Randolph Higonnet et al. (New Haven, Conn.: Yale University Press, 1987), 119.

25. Gavin, *American Women*, 78.

26. Ibid., 86.

8

Prisoners of War

Millions of military men fell into enemy hands during World War I. Airmen in action over enemy territory were aware they might fall into enemy hands, but the average soldier had no preparation for this fate. Army training did not include extensive instructions on how to behave in captivity other than to try to escape. The popular culture—with its war stories for boys and young men—offered no fictional accounts of men in prison camps. Men assumed they would fight and possibly be wounded or perish. All hoped they would return home unhurt. The shock of capture, the conditions of captivity, and the length of time many spent in enemy hands all came as a surprise.

Large numbers of men became captives, but they constituted only a minority of the troops on the western front. Out of 4 million British soldiers who served there, approximately 170,000 were taken prisoner. The average British soldier had one chance in two of being killed or wounded during his time at the front. But fewer than one in thirty fell into enemy hands. American troops conducted large-scale operations for only a brief period. Thus, only two out of every thousand Americans who served on the western front were taken prisoner.[1]

Governments also found themselves surprised. Anticipating a brief, decisive conflict, neither Germany, France, nor Great Britain was prepared to imprison or otherwise control large numbers of enemy captives. The United States had the opportunity to view the European experience during the first years of the conflict. But it too stood unready to deal effectively with the issue of prisoners when it became a belligerent.

Germany accumulated the largest number of wartime prisoners. On the western front, German forces captured approximately 535,000 Frenchmen, as well as some 170,000 Britons, and 4,000 Americans. The German homeland had to cope with a total of 2.5 million prisoners of war, most of them Russians. Those prisoners from the eastern front began to flood German camps in 1914.

France held 350,000 German military prisoners. Of that number 150,000 were taken in the closing months and the aftermath of the conflict. Great Britain's forces captured and held 328,000 Germans. The United States took over 40,000 German prisoners of war. Most of those fell into American hands during the final months of the war.

GETTING CAPTURED

Military men fell into the hands of the enemy in a variety of ways. Airmen shot down over hostile territory became captives if they survived a crash or a parachute jump. Survivors of actions at sea, if not lucky enough to be picked up by their comrades, might find themselves rescued by a hostile vessel. In these instances only small numbers of men were taken at one time.

But sometimes huge numbers became prisoners of war. Unlike Japanese soldiers in World War II, the fighting men of the 1914–18 conflict did not have rigid, permanent instructions to fight to the last man. When surrounded or out of ammunition, they often passed into enemy hands. During the German offensive in the first months of the war, 125,000 Frenchmen and approximately 9,000 Britons became German captives. While the British and French stood on the defensive during the first stage of the war, they captured 65,000 Germans by the start of 1915. In the spring 1918 offensive, the Germans overran and captured numerous British units. Half the British troops who became prisoners during the entire war fell into captivity during March and April 1918.

One eighteen-year-old British infantryman, captured the day after he entered the trenches in April 1918, described the emotion many felt in their new circumstances: "It was the most horrible thing I'd ever imagined could happen to me. It made me feel as if I was a coward. I was letting my country down, I was letting my unit down, I was letting my family down . . . I felt utterly bewildered. . . . Being taken prisoner, oh what a disgrace!"[2]

Falling into enemy hands as an individual or a member of a small group often brought humane treatment. Captured fliers and naval officers in particular recorded a cordial reception. A German U-boat crew captured Captain Norman Lewis of the Royal Navy in April 1917 and took him aboard their vessel. Lewis had commanded a heavily armed vessel disguised as a civilian ship with a mission of attracting and sinking submarines. Nonetheless, Lewis got a cordial greeting from the crew of his erstwhile target. "The treatment I received aboard U-62 during my involuntary three week's undersea trip was irreproachable," he later wrote. "Nothing but kindness was meted out to me by men and officers alike."[3]

A prisoner captured at moments like the German offensive of March and April 1918 had a different experience. The heat of battle combined with the urgent need to remove large numbers of prisoners from the vicinity of combat. Some British prisoners marched to the rear unguarded. The Germans just seized their weapons and pointed out the direction in which they were to march. This left the newly captured British to find their way to holding stations in the rear. But most prisoners were hustled out of the way with varying degrees of brutality.

One British soldier recorded the harrowing days that followed his capture in April 1918. "Captured this morning at 5.0 a.m. at Le Cornet Malo. Had no chance. Completely surrounded. Jerry relieved each of their valuables. . . . Carrying wounded until 7.0 p.m. . . . Only one doctor and one Red Cross man to attend to them. Absolute chaos, bandages made out of paper. Had no food since last night." A second British enlisted man, taken prisoner in May remembered even harsher conditions: "We were kicked, thumped, jabbed in the ribs with rifle butts and generally made to feel that we were, to say the least superfluous." Taken to a rear area, he and his fellow prisoners worked burying British corpses, which had been in the fields for weeks, then loaded ammunition trucks.[4]

Wounded prisoners could hope to receive treatment at the hands of their captors. The roughness of the procedures, shocking to a modern eye, often struck prisoners as the norm for the fighting front. One British prisoner in 1918 rescued a comrade whose elbow had been shot off and saw "his forearm was only hanging on to his upper arm by a piece of flesh no thicker than a finger." At the German first aid tent, the medical officer took a scalpel and "just cut [the] forearm off and threw it on a heap of other arms and legs." The British observer said only. "It's an awful sight to see such a pile of limbs. Unfortunately, that is what you see in war."[5] One British enlisted man in the Royal Army Medical Corps, taken prisoner at Ypres in late 1917, answered a German request to help care for both British and German wounded. He remained near the front for months and came and went freely, and his German fellow workers made him an honorary acting sergeant in the Kaiser's army![6]

During most of the war, prisoners who fell into German hands stayed in makeshift accommodations until their captors could move them to the nearest railhead. That meant days and nights in wrecked buildings, barbed wire enclosures, or even on bare ground under the sky. Feeding their new captives was a low priority for most German units, and prisoners remained in danger from their own artillery fire. The trip to Germany meant as long as two days in a railroad cattle car without food or water. Toilet facilities sometimes consisted of a tub in the middle of the car. Sometimes there were no facilities at all. One British prisoner described how "the only place we could use as a toilet was one corner of the wagon chosen among ourselves for us all to use" but the absence of drainage meant "the urine just ran out at the bottom of the truck."[7]

SETTING UP THE SYSTEM

Germany

In Germany, the flood of prisoners from the early stages of the war—625,000 of all nationalities by February 1915—led to a period of confusion and improvisation. It was possible to provide adequate food and clothing, but shelter for so many unexpected military guests was harder to arrange. Often only a tent was available for winter shelter. Primitive bathing facilities meant months without an opportunity to get clean, and prisoners suffered from body lice just as they had in the trenches. An outbreak of typhus in February 1915 showed the dangers of such a fragile system.

But the Germans went on to create a network of camps that American and other neutral observers found acceptably humane and generally on a par with those set up by the Allies. Camps in northwest Germany near the border with Holland, however, kept inmates in strict confinement to prevent escapes. Some camps were located near industrial areas with the apparent purpose of hindering enemy air attacks. Allied propaganda made much of these facts.

German camps contained a rich mixture of nationalities. Gardelagen, east of Hanover, held 4,000 Russians; 6,000 French; 700 Belgians; and 230 British prisoners in February 1915. Döberitz, located outside of Berlin, contained about 8,300 prisoners at that time: a mixture of British and Russian captives. The German system came to include 168 camps, 79 for officers, and 89 for enlisted men. Some 7,400 enlisted men lived in officers' camps where they worked as servants to those with commissioned rank.

France

The French faced difficulties comparable to those in Germany. The number of German prisoners—50,000 by early 1915—was relatively small, but the French needed to provide as well for a large number of refugees from German-occupied territory. As in Germany, housing prisoners posed an initial problem. With France itself under siege, German prisoners posed a security problem. French authorities put all kinds of

British, British imperial, and French prisoners of war in German hands. Courtesy of the Hoover Institution Archives.

buildings into service, including prisons and castles. They took care to place prison camps in remote regions of western France. Many Germans also found themselves confined in Corsica or in French possessions in north and west Africa.

Eventually, the French set up a system of seventeen camps for German officers and seventy-three for German enlisted men. By the summer of 1916, the camps in Africa shut down. Hundreds of satellite camps held prisoners assigned to labor duties. More than 100 hospitals were set up for wounded and ill German prisoners, and a number of camps were established for German invalids.

Britain

Britain faced only a minor problem of caring for prisoners during the early portion of the war. In February 1915, only 15,000 military prisoners resided in British camps. Compared to Germany, Britain met the need for prisoners' housing without undue strain. Large buildings such as factories and the homes of the wealthy in the countryside were easily converted into prisoners' dormitories.

As the numbers grew, the government set up 440 camps in Great Britain that eventually contained 164,000 prisoners. By the beginning of 1916, some of Britain's prisoners were housed in camps in France, the number eventually swelling to 184,000.

The United States

The United States had to deal with German prisoners only during the final months of the war. During its initial operations starting in the autumn of 1917, the Americans turned their prisoners over to the French. Starting in June 1918, the United States set up its own system on French soil, including ten sizable facilities. These sent prisoners out to seventy-six smaller labor camps. The construction of camps took place during the frantic months at the close of the war. Large numbers of Germans surrendered daily, but American authorities managed to build an adequate number of camps just in time.

THE HARDSHIPS OF PRISON CAMP

Robert Younger, a British judge, conducted a study during the war to determine how British prisoners, especially officers, were treated in German camps. He had the opportunity to interview 4,000 veterans of the camps: Some had been successful escapees, others had been repatriated. His general conclusion that the camps were disgraceful was apparently colored by the era's bitter emotions. Overcrowding and unpalatable food were two of the main complaints he recorded. Younger also objected to the lack of appropriate recreational facilities, because these were an important part of the normal daily life of a British officer!

Many prisoners in Germany, especially enlisted men, suffered severe and prolonged abuse. Nonetheless, neutral witnesses and recent scholars have presented a more favorable picture than the one offered by Younger. During the first portion of the war, American diplomats inspected prisoner of war camps on both sides of the battle lines. After the American entry into the conflict, diplomats from Spain and Denmark continued that work. There were numerous inspections, 200 in Germany in 1916 alone. Diplomatic observers visited every nine months, and they made frequent new visits to those where they had found poor conditions.

An official inspection of a prisoner of war camp included a visit to the barracks, the medical facility, the kitchen, and recreational areas. The senior prisoner usually accompanied the inspectors. There was also supposed to be an opportunity for individual prisoners to voice their complaints in private. The protests of inspectors helped to end abuses in individual camps, because their complaints were generally taken seriously. Any belligerent had to remember that its own countrymen were in enemy hands. Poor treatment of prisoners on one side of the battle line was likely to be matched by that meted out to prisoners on the other side.

The four main participants on the western front all voluntarily bound themselves to abide by the provisions agreed to at the Hague Conference of 1907. That gathering of delegates from forty-four countries had failed in its major goal of outlawing war. On the other hand, it produced, among other international treaties, an agreement setting standards for the humane treatment of prisoners of war. Enemy prisoners were to receive the same quality of rations and clothing as their captor's own troops; escape attempts could be punished only with strict limitations; adequate medical care and clothing were to be provided. Captured officers were paid at the rate of their counterparts in the country holding them, although such sums were likely to appear in the form of prison camp scrip. The rules allowed requiring captured enlisted men to do physical labor, and captured noncommissioned officers could be compelled to supervise them. But prisoners could not be compelled to perform work that directly aided the enemy war effort. Further agreements in 1917 and 1918 between the two warring camps expanded restrictions on the treatment of military captives.

But real prison camp conditions did not always conform to the rules, and violations were not always evident to observers. Camp directors could always create a picture that brightened reality. One British enlisted man at a camp near Münster in 1918 described the novelties displayed for visitors from the Danish Red Cross including an unusually big meal. The Red Cross representatives had no opportunity to question prisoners in private about conditions in the camp, and the British were wise enough not to volunteer complaints in front of their German captors. If they had, "we would have been punished behind the prison walls, slowly walking around with a pack of bricks or stones on your back, doubled up almost in half."[8]

Credible accounts of life in German camps show that enlisted men often received brutal treatment while in enemy hands. In his memoir of four years in enemy captivity, Able Seaman James Farrant described numerous such episodes. According to Farrant, British prisoners were regularly disciplined by being suspended from ropes for hours on end. Sent to coal mines as a particularly harsh punishment, men tried to get release with self-inflicted wounds.[9]

THE PRIVILEGES OF RANK

Officers received considerate treatment at many camps. Captain Douglas Lyall Grant of the British army recalled strolls and excursions accompanied only by a German guide or an unarmed guard. "We have parole cards that we sign and give up on our return. We go out in batches of

British prisoners of war putting on a theatrical production. Courtesy of the Hoover Institution Archives.

40 twice a week." There were also shopping trips and jaunts to the barber. On one occasion, he, two fellow officers, and a guard went off for the day to see an oculist, ending their outing with a luxurious pub lunch.[10] The British reciprocated in their treatment of German prisoners. The Germans chose not to grant such privileges to French officers. The French government, early in the war, retaliated by confining German officers to their camps.

Prison camp memoirs record an atmosphere British officers likened to being back at school: a multitude of petty rules, but a plethora of drama societies, language lessons, and sports teams. Having enlisted men as orderlies (servants) made life easier for both British and German officers. High-ranking German officers could obtain a personal orderly. An officer farther down the ladder had to share a servant. Private Norman Dykes, captured at the Somme in July 1916, left a record of serving British officers at Gütersloh and Crefeld prison camps until September of the following year. He cleaned rooms, played on an orderlies' soccer team that provided competition for the officers' team, and waited on tables in the officers' mess.[11]

Britain confined some enlisted German prisoners in camps located in France, but all German officers found themselves on British soil. Accommodations were sometimes luxurious. Prisoners confined in the mansion known as Donington Hall in Derby were permitted to wander freely through an area of ten acres, and to use part of the spacious estates for sports facilities. They had a magnificent view of the 10,000-acre estate along with its forests and grazing animals.

American authorities considered sending all captured German officers to the United States. But, in the end, they constructed an officers' camp in France, first near Brest, then around a chateau at Richelieu, southeast of Nantes. High-ranking prisoners received accommodations within the chateau. More junior officers and the group of enlisted men serving as officers' servants made do in recently constructed barracks.

The prisoners at Richelieu set up dramatic productions, choirs, and an orchestra of stringed instruments. With many teachers in their midst, the Germans at Richelieu also established a small university with classes ranging from modern languages to physics and medicine. Students were even able to receive credit for their studies from the German university system.

THE QUESTION OF FOOD

Falling into enemy hands meant sharing many of the circumstances of the enemy. British, French, and American prisoners in Germany, entitled to the same rations as members of the German military, faced the consequences of their own blockade—even when the Germans tried to honor their obligation to feed their prisoners. Officers were expected to purchase their meals, because they were being paid their salary by the German government. Early in the war, the German Ministry of War issued regulations specifying a sufficient diet for all enlisted prisoners that was to be augmented for those asked to do heavy labor. A prisoner's daily diet in the initial part of the war consisted of substantial soup made from barley, potatoes, vegetables, and sausage, along with a portion of bread and coffee.

Food parcels from home provided a welcome, sometimes crucial, supplement. In Britain, an elaborate system run by the Red Cross developed to ship parcels to individual prisoners. The Red Cross attempted to keep a list of prisoners and the camps in which they were confined. Private charities, public subscriptions, and the efforts of associations linked to certain regiments produced the necessary funds to send parcels to named individuals. British soldiers at all ranks received Red Cross parcels containing cheese, jam, canned bully beef, and stew. Regular bread supplies reached British POWs through the efforts of Lady Evelyn Grant Duff. In her contribution to the war effort, she organized the shipment of flour to Switzerland, the baking of the bread in Geneva, and its transportation by road to rail to camps in Germany. "The aim was to provide each prisoner with one 10 lb parcel and 13 lb of bread every fortnight."[12]

Many British officers relied almost entirely on their food parcels, because they found the food offered by the Germans unpalatable. The package provided American prisoners by the American Red Cross was predictably generous. It included a twenty-five-pound food supply of such items as corned beef and jam, supplemented with tobacco, sometimes candy. According to Captain Grant even when food shortages were gripping the German home front, generous food parcels from Britain passed through the German mails to prisoners.

Nonetheless, memoirs of British and American soldiers are replete with complaints of near starvation conditions. Not all prisoners were officially registered by the Red Cross and could not receive aid packages. The Germans purloined many food parcels. Moreover, conditions in Germany grew measurably worse toward the close of the war as the Germans struggled to feed themselves. Most prisoners had to get along on the meager diet the Germans could spare for their captives. One British soldier, captured in the German offensive of March 1918, painted a grim picture of hunger and deprivation in his new home. "I was so hungry that I personally exchanged my wristwatch for a slice of their bread. . . . Hunger gives you a terrible pain in your stomach. Your stomach is empty, it's got nothing to digest. . . . Some people would double up with the pain and try and be sick, but you've got nothing to bring up and that in itself is painful."[13]

Soldiers kept to work at the front suffered the most. They had no access whatever to the food parcels that continued to arrive at camps back in Germany. British captives working at the front received a daily ration of tea along with a loaf of bread for every five men. Even in Germany, the scene was often grim. After his capture, Private Charles E. Sargent of the American Thirty-seventh Division went to a prison camp there. He later recalled working twelve hours a day with soup for breakfast and a tiny piece of sausage for dinner.[14]

At first, German prisoners in France received meals comparable to those of French soldiers in peacetime: After a breakfast of bread and coffee, the other meals consisted of soup with 125 grams of meat or fish. Officers received a generous allowance for purchasing their own food. Soldiers assigned to heavy labor received a supplementary meat ration. In 1916, the French authorities altered the system, reducing the allowance of meat to the amount French prisoners in Germany were given. German prisoners also received food packages from home, although such assistance was limited by the shortages there.

Great Britain fed its prisoners a substantial diet, augmented for those doing demanding physical labor. The crisis in the British food supply, provoked by the German submarine campaign in 1917, led to a reduction in what prisoners received. Those doing manual labor received a daily allowance of 4,600 calories in the early portion of the war, subsequently reduced in spring 1917 to 3,000 calories as the nation's food supply tightened.

A German guard with Belgian prisoners of war. Courtesy of the Hoover Institution Archives.

German officers confined in Britain received a food allowance in cash. They were able to purchase food subject to what was available on the civilian market. Thus, a German officer behind barbed wire could expect at least to match the diet of a well-off British civilian. A camp canteen, such as the one at Donington Hall, offered the opportunity to buy items such as canned lobster and chocolates.

German prisoners in American hands received the same generous ration given to American soldiers. Captive Germans must what must have seemed lavish meals. Prepared by German chefs drawn from the prison population, meals for German soldiers at one camp in 1918 included corn meal, bread, and syrup for breakfast; meat, potatoes, and bread for lunch; corned-beef, bread, cheese, and bacon for dinner. Coffee was presented with all meals.

PRISON COMMANDERS AND GUARDS

The harshness of imprisonment varied from camp to camp, depending on a host of local factors: what country held the captives, the climate, proximity to foreign borders, and especially the personality of the camp commander. Small labor camps to which many enlisted men were sent were more brutal places of confinement than the larger facilities.

The German system was especially decentralized. Army corps commanders, who governed local districts, ran the local system of prisoner of war camps. They picked the camp commanders, who had broad authority. German prison camp commanders were unlikely to be sympathetic toward their charges. Normally such officers did not have distinguished military careers behind them. Some might well be brutal out of a sense of inferiority vis-à-vis their captives. Germany could spare no good soldierly material to serve as prison guards. Thus, as one British prisoner put it, "Most of the guards were young guys who were not fit to go up the line, the dregs of the German population." There were the old as well. "We also had one or two elderly men who were very, very short tempered."[15] Postwar memoirs made a number of German camp commanders notorious. The Niemeyer twins, Karl and Heinrich, appear in many accounts. They were German prison camp commanders at Holzminden and Claustal. Karl, the commander at Holzminden, was nicknamed "Milwaukee Bill" by the prisoners. He had spent seventeen years in the United States and acquired a quirky command of the English language, which he spoke with an American accent.

ENLISTED MEN AT WORK

Enlisted prisoners were subject to work assignments for their captors. All the belligerent countries set up satellite camps where prisoners were held while performing labor for their captors. The Germans began to employ prisoners of war as laborers in 1915, the French quickly followed, and the British government began the practice in 1916. The Hague Convention provided that prisoners' work should not be connected with wartime operations, but in a country mobilized for total war, such a limit was hard to enforce. Governments on all sides used prisoners for tasks that were necessary for the war effort such as unloading merchant ships.

The Germans set up many of their camps specifically to make their inmates available for industrial work. Many prisoners worked in steel mills, but the most common and feared assignment was as a miner. Some camps were placed close to the coalfields of the Ruhr and Silesia; others were located in the Hartz Mountains in central Germany. These prisoners offered a ready source of labor in a German economy desperately short of manpower. Some Allied prisoners labored in near slavelike conditions. In the final months of the war, Germany kept many newly captured prisoners close to the front to perform heavy labor. Some longtime prisoners even found themselves transferred from work sites inside Germany to haul and carry for their captors on the western front. As the

Germans retreated in the face of Allied advances, these captive laborers were forced to pull back with them.

But other prisoners were far more fortunate, especially those sent to work in farming communities. Allied prisoners in Germany sometimes found themselves virtually adopted by the farm communities in whose midst they lived. They might live with an individual family, or, if they worked on large farms, they might room in the local village meeting hall or schoolhouse.

On the Allied side, the French used prisoners in farms, factories, and mines. The hardest task—that of working in mining operations—was assigned to Germans who had been miners in civilian life. Most jobs involved manual labor. German protests that educated Germans were required to do such work led to a sympathetic French response. French authorities assigned educated prisoners who were unaccustomed to working with their hands to undemanding labor on farms.

Britain started to use prisoners as laborers in the first months of 1916. Both in the homeland and in France, Germans in British captivity worked in agriculture, unloading merchant ships, and in factories. A labor force of 30,000 Germans played a key role in bringing in the harvest in 1917. Nonetheless, a majority of the prisoners held in Great Britain were not required to perform any labor throughout the course of the war.

The United States employed German prisoners in repairing roads and unloading merchant ships. Pay varied with the level of skilled required. Tragically, in a number of incidents after the Armistice, German soldiers were killed or injured in the dangerous task of disposing of grenades and mortar shells.

MEDICAL CARE

Medical care varied substantially. In Germany, Allied enlisted men in satellite work camps suffered most from the absence of doctors. The overworked captive laborers on the western front proved especially vulnerable to the influenza epidemic that struck in the fall of 1918. Nonetheless, most prisoners in Germany survived. Deaths from malnutrition probably accounted for a substantial number toward the close of the war, but the same malady faced Germany's civilian population. In all, less than 5 percent of the prisoners held by the Germans died in captivity, mostly from diseases like pneumonia and tuberculosis.

Germany's opponents set up elaborate systems of care for sick and injured captives. At the American camp for German officers at Richelieu, the original medical arrangements were faulty, but improved care by the closing months of the war cut the sickness rate to less than 2 percent. Even in the early months of the war, the French managed to provide good medical care. At Toulouse, fewer than 2 percent of the nearly 900 prisoners were ill during March 1915. Those who needed care saw a doctor daily, and the seriously ill were evacuated to a hospital.

RELEASE FROM CAPTIVITY: MEDICAL INTERNMENT, EXCHANGES

During the war, the belligerents proved willing to release prisoners under special circumstances. In February 1915, Germany and France agreed to exchange seriously wounded prisoners whose fighting days were over. By the close of 1916, more than 11,000 such invalids, about 2,300 Germans and 8,700 Frenchmen, returned home. Less seriously injured prisoners went for medical treatment in Switzerland. After recovering, they were required to remain there for the rest of the war. Created by agreement between Germany and France in early 1916, this arrangement affected almost 27,000 French, German, British, and Belgian prisoners by the close of the year. As one scholar has put it, "The internment of invalid prisoners of war in a neutral country during wartime was an innovation unique to the First World War."[16]

Even more notable was the exchange of officers and enlisted men above a certain age. They earned their release through the length of time they had spent in captivity. An accord of May 1917 between Germany and France directed that officers over the age of fifty-five and noncommissioned officers over the age of forty-eight be exchanged after eighteen months as a prisoner of war. In addition, NCOs and enlisted men would be exchanged on a regular schedule "on a head for head" and "rank for rank" basis without regard to age.

THE MENTAL STRAIN

Mental distress formed a crucial feature of prison life. It came inevitably from camp restrictions, enforced labor for enlisted men, and enforced torpor for officers. Allied physicians held in prison camps observed that men began to deteriorate mentally after about eighteen months. "Barbed wire fever" was a term many applied to those suffering visibly from the claustrophobia of prison life. One officers' camp magazine gave a peek into such emotions in a poem that spoke of "Walking round our cages like the lions at the Zoo." It went on to describe how the captives remembered the "phantom faces" of those at home. Even a prisoner like Douglas Grant with a famously ebullient personality recognized the emotional strain of those around him. He wrote in his diary about those who lay hopelessly in bed most of the day "quite beyond doing anything." Grant went on to say, perhaps to keep his own spirits up, "The only thing is to make the best of a bad job and when down in the mouth think of Jonah—he came up all right."[17]

AFTER THE ARMISTICE: FREEDOM AND REPATRIATION

German prisoners in French, British, and American hands in November 1918 had to wait for almost a year before any could return home. One German prisoner, captured at St. Quentin on the Somme in the summer of 1918, found himself ordered back to St. Quentin with a group of his fellow captives. There was a railhead there, but hopes that the Germans were about to return home immediately disappeared. They were soon put to work repairing the damage done during the fighting. Posted on the walls were placards to remind the Germans of the situation. The German prisoner who had returned to St. Quentin described one placard that depicted "the German Emperor, bowed, humbled, surrounded by the twenty-two flags of his enemies."[18]

According to the Armistice provisions, the Germans had to free Allied prisoners immediately. Those who were prisoners at the front had the earliest opportunity to return to friendly territory. Many learned of the Armistice from their German captors and simply started to march westward. Likewise others did not wait for the Germans to act. Hundreds of British prisoners escaped from their camp in Brussels. When German officers ordered their troops to fire on the escapees, the German rank and file refused to do so. In many German camps, the guards were infected by the revolutionary fervor sweeping the country. Many who remained on duty wore red armbands—the symbol of the revolution—and took over the jobs of their former officers.

In the midst of revolution, German authorities had difficulty providing transportation for the hundreds of thousands of prisoners they held on German territory. Conditions in many camps became chaotic in the absence of any firm control by trained officers. Only the arrival of French officers, who were now permitted to cross the German border, reestablished order. It took until November 28 for the victorious Allies to form a Subcommission on Prisoners of War under the authority of the Armistice Commission.

Most prisoners remained in their camps for weeks or even months. Following Allied orders, the Germans gathered prisoners at five collection centers in various areas. Allied trains, able to carry 1,000 to 1,500 passengers, arrived and transported many of the freed captives to Baltic or North Sea ports for a sea voyage home. Prisoners close to the Rhine crossed directly to France, and those in southern Germany traveled by rail via Switzerland. All Americans were released by the close of December, and all Allied prisoners from the western front were freed by the start of February 1919.

One American's experience illustrates the frustrations former prisoners encountered. Held in a camp at Langensalza near Erfurt, he had to wait until early December before an Allied representative reached his compound. He spent two more weeks at Langensalza before trains arrived to transport his group to Cassel in central Germany, and he reached Frankfurt only on December 25. His return to Allied territory came only on January 1, 1919, seven weeks after the Armistice.

One group of British prisoners was evacuated to southern Holland. While awaiting a train to Rotterdam, they witnessed the former German Crown Prince Wilhelm entering Holland to go in exile. Other groups, containing many suffering from illness and malnutrition, traveled by railroad cattle car to the Baltic port of Stettin. There they boarded Red Cross hospital ships to Denmark and—after weeks of recuperation—took a last sea voyage to Leith in Scotland. Even in conditions of freedom, some of the former prisoners could not regain their health and perished on the way home. Both the voyage through the Baltic to Copenhagen and the second to Great Britain were punctuated by burials at sea.

Upon returning home, many British officers were required to describe how they fell into enemy hands. There was no apparent effort by the authorities to levy criticism on those who had suffered this fate. Instead, the commissioned former captives received an official letter freeing them of any blame for being taken prisoner. Enlisted men had no such inquiries to answer. They were assumed to have been under an officer's control at all times, and their descent into captivity was, by definition, not their own fault.

German prisoners in Allied hands received authorization to return to their homes much later. The Treaty of Versailles provided for their release, but only after the Treaty had been ratified. The French were in no rush to send prisoners home, because German captives were providing needed labor to repair war damage.

The American and British governments had little use for prisoners in this capacity, and they were struck by the financial burden of guarding and providing for them: 41,000 in American hands, 200,000 in British hands. The Americans and British began shipping Germans home without waiting for the Treaty's ratification. Germans in American hands obtained their release in September 1919. The British began the process in August and concluded it in October. Most German prisoners in French hands stayed in custody for eighteen months or even two years after the Armistice. At least some, who had been captured in the first months of fighting in 1914, experienced six years behind the barbed wire of a French prison compound.

NOTES

1. Statistics on the numbers of prisoners and descriptions of the prison camp system come from the definitive study by Richard B. Speed, III, *Prisoners, Dip-*

lomats, and the Great War: A Study in the Diplomacy of Captivity (New York: Green-wood Press, 1990). The most useful personal accounts of the prisoner of war experience, although confined mainly to British prisoners taken during the last months of the war, can be found in Richard Van Emden, *Prisoners of the Kaiser: The Last POWs of the Great War* (London: Leo Cooper, 2000).

2. Quoted in Van Emden, *Prisoners*, 21.

3. Quoted in Robert Jackson, *The Prisoners, 1914–1918* (London: Routledge, 1989), 15–16.

4. Quoted in ibid., 19, 23–24.

5. Quoted in Van Emden, *Prisoners*, 43.

6. Van Emden, *Prisoners*, 60–66.

7. Quoted in ibid., 47.

8. Ibid., 135–36.

9. Michael Moynihan, ed., *Black Bread and Barbed Wire: Prisoners in the First World War* (London: Cooper, 1978), 1–30.

10. Ibid., 87, 94, 107–8.

11. Ibid., 119–35.

12. Jackson, *Prisoners, 1914–1918*, 64–68.

13. Quoted in Van Emden, *Prisoners*, 124.

14. James H. Hallas, *The Doughboy War: The American Expeditionary Force in World War I* (Boulder, Colo.: Lynne Rienner Publishers, 2000), 192.

15. Quoted in Van Emden, *Prisoners*, 87.

16. Speed, *Prisoners, Diplomats*, 37.

17. Moynihan, *Black Bread*, xvii, 79.

18. Stanley Weintraub, *A Stillness Heard Round the World: The End of the Great War, November 1918* (New York: E.P. Dutton, 1985), 337.

PART II

THE CIVILIAN WORLD

9

The Home Front

From August 1914 onward, the war's effects crept into the lives of civilians in all the belligerent countries. The conflict made its influence felt at the workplace, in the home, in the world of popular entertainment, and in the schools. What individuals read and said showed the effect of governments anxious to prosecute the war with vigor. Even the world of childhood came under the shadow of the conflict.

In some belligerent countries, opportunities offered by expanding economies caused numerous individuals to resettle in new areas. The United States, for example, saw a vast domestic migration of African Americans. Inflated prices struck hard at family budgets. The shortage of wartime labor brought unprecedented numbers of foreigners—usually from other European countries, sometimes from the non-Western parts of the world—into the continent's communities.

XENOPHOBIA

Citizens everywhere needed little encouragement to vent their feelings against the inhabitants of enemy countries. And everywhere it seemed safest to indicate that one unquestionably belonged. In England, people were quick to abandon German-sounding family names. In Germany, the proprietors of the Hotel Westminster and the Café Piccadilly thought it wise to rename their establishments the Lindenhof and the Café Vaterland. Street names from a peaceful era were also awkward, and so Paris's Rue d'Allemagne became the impeccably French Rue Jean Jaurès.

As the war continued, officials at the American embassy in Berlin cautioned members of the staff against speaking English in public.

The passage of time inflamed popular feelings further. Animosity against the enemy reached deep into the arts and scholarship. Conductors like Thomas Beecham and entire French cities like Nice rejected the playing of German music. The editors of the *Cambridge Medieval History* refused to accept the contributions they had previously solicited from distinguished German scholars. A German professor at the University of Berlin, speaking in Munich, called upon his audience to "hate the very essence of everything English. We must hate the very soul of England."[1]

America's entry into the war made the spring of 1917 a moment to remove Germanisms from that country's life. It was no small task, because so much of the population of the United States had its roots in Germany. Nonetheless, the teaching of the German language was banned in many areas, and German music disappeared from the nation's concert halls. Terms with an apparent connection to the new foe like "hamburger" and "sauerkraut" or "German measles" were replaced with safe, patriotic equivalents: "liberty steak," "liberty cabbage," and "liberty measles." Living in Berlin, Iowa, posed obvious problems for that town's inhabitants until the name was changed to Lincoln.

Popular anti-German sentiment spilled over into mob violence. Five hundred members of a mob in Collinsville, Illinois, outside St. Louis, Missouri, lynched a young man in April 1918 merely because he was German-born. Those responsible for directing the crime were placed on trial, only to be acquitted in a matter of minutes by a sympathetic jury.

INDUSTRY

The busy factory with workers laboring long hours in harsh conditions became a hallmark of wartime. Prewar labor restrictions faded with the onset of the conflict and the desperate need to produce arms and ammunition. The demand for workers to meet the needs of the military brought boom times to many regions from the war's beginning. Boot orders for the expanding British army overwhelmed factories in Leicester, where the industry was centered. By the close of 1914, a report from the local labor union indicated the dimensions of the demand for workers: For the first time ever, not one of its members needed to apply for employment benefits.[2]

Factories in various countries were filled with men who had been released from military service—or excused from it—in order to take valuable roles in industry. Women in large numbers entered the labor force producing war matériel. In the United States, the need for an expanded labor force for a time pulled down the barriers against employing African Americans.

In late 1916, Germany attempted an extreme example of expanding the factory workforce. The Patriotic Auxiliary Service Law, "the Hindenburg Program," required all males from seventeen to sixty to work in war plants. But the difficulties of enforcing such a measure soon emerged, and the government exempted large categories of men such as students and civil servants. At the same time, it established boards to consider claims of extreme hardship from those men who remained affected. Many men avoided registering or else sought an exemption on medical grounds. Others falsely claimed they were farmers and hence not subject to the law's grasp.

Britain, France, and Germany all felt the jolt of factory workers downing their tools to go on strike. The essential role of miners, workers in munitions factories, and those running the transport system in a wartime economy gave them enormous leverage. During the early portion of the war, patriotism was a powerful adhesive holding such workers to key jobs, and they held back from seeking major concessions. In Britain 10 million working days were lost due to industrial unrest in 1913; in 1915, the total fell to 3 million, and it declined further the following years. In the Isère district of southern France, there were fifteen strikes in the first seven months of 1914, and only ten strikes in the thirty wartime months that followed.[3]

As the conflict continued, labor militancy revived in both France and Britain. The spectacle of entrepreneurs reaping wartime profits combined with the inflation that pinched workers' families to produce bitterness throughout the Allied home front. Labor unrest broke out in some of Britain's Welsh coal mines and Scottish shipyards as early as the first months of 1915.

In March 1917, Russian factory workers (along with mutinous soldiers and sailors) overturned the existing political order. Many workers in the other belligerent countries took this revolution as a signal to present their grievances. The year saw labor unrest in Britain over issues ranging from the employment of Chinese workers to the disparity between the earnings of munitions workers and the lesser pay given miners. In late September, there were seventy-five strikes within the space of a week. By the year's end, strikes over food prices—which sometimes escalated into attacks on food stores—took place in Coventry and Birmingham.

But the central core of patriotic devotion held steady. The Germans imposed a harsh peace on the Russians at Brest-Litovsk in March 1918, which helped block the spread of workers' discontent in western Europe. As one British labor leader wrote, even the German socialists representing the workers of that country had allowed this painful settlement to be forced on a workers' government in Russia. The Russians' willingness to stop fighting, he noted, just allowed the Germans "to carry out their annexationist programme to the letter."[4] That year, the threat posed by the dangerous German spring offensive on the western front reinforced British workers' willingness to support the war effort. Even in areas of South Wales famous for their opposition to the war, young miners rushed to enlist. Occasional strikes continued, such as the walkout of London policemen in late August 1918, but nothing took place to block the flow of men and arms to the front.

In France, too, the spring of 1917 saw a wave of labor unrest sparked in part by rising prices. If popular slogans were an indication, the walkouts also showed some workers' desire to end the war. A year later, even in the face of the German spring offensive, a more dangerous outbreak of labor unrest appeared in the crucial metals industry. The Russian Revolution of November 1917 inspired revolutionary syndicalists to call for an end to the war and for revolution in France.

Such ambitions soon faded. The government of Premier Georges Clemenceau resorted to harsh repression, arresting some strike leaders, tightening the censorship system, and even sending a number of strike leaders off to the front. But Clemenceau's success was also due to the commitment of most workers to see the war through to victory. The visibility of American troops, now landing at the rate of 250,000 a month, supported hopes that the war could be won. As one historian put it, "The reservoir of patriotism among the least privileged citizens of the Republic is perhaps the key to understanding why the French nation was able to go [to the bitter end]."[5]

In Germany striking workers also threatened the war effort. As early as May 1916, a walkout in Berlin involved thousands. Their slogan of "bread, peace, and freedom" had an ominous ring for German authorities, because it combined political with economic demands. Later strikes, whatever their immediate cause, were accompanied with even more overtly political goals. A cut in the bread ration in the spring of 1917 led to massive walkouts from war factories, first in Berlin and Leipzig, then across much of the country. In all, more than 600,000 workers struck in 1917; that was five times the number who had abandoned their work places the previous year.[6]

In January 1918, massive strikes, organized by left-wing political parties, broke out at the munitions plants in Berlin. The strikers' demands again included nonpolitical items like a call for better food supplies. But the workers also called emphatically for a quick end to the war. Neither hordes of mounted police nor the government's cry that such strikes imperiled German soldiers at the front stopped the walkouts from growing. By the last day of the month, the other major cities of Germany witnessed similar strikes, and the total number of workers who downed their tools reached 1 million. The authorities seized the strikes' leaders, put them into uniform, and sent them off to the western front. Along with the government's threat to militarize the plants—making all workers subject to military courts and paying them the same meager wages soldiers earned—this harsh response bought a period of uneasy calm.[7]

The wealth of the United States and the relatively short period it joined in the war muffled industrial unrest. By offering employers generous "cost-plus" contracts, the government encouraged them to pay high wages. As the country entered the conflict in April 1917, the government considered policies certain to inflame workers' sentiments. These included drafting workers in key industries into the army or requiring workers to remain in jobs they wished to leave. Rejecting such measures helped ensure labor peace. Moreover, the country's most prominent union leader, Samuel Gompers of the American Federation of Labor, heartily supported the war effort.

But the government kept harsh measures in reserve. Striking workers in the Pacific Northwest's logging industries—a key sector of the economy—found themselves facing such a response from Washington. The federal government crushed the radical International Workers of the World, the union to which some loggers belonged. It then put troops in civilian clothes to work cutting trees, and formed a government-operated union. To sweeten the pill, however, federal authorities arranged for improved wages and living conditions in the region's lumber camps. Even drafting workers into the military appeared to be a tool the authorities were willing to use. In early 1918, shipyard workers—and later in the year war plant machinists—were discouraged from striking by just this threat.

All in all, American workers enjoyed the benefits of boom times with plentiful jobs, high wages, and a federal government willing to accept, if not actually encourage, the growth of labor unions. They lived in an industrial world far away from the bitter and politicized labor unrest their German antagonist on the battlefield underwent.

MIGRATION AND IMMIGRATION

The war brought a wave of internal migration as workers in Britain, France, and Germany—and later the United States—flocked to areas of industrial growth. Lloyd George's Ministry of Munitions created arms factories and attracted clusters of workers to operate them in remote locations like Gretna in southern Scotland just across the border from England. The population of Paris almost doubled between the start of the war and the close of 1915. German industrial centers like Essen and Dortmund boomed.

The European workforce came to contain large numbers of foreigners. Belgians at work in Britain were one sign of an expanding industrial system. Germany pulled 600,000 Poles westward to help fill vacancies in the German farm labor force. France's desperate need for manpower led it to expand its traditional importation of European workers. That country also brought in a quarter of a million non-Europeans, creating an ethnic mixture of whites and nonwhites, as well as Christians and Moslems, unknown elsewhere on the Continent.

The United States experienced an internal migration with especially momentous consequences as African Americans left the rural South to fill industrial jobs in the North. Racist practices had barred this segment of the population from such opportunities so long as potential workers arrived from Europe. After 1914, that flow ended, and the conscription of millions into the military in 1917 and 1918 intensified the need to man the country's factories. Even before the United States entered the war, agents of industrial companies began recruiting reinforcements for the labor pool from the black population of Georgia and Florida.

More than 300,000 African Americans arrived in midwestern industrial centers like Chicago and Detroit. In response, white leaders in the South determined to stop this drain on their labor supply. Labor recruiters were harassed with exorbitant licensing fees. The mayor of one large southern city asked the president of the Illinois Central Railroad to prevent African Americans from using trains to make their way northward. Such desperate attempts to tie down an oppressed minority could not succeed, given the country's pressing need for labor. Despite discrimination by white labor unions and even race riots, the migration continued. Chicago alone saw the arrival of 60,000 black Americans from the rural South. They had been pulled by economic opportunity and pushed to leave by a harsh system that had burdened their forefathers.

Like the United States, France had imported foreign workers in large numbers before 1914. But the French continued to have access to European workers after the outbreak of the war. Moreover, the French had a sizable imperial population to tap for manpower. Many French factory workers found themselves side by side with Spaniards, Greeks, Portuguese, as well as Tunisians, Moroccans, and Indo-Chinese. These immigrants clustered in Paris and Marseilles, where there had always been large numbers of foreigners. But they could also be found for the first time in smaller cities like Bourges, Brest, and Le Havre, where new war plants attracted foreign labor. Over half a million foreign workers, in addition to some 100,000 German and Austro-Hungarian prisoners of war, contributed to the operation of the French economy.

Spaniards made up the largest group of visiting workers. Their homeland was neutral during the war, but the conflict put added economic strain on this traditionally poor country. Unlike North African and Chinese workers and other Europeans, all of whom were recruited by official French agencies, Spaniards simply crossed the border to find work in the booming French economy. And unlike the others, who were directed to places of employment by the French government, the Spanish could seek work where they wished. A French businessman in Barcelona observed a train "bursting with Spanish peasants who were going to work in France." They were leaving impoverished circumstances and "flooding full of hope to this land of milk and honey . . . with a desire to work and a confidence which were stupefying."[8]

Such immigrant workers were often downcast when they experienced life in France. Wages were high, but so too were expenses. Hardships the French accepted as the price of fighting a war to defend their country meant little to visitors. One Spaniard from Barcelona reacted to the sparse food supply in the winter of 1917–1918 by writing home that "bread of the peasants at home is better than the top quality bread here—you'd say it was bread fit for dogs."[9]

The influx of 250,000 Chinese, Indo-Chinese, and Moslems from North Africa created a different strain. French authorities organized these workers in semimilitary fashion and regulated their conduct closely. Nonetheless, numerous groups in France resented their presence. French union leaders saw them as cheap labor undercutting Frenchmen's wages. French factory workers saw them as replacements that would permit Frenchmen to be shifted from industrial duties to dangerous service in the army. And Frenchmen of various backgrounds saw them as sexual predators threatening French women. Race riots erupted in several locales during the summer of 1917, prompting the government to settle some non-European workers in isolated, fortress-like barracks outside several French cities.

INFLATION AND TAXATION

The financial burden of the war weighed upon all the belligerent populations. Prices rose—often drastically—for basic commodities. Increased taxation was less universal, but two of the wartime powers, Britain and the United States, placed greater tax burdens on their people.

Though wages rose for many in the belligerent countries, prices often went beyond what even well-paid workers could afford. In Germany, government efforts to control prices failed. They could have little effect when the black market controlled much of the food supply. An eloquent cry of pain came from an association of German roof-makers in the closing months of the war. They noted that prices overall had tripled or quadrupled in the last two years alone, whereas their wages, from 1914 to the summer of 1918, had increased only 50 percent. "It gets worse every week. Various articles have increased twenty times in price, earnings by only a half. We can no longer go on. We have come to the end. . . . Our cupboards, our boxes are empty, our savings lie in the money bags of the usurers."[10] Germany's civil servants, including judges and university professors, and its white-collar workers, who did not enjoy

Poster encourages the French people to buy war bonds. Courtesy of the
Hoover Institution Archives.

the pay increases given out to munitions workers, were impoverished as
well.

British workers echoed these sentiments. By mid-1917, shipyard workers in Scotland and textile industry workers in Yorkshire were pointing
to an inflated cost of living to justify their wage claims. Both groups
declared that prices had doubled since the outbreak of the war, and both
claimed that their pay increases covered only half—or even just a quarter—of their growing expenses. In 1918, however, effective food rationing in Britain muffled at least some of the discontent. In France as well,
prices for basic commodities began to rise steadily from the middle of
1915. The cost of most foods doubled by early 1917 and tripled by the
close of the year. Here, too, food rationing removed some of the pain of
higher prices as the war moved toward its conclusion.

Higher taxes also brought the cost of the war home to many. The
British government put a heavier tax burden on its people from the war's
start, and the increases continued down to be included in the 1918 bud-
get. The authorities doubled the income tax and levied heavy taxes on
consumer goods. Higher taxes on beer and tea caused daily pain in a
population that found both items indispensable. These levies were soon
joined by higher taxes on matches and tickets to the movies and the
theater. An excess profits tax forced businessmen prospering as a result
of the war to disgorge some of their riches. More and more factory workers became subject to the income tax, formerly a burden only the groups

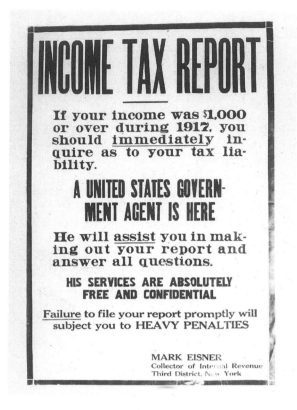

United States tax poster. Courtesy of the Hoover Institution Archives.

higher on the social ladder had to pay. At the same time, an expanded estate tax as well as the growing income tax made it harder for the landed elite to survive the war with their wealth intact.

In bumpier fashion, the American government made its citizens cover some of the cost of the war in taxes. Some Congressional leaders hoped to meet half the cost of the war with an expanded income tax, greater taxes on corporate profits, as well as taxes on luxury goods like automobiles. This proved politically impossible. In the end, the explosive cost of the war meant that most of the money to finance the conflict had to come from war loans. But legislation at the end of 1917 raised both corporate and individual income taxes. Much to their surprise, more Americans than ever before found themselves paying a tax on their income.

The German government rejected a general increase in taxes, in part because of fears of its effect on morale. Thus, more than 80 percent of the war's cost came from borrowing from the German population, and the government hoped that defeated enemy countries would be compelled to pay off the loans. In the meantime, the government expanded the money supply, and the resulting inflation only added to the woes of the average citizen. The Germans could console themselves by observing that France had chosen the path of borrowing instead of taxation as well.

CENSORSHIP AND RUMOR

All the belligerent countries moved to restrict what newspapers could print and what individuals could say. From the first days of the war, French readers found blanked out sections of their newspapers. In all the belligerent nations, the horrors of war, such as pictures of soldiers who had lost a limb, were specifically banned. Even in the war's final weeks, with German armies being pressed relentlessly backward toward the homeland, the country's newspapers highlighted the failure of local Allied attacks.

In the absence of uncontrolled news, civilians fell back on sources that seemed more personal and arguably more reliable. The soldier returning from the front, if he could be prevailed upon to discuss his experiences, offered an alternative to the communiqués of the high command. Rumors also shaped the day-to-day views of civilians. Some rumors kept spirits up with optimistic tidings. Many more explained dangers and failures, often by pointing to mysterious and traitorous activity both at home and in the military. Early in the war, rumors spread, often speedily, through private conversations. Later, when crowds gathered in food lines or in front of posted military casualty lists, bitter accounts of "what was really happening" leapt from mouth to mouth in lightning fashion.

From the first weeks of the war, Britain saw a wave of rumors. The First Sea Lord, Louis of Battenberg, whose family originated in Germany and Austria, was alleged to be a German spy. Some even claimed he had been arrested at the war's beginning and confined to the tower of London. Large numbers of Russian troops, "with snow on their boots" despite the August heat, had been seen disembarking in Scotland or perhaps in Yorkshire en route to the western front. The first British troops to clash with the Germans—at Mons in the third week of August—had been saved from defeat by angelic hordes fighting by their side. Suspicious individuals were supposedly buying poisonous substances in drug stores, and some had been caught trying to poison local water supplies. Enlisted men in the Territorial Army (the British equivalent of the American National Guard) were dying during forced marches to their duty stations. When zeppelin raids began in January 1915, word spread that they were being guided to their targets by automobiles with their headlights on.

The growth of the British munitions industry led to a spate of ugly stories. Munitions production, it was bruited about, remained low because of drunkenness among the workers. The new women workers operated their machinery too rapidly allegedly in order to make as much money as possible. On the other hand, women workers also sabotaged the machines when they wished to have an unscheduled rest period.

The death of Minister of War Horatio Kitchener en route to Russia on a Royal Navy cruiser was said to be the result of treasonous plotting among members of the high command. Pursuing betrayal in other quarters, some alleged that the twenty-eight cafés set up in central London by Belgian refugees were in reality a gathering place for spies.

In early 1918, one sweeping rumor came from Pemberton Billing, an eccentric Member of Parliament. His rabble-rousing journal *Vigilante* published articles hinting darkly that the Germans possessed a "Black Book" listing the sexual misdeeds of leading members of British society. This purported record of bad conduct, according to Billing, gave the Germans the power to blackmail the influential and to shape how Britain conducted the conflict. In fact, it explained what Billing dubbed "all the regrettable incidents' of this war."[11] Even Prime Minister Lloyd George promoted rumors of hidden enemies under the nation's bed.

In Germany, the spread of pessimistic rumors proved so alarming that the military tried in vain to punish those who spread them. They had more success in just getting civilians to report rumors to the authorities. Some widely circulating tales had a positive cast: The food supply would soon improve, a general peace or at least peace with one of Germany's adversaries was in sight. Even these happy tales struck officials as alarming, because their inaccuracy was certain to be evident in short order.

Most rumors had a darker tone. German civilians heard through the grapevine that officers in rear areas were wallowing in luxury while troops at the front lacked decent rations. One particularly disturbing rumor had it that many families were being told their loved ones had died in battle. In reality, the soldiers had gone insane or been horribly disfigured and placed in hidden institutions. For Germans facing daily food shortages, it might have seemed plausible when a friend or neighbor told them that hundreds of civilians were dying of starvation each day in Munich and Berlin. The authorities were carrying off their corpses in streetcars. Such Germans were doubtless enraged by rumors that food from their country was being diverted to the enemy. Supposedly, British ships sunk by submarines had left crates of eggs and sacks of flour floating on the waves. The various packages showed marks indicating their origin in Germany.

One rumored explanation for the failure to win the war illustrated the growing shakiness of Kaiser Wilhelm II's public image: Word spread that the Emperor was at heart loyal to his English relatives. He had all his money stashed away in English banks! In the war's closing weeks, rumors spread that General Erich Ludendorff, the strongman in the military high command, had taken his life.

PROPAGANDA

All governments stimulated and channeled popular feeling in support of the conflict. The casualty lists mounted. The war fever that had appeared in the conflict's early months faded. Increasingly governments manipulated the civilian population to keep morale high and the war effort in full force.

At the very start of hostilities, French and British publicists set the tone for propaganda on both sides. Germany had clearly violated international treaties by invading neutral Belgium, but it was easier to rouse emotions with stories of German soldiers who decapitated infants and chopped off the hands of young Belgian boys. Another theme guaranteed to linger in the memory was the sexual molestation of civilian women. When German battle cruisers killed civilians during attacks on the ports of eastern England, the British immediately dubbed the enemy "baby-killers." The Germans countered with stories of Belgian priests luring German soldiers into ambushes, British soldiers using dumdum bullets on the battlefield, and British repression in Ireland. They added that German prisoners of war were dying in huge numbers as a result of conditions in British prison camps.

British propaganda benefited from the talents of fine civilian writers. Most German efforts to influence public opinion came from cautious bureaucrats in the War Press Office, a part of the War Ministry. Thus, German air raids on Britain, with the resulting civilian deaths, permitted British writers to portray Count Zeppelin, the German inventor of the airship, as a "wholesale contriver of murder." Allied bombing raids against cities like Karlsruhe in western Germany also killed numerous civilians including young children, but War Ministry censors blocked the publication of news reports about these horrors.[12]

Visual propaganda had even greater force. The wartime poster could rouse emotions in short order, and the British government issued over 100 during the first year of the war. Presenting the enemy as a hulking monster about to ravage the homeland was guaranteed to evoke a response. So too was the image of the enemy as a sexual predator. A notable British propaganda poster of 1917 responded to the German decision to deport French and Belgian civilians for labor service in Germany: It showed a brutish German soldier abducting an innocent young girl.

The American government's Committee on Public Information flooded the workplace and other public gatherings with its "Four Minute Men." Recruited for their speaking ability, these individuals presented pep talks heard by millions in support of the war. In a nation filled with recent immigrants, the committee found recruits able to deliver their patriotic speeches in a variety of tongues, and the committee published its propaganda pamphlets in languages including Yiddish, Swedish, and Spanish. The committee also moved enthusiastically into the new medium of film. It produced some itself and publicized others from private moviemakers. Some, like *Pershing's Crusaders*, glorified the men of the AEF. Others, like *The Kaiser, the Beast of Berlin*, presented an appropriately evil view of the enemy.

The French government boosted morale during the final years of the war by tapping the energies of local elementary school teachers. They conducted educational conferences on the war in farming towns to attract members of the surrounding peasant farms. Because country folk were usually too exhausted or too apathetic to attend, such efforts drew mainly townspeople. In 1918, the teachers moved out into the villages, and by the middle of the year peasants in all but the tiniest and most remote French communities had at least one lecture on the war's features. Equipped with teaching guides from the central government, the teachers faced the inevitable questions of why the war went on interminably, why prices continued to rise, and what difference Russia's departure from the war and America's entry into it would make. To all of those, they offered the most optimistic responses they could contrive.

Propaganda campaigns accompanied important shifts in policy. When Germany began unrestricted U-boat operations in early 1917, the new offensive offered the chance to win the war quickly but inevitably meant bringing the United States into the conflict. The German propaganda machine launched an energetic campaign to secure popular approval. The public was flooded with millions of copies of pamphlets with optimistic titles like "To the Final Battle" or bracing ones like "We Must Win."

POPULAR CULTURE

Making a top military or government leader into a familiar figure assured the population of a warring country that the conduct of the conflict was in good hands. The mustachioed features of Field Marshal Kitchener looked out from millions of recruiting posters to tell the nation's male civilians "I Want You." In Germany, Field Marshal Paul von Hindenberg took on a similar role. Wooden statues of the husky, unflappable military leader—first the commander on the eastern front, then the nation's supreme military commander—appeared in numerous city squares. Germans showed their patriotic devotion by paying a small sum to drive a nail into the statue, the money going to support the war effort.

Companies marketed the by-products of the war to those at home.

German patriotic postcard. Courtesy of the
Hoover Institution Archives.

With the fighting only a few weeks old, advertisements in British
women's magazines for a well-known beauty treatment presented an
urgent message: "Do not neglect your appearance. At times like the present the country should see their women-folk looking their best."[13] Soon,
advertisers offered British women the chance to purchase a small medal
showing that a family member was in uniform. As women moved into
factory work, the advertisers followed. Yen Yusa, the "Oxygen Face
Cream," was publicized as the answer to the strain on the skin from "the
grit and grime of the munitions factories, exacting hospital work, and
exposure to sudden weather changes."[14]

In Germany, chess sets and children's games were modeled after the
structure of armies. Popular gifts for children included miniature cannon
and mechanical soldiers who fought each other with hand grenades.
German publishers flooded the market with cheap wartime adventure
novels and wartime playing cards. The latter put a picture of Emperor

— Tiens, le poilu qu'a un casque comme le mien.

French postcard showing a child identifying with a soldier. Courtesy of the Hoover Institution Archives.

Wilhelm II on the ace, and his leading military commanders appeared on the other face cards. When a German submarine sank the British ocean liner *Lusitania* in May 1915, a company issued a postcard celebrating the event. It showed the ship along with a small picture of Admiral Alfred von Tirpitz, the father of the modern German navy.

In France, the wartime postcard, produced by more than seventy different companies, let people send a private message accompanied by an expression of concern about the war. Subject to government censorship, they nonetheless delved into vulgarity—a child urinating into a German helmet—and even mild criticism of the war effort—a baby leaving an egg, viewing the battlefield around him, and stating "If this is life, I prefer to go back inside."[15] One French company, Pellerin in the city of Épinal, prospered during the war by marketing colorful posters with

—Fusillez-moi, je suis le maire, mais
relâchez notre bon vieux curé.

French postcard showing children playing at
war. Courtesy of the Hoover Institution Archives.

glamorous scenes purporting to show what combat on the western front
was like.

Wartime themes came to the stage. In the first months of the war, a
French, German, or British theatergoer found playbills filled with productions touting patriotism and national solidarity. In London, plays like
Tommy Atkins and *England Expects* were on offer. Numerous German
productions showed the new willingness of labor and management to
put aside their grievances. They began with scenes of conflict between
the upper and lower classes, and invariably presented a final scene with
everyone standing in patriotic harmony, sometimes on the battlefield.

But the growing human cost of the war and the resulting change in
the popular mood made the public look to escapist productions. Light
comedies and detective stories were the rage in all countries by the summer of 1915. German musicals set in the present offered such themes as

the faithful wife and equally faithful spouse at the front. German soldiers appeared fending off the advances of loose French women. The tone of the London theater pushed one prominent British general to complain about the vulgarity and suggestiveness to be seen on the stage. The German stage remained more cosmopolitan than its counterparts across the battle lines: The works of William Shakespeare, George Bernard Shaw, and Oscar Wilde continued to appear throughout the war.

Those who wanted to leave the war behind for a few hours found it increasingly hard to do at the theater. As the war went on, performances in Paris were limited to three a week. Germans had to sit in unheated halls to watch casts perform. There were increasingly strained efforts to make light of wartime shortages. German plays examined the power of saleswomen, maids, and cooks. They now outranked their patrons by their ability to find and distribute scarce goods. By the final months of the conflict, some German theatrical productions reflected true desperation about the food shortage.

CHILDREN, SCHOOLING, DELINQUENCY

Children saw their lives change as well. Many of their male teachers left for military service. With one out of every three German school teachers gone, children attended school only a few days a week and sat in combined classes that held as many as eighty students. The army regularly requisitioned German schoolhouses, and a child was likely to attend classes in a makeshift and uncomfortable location provided by local government or religious authorities. School curricula everywhere included topics connected to the war, and children became the objects of official propaganda. German schoolchildren received lessons in the vital area of food conservation. History and geography were obvious areas for wartime, patriotic themes. But, with a little imagination, a teacher could use a mathematics lesson as well. Asking a class to convert the 200 marks a German prisoner of war in England received from his family into English pounds was one approach teachers used.

Starting in 1917, war study courses appeared in American schools. Elementary school children learned that the United States was at war with Germany to protect the victims of German aggression in Europe. A more emotional theme certain to make an impression on a young child also appeared in the syllabus: American soldiers were fighting "to keep the German soldiers from coming to our country and treating us the same way."[16] High school students received much the same message prepared by Samuel B. Harding, a professor of History at Indiana University. David Kennedy has summarized Harding's message as declaring "that Germany alone had caused the war, that German soldiers fought cruelly without regard to the laws of God or Man . . . and that the Allies sincerely wished peace, which the Germans callously scorned."[17]

In 1915, German school children were asked to draw their impressions of the war for an exhibit in Berlin. Whereas many elementary school girls sketched an absent father, male students of that age produced detailed and accurate drawings of submarines, guns, and zeppelins. Children in the ten- to fourteen-year range showed their awareness of the gritty side of the war with violent combat scenes and images of battlefield casualties. By early 1917, teachers were dazzling school children with stories of heroic U-boat commanders and their promising efforts to win the war for Germany.

French children were presented with a curriculum that integrated the war into every subject. Essays made up a large part of the school routine, and they offered a chance for children to hail French heroes like General Joseph Joffre, to express pride in the fighting men at the front, and, most striking, to articulate their hatred for the Germans. One French schoolboy in 1916 wrote of that hatred that "will always exist between the French nation and the German nation, for what they have done is unforgivable and unforgettable."[18] On the other hand, a youngster's willing immersion in wartime feelings did not always last. By the final year of the war, French schoolteachers reported that many children were indifferent to the conflict's events. Some even expressed pacifist sentiments.

The strains on the school system combined with a wealth of job openings to pull older children into the factories. Meanwhile, the departure of fathers and school teachers, along with the general disruption of peacetime routines, led to a surge in juvenile crime. In Germany, unexcused absences from school became common, and the number of adolescents convicted of crime in 1918 stood at twice the prewar figures. Adolescent boys found their labor in high demand in wartime industry. The resulting high wages gave them a freedom the authorities found dangerous and disturbing. Such young men were much in evidence in Germany's bars, tobacco shops, and movie theaters. They were reputedly frequent clients for the country's prostitutes.

German authorities approached the problem with a variety of measures. An employed teenage boy was likely to encounter one of the growing number of youth-welfare workers, and he also faced recruitment into an officially sponsored paramilitary organization, the "youth army," designed to prepare him for life in uniform at a later age. He faced a curfew in many areas and often found himself forbidden to smoke in public. His freedom to visit bars after nine o'clock in the evening and even to attend the movies without an adult was also subject to official restrictions. Starting in 1916, many workers younger than nineteen saw the bulk of their wages placed in bank accounts, which they could tap only with official permission.

In Britain, the delinquency of young females stirred concern, especially during the early part of the war. The sudden expansion of the army meant that military camps were springing up all over the country. The dislocation of the nation's young men was matched by blows to the routine lives of young working-class women, many of whom lost their jobs as the war disrupted civilian industry. Alarmed middle-class observers saw many of these young women turn into so-called "Khaki girls," who clustered around military camps and sought relationships with new army recruits.

The fear of "Khaki girls" reflected a mixture of concerns: over the spread of venereal disease, over the new social freedoms being seized by lower-class women and girls, and especially over the possibility that these practices would move up the social ladder to provoke similar behavior from young females in "better" families. An image of wild girls corrupting innocent young men in uniform appeared in some commentaries. One writer described a group of soldiers pursued by young girls like "tigresses at their heels." An even more alarmed observer worried that "impressionable, undisciplined girls, hardly more than children, . . . have often ended by entangling themselves and their soldier friends in actually vicious conduct."[19]

Creating British women's police patrols became one remedy for the problem. Once established, these enforced middle-class moral standards in public places. Some women's police organizations eventually became integrated into regular police forces. During the war, their stated aim, as one spokeswoman put it, "was to act as a steadying influence on girls and young women, and in general to look after their interests."[20]

The danger faded as the conflict continued. The growing war effort provided abundant places for potential "Khaki girls" in war industries, health services, and eventually in women's auxiliaries to the armed forces. The Girl Guides, founded before the war as a sister organization to the Boy Scouts, seemed to offer a healthy outlet for young women's exuberance and energy. Their numbers almost doubled during the course of the war—from 40,000 to 70,000 members—and observers saw them turning potential "Khaki girls" into upstanding junior citizens.

NOTES

1. Quoted in John Williams, *The Other Battleground: The Home Fronts: Britain, France and Germany, 1914–1918* (Chicago: Henry Regnery, 1972), 161.

2. Trevor Wilson, *The Myriad Faces of War: Britain and the Great War, 1914–1918* (Cambridge, Eng.: Polity Press, 1986), 149.

3. Ibid., 221; P.J. Flood, *France, 1914–1918: Public Opinion and the War Effort* (Houndmills, Basingstoke, Hampshire, Eng.: Macmillan, 1990), 115.

4. Quoted in Wilson, *Myriad Faces*, 655.

5. James Mcmillan, *Twentieth-Century France: Politics and Society 1898–1991* (London: Edward Arnold, 1992), 72.

6. Laurence Moyer, *Victory Must Be Ours: Germany in the Great War, 1914–1918* (New York: Hippocrene Books, 1995), 209–10.

7. Roger Chickering, *Imperial Germany and the Great War, 1914–1918* (Cambridge, Eng.: Cambridge University Press, 1998), 161.

8. Quoted in John Horne, "Immigrant Workers in France during World War I," *French Historical Studies* 14, no. 1 (1985), 64.

9. Quoted in ibid., 69.

10. Quoted in Jürgen Kocka, *Facing Total War: German Society, 1914–1918*, trans. Barbara Weinberger (Leamington Spa, Eng.: Berg Publishers, 1984), 25.

11. Wilson, *Myriad Faces*, 641–42; also Panikos Panayi, *The Enemy in Our Midst: Germans in Britain during the First World War* (New York: Berg, 1991), 176–80.

12. Moyer, *Victory*, 196.

13. Quoted in Susan Kingsley Kent, *Making Peace: The Reconstruction of Gender in Interwar Britain* (Princeton, N.J.: Princeton University Press, 1993), 15.

14. Quoted in Gail Braybon, *Women Workers in the First World War: The British Experience* (London: Croom Helm, 1981), 163–64.

15. Marie-Monique Huss, "Pronatalism and the Popular Ideology of the Child in Wartime France: The Evidence of the Picture Postcard," in *The Upheaval of War: Family, Work and Welfare in Europe, 1914–1918*, ed. Richard Wall and Jay Winter (Cambridge, Eng.: Cambridge University Press, 1988), 336.

16. Quoted in David Kennedy, *Over Here: The First World War and American Society* (Oxford: Oxford University Press, 1980), 55.

17. Ibid., 56.

18. Quoted in Stephane Audoin-Rouzeau, "French Children as Target for Propaganda," in *Facing Armageddon: The First World War Experienced*, ed. Hugh Cecil and Peter Liddle (London: Leo Cooper, 1996), 771.

19. Quoted in Angela Woollacott. " 'Khaki Fever' and Its Control: Gender, Class, Age and Sexual Morality on the British Homefront in the First World War," *Journal of Contemporary History* 29, no. 2 (1994): 330–31.

20. Quoted in ibid., 335.

10

Civilian Hardships

Numerous civilians felt the sharp edge of the war's harshness. In 1914, the German army occupied densely populated areas of Belgium and France. Swarms of refugees fled from the fighting and the danger of falling under German control. But larger numbers, unable or unwilling to leave their homes, found themselves living under enemy occupation for years to come. The invaders compounded the inevitable disruption of normal life with a deliberate policy of intimidation. German control meant hostage-taking and bloody reprisals for alleged acts of resistance.

Civilians became the targets of weapons in enemy hands. The grim innovations scientific and technological progress had brought into the war put noncombatants in immediate danger. Aerial bombing could strike large areas of the home country. The German submarine war against Allied merchant ships meant passengers traveled at the risk of their lives.

Prewar Europe had permitted wide freedom of movement across international borders. Tourists traveled without passports or significant restrictions. A citizen of one country often settled in another—to study, to work, even to marry and start a family. Members of both groups were now exposed to being declared unwelcome aliens, citizens of an enemy society. Such individuals and families faced the hostility—often violently expressed—of their neighbors. Newly suspicious officials restricted their travel and living arrangements. Male aliens were likely to suffer confinement, often for the full four years the war lasted.

INVASION AND OCCUPATION

The German sweep westward in 1914 put almost all Belgium under occupation. In France, the Germans held portions of fourteen departments temporarily, and, after their pullback to strong defenses, they kept ten entire departments under their control. More than 2 million members of the French population were under German military authority for the next four years. Virtually the entire Belgian population of 7.6 million likewise experienced an oppressive German presence.

In order to stifle resistance and to limit the need for large garrisons, German commanders adopted a policy of exemplary brutality toward civilians in the war zone. The tales of German atrocities that soon circulated in Britain and the United States included fictional elements. But reality was enough to shock. And the Germans permitted journalists from neutral countries to accompany their armies. This made the stories from the occupied lands available quickly and exposed them to a wide audience.

To control the population, the invaders identified leading figures in occupied communities and deported them to Germany. During its brief occupation of the strategic French city of Amiens, the Germans abducted 1,500 of its citizens. A more brutal device was to take—and often to execute—hostages in reprisal for real, anticipated, or imagined resistance to German forces.

In August 1914, both the German army and the German press encouraged soldiers to fear resistance from armed civilians: cowardly snipers, torturers of helplessly wounded German soldiers. Whether armed civilians—akin to the "franc-tireurs" who had opposed the German invasion of France in 1870–71—existed remains uncertain. Nervous German troops firing at one another may have been the real cause of rumors, but the brutal response came quickly. The Belgian frontier village Warsage was one of the first locales in which hostages were shot, and nearby Battice was an early example of an entire village burned to the ground.[1]

With the permission of its high-ranking officers, the German army executed more than 5,000 Belgians and destroyed some 16,000 buildings in the provinces of Luxembourg, Namur, Brabant, and Hainault. The most visible atrocities took place in Brabant. There, much of the city of Louvain, including historic buildings that were part of its ancient university, was vandalized and destroyed. The killing went on for days at a time, and even distinguished members of the university faculty who pleaded for their lives in fluent German were gunned down.[2]

German soldiers' diaries confirm that such bloody reprisals occurred in Belgium and the border areas of France. German apologists for their army's conduct cited the military's justifiable response to civilian resis-

Advertisement for a French exhibition on
German war crimes. Courtesy of the Hoover
Institution Archives.

tance, but the scope and brutality of German actions remains jarring. In
Schaffen, near Louvain, fifty civilians were executed on August 18. Their
crime was to have sought shelter in a church tower the Germans identified as a source of hostile machine-gun fire. Two hundred Belgians
were shot down and their village of Leffe, located near Dinant, destroyed
by fire. At Nomény, a border town in Lorraine, the victims were French.
There, German soldiers experienced a single artillery shell exploding in
their midst. In response, their regimental commander ordered the male
population of Nomény to be executed, the women and children driven
into exile.[3]

Targeting Catholic priests was a particularly ugly aspect of German
reprisal policy. Anti-Catholicism among German Protestant soldiers
combined with lurid stories that Belgian and French priests were or-
chestrating resistance to the German advance. Many in the advancing

German ranks saw priests as the leaders of "franc-tireur" activity. Rumors ran wild that priests were using their churches as torture chambers to mutilate wounded German soldiers. The Germans viewed church bell towers as likely sites for enemy communication posts and machine-gun nests. Soldiers' war diaries confirm the execution of individual priests, sometimes with large numbers of their parishioners. Belgium's bishops claimed that the Germans murdered fifty of their priests at the start of the war.

The initial wave of bloody atrocities did not go on long. The occupation in both Belgium and German-held France now took a largely non-violent but oppressive form. In Belgium, the Germans left the domestic civil service intact. In occupied France, they put the upper levels of the government in their own hands. Thus, France's prefects and subprefects no longer had a role to play in directing the life of the civilian population. It was the local mayor and city councilors who dealt with the Germans. French civilians found themselves tied to their home communities. German authorities had to give special permission before a French citizen could leave his town for any reason. Those who sheltered French or British soldiers learned that they risked execution at the hands of the Germans.

German control created a painful and isolated way of living for the occupied population. Families were cut off from word of their loved ones on the other side of the fighting front. The barrier of the trenches hid the fate of the young men who had escaped to join the French army. Family members could only turn to the German-controlled newspapers available in the occupied zone such as *Le Bruxellois* or *La Gazette des Ardennes*. These published lists of prisoners of war and identified French captives who came from occupied communities like Lille, Tourcoing, and Roubaix who had fallen into enemy hands. Many in those cities had no word from loved ones during the entire fifty-two months of enemy control.

These communities faced a daily dose of tedium, uncertainty, and petty regulations. Ruled by foreigners, they were now largely populated by females, boys, and old men. A German-produced French phrase book for use by occupation troops put all verbs in the imperative form; Germans would speak to the French only in the tone of superiors addressing inferiors.[4]

German pressure on the civilian population included massive seizure of property. Soon after arriving, the invaders demanded five-sixths of the harvest to feed their soldiers and their home population. Most French families in communities like Roubaix were permitted to keep their homes, but the Germans seized mattresses and other material useful for their war effort. In order to keep warm in the bitterly cold winters of northern Europe, families gradually demolished the interiors of their own dwellings. They tore apart bookcases, staircases, and other wooden structures for firewood. People lived on the floors for lack of furniture.

A shortage of food added to the drabness of life. German authorities refused to accept any responsibility for feeding the populations under their control. Belgian groups, aided by an American relief service established by Herbert Hoover in October 1914, kept a flow of food arriving for that country. Starting in April 1915, Hoover took on the task of aiding the population of occupied France. But these efforts, directed by an inspired and talented administrator, provided only one meal a day. People ate in the early evening and found that the meal offered just enough nourishment to keep them alive. The topic of food dominated most conversations for the millions under German control. Many discussions contained bitter comments about the black market when people grew aware that some of the food arriving from abroad was being diverted for illicit sale.

German authorities began at once to seize laborers from the French civilian population. Potential workers, males from ages seventeen to fifty, had to report regularly to the authorities, and the occupiers pulled them away frequently and for extended periods of time. In the spring of 1915, a group of 1,500 men drawn from twenty communities was placed at Péronne, near the fighting front. They remained there and in adjacent areas until the Armistice in November 1918. In some cases, drafted workers found themselves deported to Germany. Women were also subjected to involuntary labor, and the young among them were subjected to sexual advances from their guards. According to Annette Becker, all those called up faced humiliating physical examinations, and some were even conscripted to serve as prostitutes for German soldiers.[5]

In October 1916, the Germans moved harshly against unwilling Belgian workers. Those who would not volunteer to take jobs in Germany or to work in Belgium to aid the occupiers faced deportation. The Germans tore about 120,000 such individuals from their everyday lives, shipped them to Germany, and forced them to perform labor service there. To the disappointment of the authorities, the levies raised only one-quarter of the hoped for numbers. An international outcry, led by Belgian Cardinal Mercier and joined by socialist deputies in the German Reichstag, forced the program to shut down. By the following summer, virtually all those seized in this summary fashion had been returned home.

Those in occupied territory had no reliable news about the course of the fighting, but they could not escape a nervous awareness of great battles taking place. All of occupied France stood within twenty miles of the front lines. The sounds of artillery thundered in communities like Lille. The railroad system supporting much of the German effort on the western front ran though occupied Belgium and France. Aware of in-

creased train traffic, civilians in the occupied zone sensed the preparations for an offensive—and then heard the trains carrying loads of
casualties back to Germany.

The presence of German military police—the *Feldgendarmerie* whom
the oppressed civilians called "green devils" because of the color of their
uniforms—was an everyday torment. The *Feldgendarmerie* patrolled with
their large police dogs, conducting the requisitions of goods and people
that drained the occupied zone. They hunted down members of the population who appeared to be engaged in active resistance. In occupied
France, the authorities compelled pigeon breeders to give up their birds,
because the animals could be used to send messages. Several breeders
who tried to evade the seizure—perhaps to help the Allies, perhaps
merely to treasure their pets—were caught and executed.[6]

Hunger and cold augmented by the humiliation of living under harsh
foreign control came to seem intolerable. As one Frenchwoman described
the situation, "Every day it felt as if we had reached the pit of human
wretchedness, and then the next day we saw there was more to come."
In the midst of the harsh winter of 1916–17, her home city of Lille had
become a dreary and idle community in which most citizens went to bed
at five in the afternoon. "All you see in the streets," she recorded, "are
yellow faces, shrunk by privation and tears."[7]

As Richard Cobb has pointed out, military occupation had other consequences. With the passage of time, both civilians and the soldiers gar-
risoned among them had a shared weariness with the war and its
hardships. A population of young German men without women side by
side with a French population largely composed of women without men
led to sexual liaisons and a wave of childbirths. Cobb suggests that such
human ties crossed the barriers of nationality, and perhaps mitigated the
harshness of the occupation.

The Germans decided against sealing off the occupied zone completely. Instead, they permitted the repatriation of thousands of French
citizens from the occupied departments: the very young and the very
old, in particular. Thus, they sought to make those who could not help
the German war economy into a burden on the government in Paris. In
a gesture that smacks of cruel insult, they sent the prostitutes of one city
back in to unoccupied France.

Sadly, Frenchmen and Frenchwomen of all stripes uprooted in this
summary fashion found themselves unwelcome—and even suspected—
figures when they reached freedom. In southern areas of France where
many settled, some local inhabitants believed that the refugees had aided
the German war effort. Thus, the strangers were accused of helping to
prolong what the locals called *"votre guerre"* (your war). Many of their
compatriots applied the harsh appellation *"Les Boches du Nord"* (the
Krauts of the North) to refugees from occupied France, demonstrating

French refugees flee the advancing German army. Courtesy of the National Archives.

their contempt for Frenchmen whom they considered Germany's accomplices.

REFUGEES

Floods of civilians fled the assault of the German armies on the western front in 1914. As many as 1.4 million Belgians left their communities during the chaotic first days of the war, many to take shelter behind the fortifications at Antwerp. Most of these people eventually returned home. But hundreds of thousands of Belgians chose to leave or felt forced to depart. Many hiked across the border into France or neutral Holland. Others ran from one seaport to another—Antwerp, Ostend—before boarding a ship for Britain.

Later military operations also created numerous refugees. As German shells rained down on the Ypres salient in April 1915, members of the population who had dared to stay on after the start of the war picked up and left. When the German assault on Verdun began in February 1916, French authorities ordered the city's civilians to evacuate within five hours.

From the war's start, observers were struck by the sight of pitiable families, hauling possessions selected in a moment of panic, racing to escape the advancing Germans. A French civil servant in Paris watched Belgian civilians of all ages, "weeping with weariness, pushing carts and barrows and children's prams," their choice of what to take at a moment's notice "revealing to all their scale of values concerning their intimate possessions." Perhaps they had turned away from the practical choice of bedding in order to salvage "the old family clock."[8]

By late 1914, some 200,000 Belgians had settled in Britain. Many arrived directly. Others had taken temporary shelter in Holland, and they left when the Dutch government persuaded Britain to accept this added burden of refugees. Placed suddenly in Britain, many Belgians had a difficult adjustment to make. The very first to arrive tended to be the wealthy and educated, often with personal contacts in Britain. But most refugees came from working-class families. With no knowledge of English, they found themselves strangers. They had taken refuge in a Protestant country where their Catholicism marked them as outsiders. They were coffee drinkers in a country where all activity stopped in the late afternoon for tea. They were lovers of good food in a country where outsiders found the manner of cooking appalling.

The British attitude toward these unexpected visitors evolved from an open-armed welcome to an increasing sense of discomfort. People offered accommodation to strangers in their homes, but they thought better of their pledge when the cost and duration became clearer. H.G. Wells's novel *Mr. Britling Sees It Through* expressed the difficulties in remaining a sympathetic host to a long-term foreign visitor.

In time, the shortage of workers in arms factories created enough job opportunities to absorb many of the immigrants. The establishment of Belgian communities—with various forms of communal housing—in the factory regions of central England helped as well. It eased the strains of having a substantial foreign contingent suddenly placed within the British population. Stories of spectacular adjustments—such as the Belgian poet who now worked at a shell factory—put a sunny façade on a grim reality. Less favorable material for upbeat press coverage were the Belgian physicians who had difficulty in qualifying to pursue their professions, and the Belgian attorneys who found it impossible.

Belgian refugees endured four years of exile and uncertainty about relatives and friends back home. They remained restricted aliens in British society, limited in where they could reside and required to notify the police of every journey they took. By the war's conclusion, more Belgians were settled in France than in Britain, and the zone of territory near their home where they concentrated became known as "little Belgium."

COMBAT FATALITIES: ON LAND

Much of the war's combat took place in populated regions, and this placed civilians in peril. Even when not the intended targets, civilians could become casualties of wartime weapons. Some of the first such victims were the citizens of the Belgian city of Ypres and the masses of refugees who had fled there. As the Germans closed in on this crucial British stronghold in the fall of 1914, their artillery and aerial bombing leveled much of the city. The local priest recorded what it was like. "Today, 3rd November, the first shells fell on the hospital of Notre Dame causing terrible damage. Arthur Debos was mortally wounded. He died a few minutes after receiving extreme unction." The following day, he added: "The exodus of inhabitants continues. . . . The great shells continue to rain down. . . . Oscar Seghers was killed, also a woman. Many, many wounded."[9] Sometimes, civilians suffered from both enemy occupation and their city's location near the battle lines. The city of Soissons, occupied by the Germans at the war's beginning, came under intense Allied artillery fire from September 1914 to February 1915.

Fire from friendly guns could be deadly. In Ypres in July 1917, Allied antiaircraft artillery fired at German bombers but missed their targets. As the spent shells fell to earth, fragments struck the home of one Belgian family. A young child was killed instantly by the deadly metal. The mother of the family lost a leg and, after being evacuated to a military hospital, perished from her injuries.

Sometimes innocent civilians were deliberate targets. In December 1914, German warships slipped through the British fleet dominating the North Sea to bombard three cities—Hartlepool, Scarborough, and Whitby—along the eastern coast of England. Hartlepool suffered the worst damage when German battle cruisers attacked from two miles offshore. Starting around eight o'clock in the morning, German naval guns fired for half an hour. They killed 86 and wounded 424. Local military units were on the scene, but inevitably the victims were mainly civilians.

The naval bombardment shook the sense that Britain's population at home was free from the threat of enemy attack. The stalemate at sea released German naval zeppelins to conduct raids against the enemy's homeland. With the onset of German aerial attacks, that sense of security vanished for the duration of the war. Starting in January 1915, zeppelins bombed London and parts of southeastern England. Over the following two years, they widened their range of operations reaching the English Midlands, the West Country, and even southern Scotland.

The zeppelin assault produced only a limited number of deaths and injuries. A series of nine raids between June and October 1915 resulted in only 127 fatalities and 352 injured.[10] Nonetheless, the zeppelins constituted a visible sign of the homeland's vulnerability. They attacked on dark nights and cruised above the altitude at which British fighter planes or ground fire could reach them. There were attempts to put a humorous interpretation on the attacks: Theaters advertised that performances would take place on "full moon" nights, that is, times during which zeppelin attacks were unlikely. But such forced levity showed how the attacks penetrated the popular mind.

German newspapers reflected the new weapon's successes, but with a tone of jubilation. "The City of London, the heart which pumps the life-blood into the arteries of the brutal huckster nation has been sown with bombs by German airships," crowed one Leipzig newspaper. "At last, the long yearned for punishment has fallen on . . . this people of liars and hypocrites." By late 1916, however, British defenses, which included fighter planes armed with a powerful explosive type of ammunition, were downing the attackers regularly.[11]

But airplanes constituted a more potent danger. They could defend themselves more effectively than the zeppelins, and several together could carry the equivalent of an airship's heavy bomb load. Civilian populations on both sides of the battle line faced this threat. Allied bombers operating from bases in eastern France could reach western German cities, including Cologne, Mainz, Karlsruhe, and Freiburg. American bombers augmented attacks by the French and British bombers by the closing months of the war. A total of 768 Germans died as a result of such air raids from 1914 through 1918. A citizen of Freiburg who resided in that university community throughout the war found his city under aerial attack on twenty-five occasions. Thirty-one of his fellow citizens died as a result of these assaults.[12]

The location of the fighting fronts and the range of World War I aircraft placed the largest British and French cities at greater risk. Targets for air attack included the two national capitals. The first attack on London by an airplane came in late November 1916. Only minor harm resulted: a few wrecked buildings near Victoria Station and ten injured citizens. To reassure the public, military authorities announced calmly that "this morning six bombs were dropped on London by a hostile aeroplane flying at a great height above the haze," adding that "[t]he material damage is slight."[13]

In June 1917, German bombers began a potent assault on the British capital. The initial attacks came in daylight when many of London's inhabitants were at work or at school. The first raid took a grisly toll: 162 fatalities and 432 injured. Public outrage sharpened when Londoners learned that sixteen of the dead were school children no more than five years old. Their attempt to shelter from the raid in a cellar failed to save them. A young British officer on leave from the trenches noted that "the German air raids had almost persuaded my London friends that London was the sole battlefront."[14]

In response to stiffened British defenses, the German attackers began operations at night. By September, the first type of German bomber, the Gotha, had been supplemented by a few Giant (Riesen) planes. These approximated the size of the American B-29 bomber of World War II and carried more than a ton of bombs. Together, the Gothas and Giants impelled thousands of Londoners to desert the city. Those who stayed found safety in subway stations far below ground, but relocating there for the night added to the physical and mental anguish of a multitude of Britons. And panic brought on by sudden air raids led to deadly tragedies. A crush outside two shelters saw fourteen people trampled to death. Air attacks continued on London and other parts of Great Britain until May 1918.

Paris, closer to the battle line and less well defended than London, also experienced several varieties of attack from the air. A German airplane first struck in September 1914, resulting in only one casualty. Paris also faced attack by zeppelins, the initial raid taking place in March 1915. President Raymond Poincaré was able to see the airship from the Elysée Palace, describing it as "a gigantic golden shape in the sky." The initial attack did no damage, but in January 1916, a second attack killed twenty-four people. Although the airships did not return, the prolonged fear of attack continued. One observer in Paris at Christmas-time in 1917 noted "there was constant fear of the Zeppelins."[15]

By that time, German bombers were the greater threat. Starting in January 1918, squadrons of Gotha bombers struck Paris. Dozens of additional attacks took place through the spring and early summer. The raids in March alone resulted in 120 fatalities. Communal air raid shelters and private cellars became a second home for many of the French capital's citizens.

By 1918, long-range German guns also threatened the citizens and buildings of Paris. Located at Crépy-en-Laonnais, approximately seventy-five miles northeast of the French capital, these mammoth German artillery pieces began their assault on March 23. For seven hours on the first day, explosions erupted in more than twenty locations. The blasts created several bomb craters in central locations such as the Tuileries Gardens and the Place de la République. It took some time for the authorities to examine the shell fragments and to conclude that they were fired from cannon rather than the remnants of an aerial bombardment.

There followed forty-four days of this random artillery assault. The Germans coordinated their attacks with their final ground offensive in the spring of 1918. Carefully censored French press reports made it clear that the shells were not coming from short-range cannon. Thus, Parisians could take some comfort from the fact that the enemy was not yet on the city's doorstep. Nonetheless, with no way to aim precisely, the Germans were out to demoralize the inhabitants of the French capital with the threat of sudden and unpredictable explosions. Herbert Hoover, the American Food Director, visited Paris in the summer and witnessed one such sudden eruption at close range.

The final toll of casualties reached 256 fatalities with another 625 peo-

Funeral for victims of the *Lusitania*. © Hulton-Deutsch Col-
lection/CORBIS.

ple injured.[16] Some observers spoke of the city's population taking the
shelling in stride. In time Parisians learned to avoid the swath of territory
where shells regularly struck. Nevertheless, combined with the approach
of the German army, the cannon fire propelled many to take their money
from their banks, rush to the railroad stations, and flee the city. There
was an exodus of some 500,000 people from the capital before the final
cannon shell arrived on August 9.

DEATH AT SEA: SUBMARINE ATTACKS

With Germany's expanding use of submarines, the naval war imperiled numerous civilians. The established law of the sea required navies
to respect the lives of civilian crews and passengers even when destroying the vessels on which they traveled. This meant warning those on a
merchant ship before sinking it. It also required taking steps to ensure
the safety of noncombatants on such a vessel. But the fragile structure
of submarines made such measures risky. It was too dangerous for a
submarine to warn a merchant vessel that it was about to be sunk: a
single shot from a merchant ship's deck gun could fatally damage the
sub. The cramped spaces of the submarine made it impossible to carry
more than a few of the survivors from a sunken vessel to safety.

Civilians traveling on a merchant ship or passenger liner as well as
the vessel's crew sailed at their peril. Professional merchant seamen were
accustomed to the risks of ocean travel such as storms, collisions, and
navigation in shallow, poorly charted water. But they now faced an

armed enemy who intended to sink their vessels by shell fire or torpedoes. For civilian passengers, there had been only negligible risks in modern sea travel, the most recent example being *Titanic*'s collision with an iceberg in April 1912. But these noncombatants, too, faced an armed enemy willing to endanger their lives by sinking the vessels on which they sailed.

The 500 civilian passengers on the English Channel steamer *Sussex* experienced such a submarine attack in March 1916. A torpedo blew off the ship's bow, killing everyone in the first-class dining room. One passenger recalled the sights and sounds: "There was a terrific bang and . . . I was blown on to the top deck. When I came to I saw a woman's dead body, a piece of something gruesome near me, and a solitary man standing by the davits staring down at the sea."[17]

When Germany declared unlimited submarine warfare in early 1917, no ship sailing the waters around Great Britain was secure from attack. Numerous American civilians began to experience the shock of a torpedo attack. An American newspaper correspondent, Floyd Gibbons, described the sensation he felt on Sunday evening, February 25, on the *Laconia*. The Cunard liner was bound for Liverpool when, all of a sudden, "the ship gave a sudden lurch sideways and forward. There was a muffled noise like the slamming of a door at a good distance away." Departing from the listing vessel, Gibbons watched as *Laconia* "sank rapidly at the stern until at last its nose stood straight in the air. Then it slid silently down and out of sight like a piece of disappearing scenery in a panorama spectacle."[18]

Death from drowning was the most immediate danger for those whose ship was a victim of the submarine. The American freighter *Aztec* with a cargo of food was approaching the French port of Brest when its captain saw "a brilliant flash forward," felt the vessel shudder, then list badly. More than half its crew—twenty-seven seamen—were lost. [19]

The total of fatalities in the spring of 1917 was gruesome: 630 merchant seamen dead in March alone. Some perished from the impact of the torpedo, and some from drowning. But reaching a lifeboat offered no guarantee of safety. The wife and sister of an American businessman in London perished in one of the *Laconia*'s lifeboats. They froze to death in the brutal cold of the North Atlantic. So too did sailors from the torpedoed American merchant ship *Vigilancia*. Sunk off the Scilly Islands near the southwestern tip of England, survivors of the crew drifted for two days before being rescued more than 140 miles from land. But fifteen crewmen died, many from exposure to the elements.

When 139 crewmen and passengers from the liner *Alnwick Castle* departed the torpedoed ship more than 500 miles out in the Atlantic, they could not have known that two of their lifeboats would disappear completely. The first boat carrying survivors to reach land came ashore in

Spain only after a nine-day ordeal. It left eight of the boat's occupants dead and twenty-one close to death.

In the heat of action, German U-boat commanders went beyond endangering the civilian survivors of torpedoed vessels. Some resorted to outright murder. On two occasions in April 1917, Lieutenant Wilhelm Werner took on board the skipper of a vessel he had just torpedoed. He then compelled the remaining members of the crew to line up on the deck of his U-boat and submerged, leaving them all to drown.

ALIENS AND INTERNEES

What aliens and internees experienced did not involve a massive loss of life. Nonetheless, tens of thousands of individuals found the pattern of their lives overturned. Surrounded by hostile neighbors, they underwent profound psychological shock. For many, a grim and prolonged confinement followed.

In pre-1914 Europe freedom of movement across international boundaries remained easy. Foreign countries welcomed the student who wanted to pursue a program of learning. The worker who wanted to put in a few years—or even to buy a business and settle—in an alien land was often able to do so. Thus, the outbreak of war caught thousands of civilians on the wrong side of the fighting lines. Women and children struggled to find transportation back to their native countries. Men of military age were subject to confinement.

An American official at the Paris Embassy witnessed the pain and disorientation felt by civilians from the Central Powers whose world had suddenly broken apart. "Last week they were everywhere treated with respect and politeness, today they are looked upon with suspicion and hostility. They are hungry, and they have no money. . . . Many have lost all their worldly goods and possess nothing except the clothes in which they stand."[20]

ALIENS IN BRITAIN AND GERMANY

Political, religious, and especially economic motives had created a community of over 53,000 Germans in Britain by the eve of World War I. More than half of them lived in metropolitan London. Waiters had a strong incentive to live in England, because a command of English improved their employment prospects in many parts of the world. Immigrant Germans worked frequently as bakers' assistants until they had learned the trade. Some of these Germans preferred to remain in England. Despite the fact that many retained their German citizenship, they married English women and had children in their adopted homeland.

Germany too was a gathering place for foreigners. Its advanced industries offered jobs to engineers and technicians from abroad. Distinguished German schools and universities attracted students from both sides of the Atlantic, and Germany's burgeoning interest in sports led various professional players to settle there for a time. German ports were always filled with foreign vessels and their crews. Summer holidays and an established German tourist industry brought thousands of short-term visitors to the Reich. At the same time, some Germans within Germany found themselves considered foreign aliens. They had been born to German parents residing temporarily in Britain or another foreign country. Some were German-born children of British citizens who had taken up permanent residence in Germany.

In Britain, many workers in hotels and restaurants—even King George V's chef—were enemy aliens who rushed to flee the country. Those who stayed were compelled to register with the police, and the government forced some 19,000, either immediately or soon after, into internment camps. Naturalized English families of German origin found it advisable to turn suddenly harsh sounding labels like "Steindecker" or "Stohwasser" into impeccable English surnames like "Stanley" and "Stowe." In October 1914, the government responded to nativist outrage expressed in newspaper editorials and letters to the editor columns and restricted such name changes without official permission.

In Britain, aliens from hostile countries, and even those from neutral nations, faced a network of restrictions. They were to register with the police, and they could not venture outdoors between nine o'clock in the evening and five o'clock in the morning without police permission. The authorities regarded aliens' travel with suspicion and barred them from militarily sensitive areas, especially seaside regions. Hotels and boarding houses were required to register and report the presence of foreigners.

Starting in August 1914, government orders required the internment of male German residents of military age. The government's first impulse was to confine all such Germans (and Austrians). But, at first, only those who seemed a threat to national security went behind bars. By the close of the month, 4,800 found themselves in custody. Harsh feelings at the war's beginning hardened further over time. Representatives of some fifty golf clubs met in late October 1914 to apply social sanctions on foreign-born and presumably dangerous elements. With only a single dissenting vote, they resolved to allow no naturalized German or Austrian players from using their courses for the duration of war. Enemy aliens received the harsher penalty of outright expulsion from their golf clubs for the duration.

Internees released from some provincial areas moved to London, and the public and press worried vocally about German military reservists wandering about in the nation's capital. The sinking of the British liner *Lusitania* by a German submarine in May 1915 escalated public hostility toward enemy aliens. The large, sudden loss of civilian life in the tragedy provoked a wave of popular anger, which the country's newspapers inflamed. Crowds looted German stores in London's East End; London business exchanges expelled German-born brokers, including those who had taken English citizenship; and even the German butchers in Smithfield market found themselves forced out of business by their British colleagues. Mobs wrecked the shops of German and Austrian bakers, who supplied much of the bread for east and south London. The government announced that virtually all male enemy aliens of military age still at large would be interned; older aliens, women, and children were to be forced to depart the country.

Many German aliens, aware of their precarious situation, applied voluntarily at their local police stations for internment. The recent riots showed them the danger they were in. Others reacted in opposite fashion to the outbreak of violence by going into hiding. The London police, especially in the East End where many aliens resided, put in extra hours to run down those who could not be readily located.

A final wave of hostility toward anyone with German links occurred during the tense summer of 1918. The strain of the long, costly war combined with news of the frightening German spring offensive to heighten popular xenophobia. Local officials in London moved to replace street names that seemed too unpatriotic in wartime: Hanover Street became Andover Street, for example. The scientific world responded as well: London's prestigious Royal Society voted to expel enemy aliens. Meanwhile, huge crowds gathered in central London in response to stories of the continuing presence of unconfined enemy aliens. David Lloyd George, the prime minister, threatened those with German connections. The final German offensive in France was still in progress when he spoke in the House of Commons on July 11. In his talk, he claimed that any British setback brought him "anonymous letters written by Germans in this country crowing over it." With the full prestige of his powerful office behind him, he asked, "Where are they?" and called out, "I feel that sort of thing has got to be stopped."[21]

In Germany, the authorities arrested large numbers of male Britons immediately upon the outbreak of the war. Merchant seamen caught in German ports in early August were some of the first targets. Other men with British citizenship remained free for a time, but they were required to register with the local police and report to that authority regularly. Female aliens from Britain kept their liberty throughout the war. If they rejected repatriation home via Holland, however, they were obligated to keep in contact with local police agencies.

Unlike Britain, Germany did not experience significant public outbreaks of anti-alien violence. But the German government acted quickly in demanding that all German detainees in Britain be released. When that call was not answered, the Germans took sweeping measures to intern male aliens of British nationality.

THE EXPERIENCE OF INTERNMENT

In German Confinement

British men who had not been taken into custody by November 6, 1914, now entered confinement as "detainees." Their new homes were civilian internment camps, the most famous of which was Ruhleben, a former racetrack in suburban Berlin. At Ruhleben, a camp population ranging from 1,000 to a peak of 5,500 spent the entire war. British subjects were ordered to Ruhleben if they were male and between the ages of seventeen and fifty-five.

Their predicament brought together a diverse group at Ruhleben. They included "company directors and seamen, concert musicians and factory workers, science professors and jockeys. Few had ever met previously; their only bond was their British citizenship."[22] The principal hardships, beyond the psychological strain of confinement, were cold, uncomfortable living quarters and poor food. The food situation eased in February 1915 when the British government began to provide four marks per week for each detainee. Thus enriched, individuals could supplement the meager rations provided by the German authorities; the Germans provided a daily payment of only sixty-six pfennigs per person.

Confinement at Ruhleben meant living behind barbed wire while German soldiers stood on alert to prevent escapes. The camp, located on drained marshland west of Berlin, consisted of ten acres. A tolerable place in summer, "in winter it was damp, dreary, and windswept." Educated inmates who sought to pass the time reading soon discovered that, appropriately enough for a stable, there was a shortage of indoor lighting. Toilets located some distance from the improvised barracks created an initial hardship. Constructing new ones in June 1915 scarcely alleviated the problem. Given the damp soil and poor drainage, no sanitary system could remove body wastes efficiently. Veterans of Ruhleben remembered the smell of the place long after they had been freed.[23]

Like imprisoned military officers, the detainees at Ruhleben did not have to labor for their German captors. This left them the task of making the time go by. Detainees slept in six-person horse "boxes," and these groups became the functioning core family for social interaction. The involuntary community contained numerous talented individuals and gave rise to a range of activities: Musicians created an orchestra, university professors taught classes, athletic types set up football competitions, and theatrical groups put on stage productions. Chess, checkers, cards, and raffles helped pass the time for those forced indoors by rainy

German winters. The detainees soon developed their own camp administration, prompting one German observer to declare: "You English seem to set to work as if you were founding a new colony." German officers in charge of the camp met with a flood of requests for improved living conditions. They often replied to their charges with frustration by stating, "You are forgetting that you are prisoners."[24]

Confinement led to waves of rumors. A tale that the British had captured the Belgian ports was one favorite, and word that the Royal Navy had sunk much of the German High Seas Fleet was another. But more solid information was available in the German newspapers sold in the camp. Moreover, there was a regular supply of smuggled English newspapers. Thus, morale benefited from a reasonable amount of information about the course of the war. Notwithstanding the mental strain of confinement, there were relatively few instances of serious emotional breakdowns. But some men did lose their mental bearings. For them, the constant but frustrated hope of release was too much to bear. Some of the younger men were depressed by being cut off from the military service their generation was offering the home country. It was alienating to be relatively safe at a time when their contemporaries were in the maelstrom of the western front.

In British Confinement

The British government had no plans for interning large numbers of enemy aliens. Nonetheless, by midsummer 1915, it had almost 46,000 German and Austro-Hungarian males on its hands in camps run by either the Home Office or the War Office. Initially, the authorities confined prisoners in hastily converted factories, tents, or even prison ships. Armed guards made it clear that the inmates, although civilians, would receive no undue freedom. One Austrian detainee recalled his introduction to a camp on the Isle of Man. The elderly camp commander told them: "If you will obey my orders I will treat you with kindness and consideration. Anybody attempting to escape will be shot."[25]

Inmates recalled their entry into camp with some bitterness. It featured an examination of their personal possessions, and the military guards seized anything and everything they wished. Occasional harsh incidents in the camps created a sour and fearful atmosphere. In November 1914, five internees were killed in a fusillade of gunfire. The bloodshed followed a dining hall riot at the Douglas Camp on the Isle of Man.

Nonetheless, German internees underwent an experience similar to their British counterparts at Ruhleben. Most of the Germans were confined in camps on the Isle of Man, an island in the Irish Sea. Theater groups, lecture series, and a camp school emerged as antidotes to the tedium of confinement. The mortality rate matched that of any similar age group in peacetime. The chief sources of pain came from the confinement itself, the lack of privacy, and separation from loved ones. As one prisoner recalled, "No privacy, no possibility of being alone, no possibility of finding *quietude*. It is inhuman, cruel and dreadful to force people to live in closest community for years."[26]

Those internees confined in London had the bittersweet privilege of access to their families. These camps mainly held German men with British wives. Once every two weeks, the internees could meet their families for a brief moment. One observer wondered whether such a rendezvous alleviated mental anguish, because these were visitors "bringing solace to some and tearing open the wound of others." He himself was content not to have visitors, because "it seemed cruel to allow the wretches to have their world so near to them only to be snatched away after a few moments."[27]

NOTES

1. Barbara Tuchman, *The Guns of August* (New York: Macmillan, 1962), 172–74.

2. E.H. Kossman, *The Low Countries, 1780–1940* (Oxford: Clarendon Press, 1978), 522–23; Mark Derez, "The Flames of Louvain: The War Experiences of an Academic Community" in *Facing Armageddon: The First World War Experienced,* ed. Hugh Cecil and Peter Liddle (London: Leo Cooper, 1996), 618.

3. John Horne and Alan Kramer, "German 'Atrocities' and Franco-German Opinion, 1914: The Evidence of German Soldiers' Diaries," *Journal of Modern History* 66, no. 1 (1994), 7, 10–11, 17.

4. Richard Cobb, *French and Germans, Germans and French: A Personal Interpretation of France under Two Occupations, 1914–1918/1940–1944* (Hanover, N.H.: University Press of New England, 1983), 11–12; Annette Becker, *Oubliés de la Grande Guerre: Humanitaire et Culture de Guerre: Populations Occupées, Déportés Civils, Prisonniers de Guerre* (Paris: Éditions Noêsis, 1998), 42.

5. Helen McPhail, *The Long Silence: Civilian Life under the German Occupation of Northern France, 1914–1918* (London: I.B. Tauris, 1999) 45, 172–73; Annette Becker, "Life in an Occupied Zone," in *Facing Armageddon,* ed. Cecil and Liddle, 635; also Becker, *Oubliés,* 69–73.

6. McPhail, *Long Silence,* 51.

7. Quoted in ibid., 109.

8. Quoted in ibid., 13.

9. Quoted in Lyn Macdonald, *1914* (New York: Atheneum, 1988), 408–9.

10. Trevor Wilson, *The Myriad Faces of War: Britain and the Great War, 1914–1918* (Cambridge, Eng.: Polity Press, 1986), 157.

11. Quoted in Raymond H. Fredette, *The Sky on Fire: The First Battle of Britain, 1917–1918 and the Birth of the Royal Air Force* (New York: Holt, Rinehart and Winston, 1966), 32.

12. Roger Chickering, *Imperial Germany and the Great War, 1914–1918* (Cambridge, Eng.: Cambridge University Press, 1998), 100.

13. Fredette, *Sky on Fire*, 4–5.

14. Ibid., 53–61; John Williams, *The Other Battleground: The Homefronts: Britain, France and Germany, 1914–1918* (Chicago: Henry Regnery, 1972), 196.

15. Williams, *Other Battleground*, 77, 146, 222.

16. Ibid., 267–68.

17. Quoted in Lyn Macdonald, *The Roses of No Man's Land* (London: Michael Joseph, 1980), 139–40.

18. Quoted in A.A. Hoehling, *The Great War at Sea: A History of Naval Action, 1914–1918* (New York: Crowell [1965]), 185–88.

19. Ibid., 193–94.

20. Quoted in Richard B. Speed, III, *Prisoners, Diplomats, and the Great War: A Study in the Diplomacy of Captivity* (New York: Greenwood Press, 1990), 142.

21. Quoted in Wilson, *Myriad Faces*, 643.

22. J. Davidson Ketchum, *Ruhleben: A Prison Camp Society* (Toronto: University of Toronto Press, 1965), 3.

23. Ibid., 13–18.

24. Quoted in ibid., 29–30.

25. Quoted in Speed, *Prisoners*, 146.

26. Quoted in Panikos Panayi, *The Enemy in Our Midst: Germans in Britain during the First World War* (New York: Berg, 1991), 128.

27. Quoted in ibid., 129.

11

Food

In each of the belligerent countries, the war had a profound effect on what most of the population ate. The need to apportion national resources, the strains of the war effort, and even the direct assault of the enemy on the food supply reached into kitchens and dining rooms everywhere. In food more than in any other area of daily life, individuals in Britain, France, the United States, and Germany felt the new role of government in regulating personal behavior. In Germany, the impact was especially acute. There, the pain of daily hunger and the humiliation of standing in food lines, scavenging, and participating in the black market struck the entire population.

Even assuming a high level of cooperation, directing a nation's food habit was enormously complex. In Germany, a population of 65 million drew most of its food from the labor of 5 million German farm families. Most farms were small operations, and firms that processed farm products, like the 341 plants that processed sugar beets, also operated on a limited scale.[1]

Government officials who tried to alter a national diet soon learned that they would evoke widespread resistance. "Food cultures" formed a high barrier for regulators to surmount. In general, few people were willing to give up the foods they had eaten since childhood for new, often unpalatable substitutes. Moreover, many clung to a certain kind of diet as a mark of one's social status—or one's social aspirations.

DIET AND FOOD SUPPLY IN 1914

In three belligerent countries—Germany, Britain, and the United States—widening economic prosperity had created a richer, more varied diet for much of the population. France had seen more gradual change in the same direction. The decades before 1914 brought many people the opportunity to consume more meat and dairy products. And for many it was now possible to reduce somewhat a dependency on bread and cereals.

At the same time, the science of nutrition—rooted in Germany but spreading in Britain and the United States—was developing rapidly. Some of its advocates preached the virtues of a simpler rather than a richer diet. The new knowledge of food values suggested that it was possible to replace one food for another in several categories. The shortages and food crises of the war gave the nutritionists an opportunity to win governments over to their program.

The diet of many Germans had changed with the decades of affluence prior to 1914. The domestically grown potato remained a staple food for most of Kaiser Wilhelm II's subjects. Nonetheless, consuming large amounts of animal products, especially pork and butter, was becoming a mealtime habit for much of the population. Another sharp change occurred in the bread supply. Bread made from rye—a domestic crop—had increasingly given way to white bread containing wheat from abroad. The term "German diet" had come to mean consuming more than three meals daily.

Although Germany had a highly productive farming economy, the country was deeply dependent on regular shipments of food from abroad. Quantities of meat, fish, eggs, dairy products—constituting approximately 25 percent of the nation's food supply—came from foreign sources. Besides potatoes, German farms and orchards produced carrots, beets, asparagus, as well as apples, grapes, and strawberries. But much of the fruit and vegetables the population consumed came from Italy and Greece. The turnip was the only vegetable that could be produced domestically in quantities comparable to that of the popular potato.

In Great Britain as well, a shift away from starches symbolized rising national wealth. For many, change was only gradual. The staples for working-class families remained potatoes and especially bread. The average working-class Briton consumed far less meat, fats, and milk than the national norm. The working-class diet had only a limited place for fruit, eggs, and vegetables. Nonetheless, more Britons than ever, including the upper levels of the working class, had access to a diet with significant amounts of meat, milk, cheese, and butter. The nation's supply of meat had grown with the spread of refrigeration. This allowed frozen meat to be transported from distant locations such as Argentina and

Australia to British dining rooms. Poorer Britons ate lower-quality meat from such sources, whereas more affluent members of the society depended upon better-quality cuts coming from domestic sources

The national preference for white bread made from wheat underlined the importance of Britain's ties to the outside world. In the previous century, the country had transformed itself into an industrialized and urbanized society. That change took place in parallel with the decline in British agriculture. As a result of changes in the four or five decades prior to 1914, fully 60 percent of the calories Britons consumed were imported. Most of the fruits and vegetables in the national diet had to be imported, and 80 percent of the wheat that went into British bread came from abroad. So, too, did Britain's crucial supply of sugar; the average Briton consumed almost two pounds a week, and working families bought as much as they could. As Margaret Barnett put it, "It was commonly believed by the working classes that children would die unless they ate a pound of sugar a week."[2]

In the United States, the population was increasing its consumption of fresh meat, eggs, and butter. With its multicultural society and various regions, the United States presented an especially complex dining picture. Nonetheless, eating meat and butter along with drinking milk came with growing prosperity for much of American society. Imported coffee and tropical fruits like bananas, signs of an elite lifestyle back in Europe, became accessible to large numbers of Americans. Canned fruits and vegetables, mostly from domestic producers, were increasingly available, even for those with modest incomes. With the advent of refrigerated railroad cars after 1869, fresh fruits and vegetables from rural regions in California, Texas, Georgia, and the Midwest became increasingly available. Even the poorest Americans could afford apples, the most commonly available fresh fruit.

Conspicuous consumption marked upper-class social life. In April 1913, a society dinner to honor the architect who had designed the new Woolworth Building in New York illustrated the trend. A partial list of the foods to which guests were treated included "[c]aviar, oysters, turtle soup, Turban of Pompano with Austrian potatoes, breast of guinea hen with Nesselrode sauce" along with appropriate wines and desserts. Meanwhile, many immigrant workers at the other end of the social scale enjoyed a diet reflecting a society of abundance. A typical steelworker in Pittsburgh just before the outbreak of the war in Europe was likely to consume a diet that included eggs and butter along with oatmeal or pancakes at all breakfasts. He took a substantial lunch along to his workplace, and his dinner invariably included meat, potatoes, and fruit. Working-class families with surplus funds to spend on food signaled their prosperity by purchasing fresh fruit and milk, along with sweets in the form of cakes and rolls.[3]

Unlike the other major belligerents, the United States not only produced most of the food its people ate, it exported great quantities of grains and meat. That role expanded as Europeans waged their conflict. During 1916, the surplus from the previous year's bumper crop allowed the export of a particularly sizable amount. Nonetheless, a rapid rise in the price of food staples in the winter of 1916–17 led to riots in major eastern American cities. Even before the government declared war against Germany on April 6, 1917, a food shortage smacking of wartime circumstances was becoming evident.

Of all the western front's key belligerents, France had gone through the most gradual change in its food habits in the years prior to 1914. Much of its population remained tied to a diet in which the daily loaves of bread were the centerpiece. The average French citizen still ate only about 4 ounces of meat per day. But the wheat for his bread came from within the country; so too did most other products—including fruits and vegetables—the population consumed. France did not export large amounts of food, but France alone among the major European powers on the western front produced most of what was needed for the nation's stomachs—at least in peacetime.

WARTIME DISRUPTIONS OF THE FOOD SUPPLY

The large-scale and costly war soon struck at the food supply of the European belligerents. Soldiers at the front needed a richer diet than those men had consumed as civilians. Numerous workers performing demanding labor in arms factories added new demands on the nation's food supply. As the war went on, the example of tsarist Russia made governments alert to the dangers of a hungry population: Women protesting food shortages in the capital city of Petrograd had set off the chain of violence that toppled the monarchy. Even before those dramatic events in March 1917, food shortages had driven part of the population in Britain and France into the streets to protest.

Despite its apparent self-sufficiency, Germany soon showed its vulnerability to food shortages. German domestic production depended upon large quantities of foreign fertilizers for its fields; the country also required fodder from abroad to maintain its farm animals. Calling millions of able-bodied men into the military drained farm labor and caused diminished production. So too did the absence of hundreds of thousands of farmworkers from Russian Poland, who came in peacetime years to bring in the grain harvest in eastern Germany. The enemy put Germany under increased economic pressure by blocking its ports. Moreover, the Allies now treated food carried in neutral ships to Germany as "contraband," that is, war materials subject to seizure.

The action of Germany's great maritime enemy diminished Germany's food supply in other ways. The British threatened action against Denmark and Holland—two traditional food exporters to Germany. As a result, those countries dared to send only limited amounts of food to Germany. The British insisted on a level of such food transfers no greater than in peacetime. In all, the effects of the British blockade reduced German food production by 25 percent.

Britain's vulnerabilities became evident more slowly. Nonetheless, an early crisis emerged over sugar. Sugar had become an accepted part of the population's diet, and the British had to import their entire supply. Austria-Hungary, now an enemy state, was the country's main pre-1914 supplier. As a result, panic flared up. Hasty buying in the beginning days of the conflict pushed up prices for sugar as well as other items, and gave food store owners a sudden windfall of profits. Buyers came equipped with trash cans and tubs to fill with food; one woman reportedly bought 144 pots of jam and a ton and a half of flour. Chauffeur-driven limousines were parked in rows outside food shops as the servants of the wealthy purchased stocks of food for their employers. Although the initial panic faded, prices for many items continued to rise.[4]

In early 1917, the Germans used submarines to cut the British off from foreign food supplies. A national crisis soon developed as the grains and meats upon which the country depended came under enemy attack. The Germans began to sink one out of every four merchant ships sailing from a British port, and Britain's wheat reserves fell far below normal. Official government statistics had to be censored to prevent public knowledge of the decline in wheat imports.

Despite France's rich agricultural resources, that country found itself facing an increasing food deficit. One out of every four of France's 5.2 million farmers and farm workers was mobilized in 1914. Ten departments in northeastern France, which provided a significant part of France's food, fell under enemy occupation. The military requisitioned many of the horses that provided motive power on French farms, and the jammed railroads were unable to deliver the usual supply of fertilizer. A shortage of gasoline made it difficult to operate tractors, and a shortage of coal hindered the operation of grain threshers. Additional pressure on the food supply came from the country's huge army. French soldiers at the front required a diet that included 11 ounces of meat daily.[5]

By 1917, the decline in French agriculture had become a national crisis. In Isère, a department in southeastern France, the labor shortage put two out of every five farms out of operation. The women, children, and old men of the community had found it impossible to meet the physical demands of tilling the fields. That same year, French wheat production

American food poster. Courtesy of the Hoover
Institution Archives.

fell to only 40 percent of its prewar level. Like Britain, France faced
starvation without massive help from abroad.[6]

The American situation differed dramatically. Wartime demands on
the food supply began only in the winter of 1916–17 when the country
was about to enter the conflict. The United States enjoyed a traditional
abundance of food and an established role as an exporter of foodstuffs.
Now, it needed to gather and ship as much food as possible to America's
European allies. This required creating an even larger surplus than usual
by getting the American population to cut down on its consumption of
key items like meat and wheat.

THE FORCES OF NATURE

None of the belligerent countries could escape factors like the weather
and the difficulties it brought to the harvest. The poor harvest of 1916,
noticeable throughout the world, created problems for all the warring
powers. For Germany, it brought the onset of serious crisis. German
grain production fell to a dramatic low, and the population began to feel

a crisis in the food supply far greater than the mere shortages of the years just past. While other countries suffered, the Germans faced desperately bleak prospects for their food supply.

The heavy rains of late 1916 combined with a cold winter to cripple Germany's agricultural production. The potato was a staple of the German diet, in good times and bad. Municipal workers in 1915 Berlin and their families, for example, depended on a supply of one pound of potatoes per person per day. The adulterated bread of the wartime years—"K brot"—contained a large component of potato flour.

When the weather's vagaries wrecked the potato crop, Germans felt the impact with particular force in the first months of 1917. Animals as well as humans depended upon the potato, and the precipitous fall in potato production—almost half of the winter potato crop perished—overturned German eating habits. The turnip, an unappetizing vegetable and a meager source of nutrition, became the keystone of the German diet in the "turnip winter" of 1916–17. The resulting food crisis was massive and jarring, the worst to date for any of the major belligerent countries on the western front. But other nations faced difficulties that were comparable in kind if not intensity. The wheat crop in Argentina also failed, and the government halted all exports. Britain and France, who depended upon this source, now faced a deteriorating bread supply.

ADJUSTING TO CRISIS

Germany

German authorities took the first steps among the major belligerents to regulate the wartime food supply. A system of price controls for bread, milk, and potatoes went into effect almost at once. By the start of 1915, the national government began to ration bread. But such measures soon appeared ineffective to much of the population. A physician and member of the German Parliament, Alfred Grotjahn, expressed his concern in his diary in February 1915: "Slowly but surely we are slipping into a, now still well organized, famine."[7]

Germany's wartime government depended upon the senior military officers present in the country's twenty-four military districts. They controlled food policy, including prices, at the local level. Because each set up his own rules, the system quickly showed its faults. Farmers and middlemen, acting in their own self-interest, shipped food to those districts where they could get the best price. Farmers reacted to a cap on grain prices by feeding their animals with the grain, transforming one food product into a second, more lucrative one. An attempt to set up a more centralized system in the summer of 1916 failed to cut through the welter of local authorities and the silent opposition of Germany's farmers.

Alone among the major belligerents on the western front, Germany developed a large and notorious black market. In Berlin, it was common knowledge that those with wealth and connections could obtain lavish quantities of food. Black marketeers even advertised in the newspapers. Although forbidden by law, many city dwellers spent spare hours or days traveling into the countryside to find food. Many in the German population had only recently moved from rural to urban areas, and lots of Germans still had close contacts with those left on the farm. But others, without money or connections, increasingly went hungry as the government proved incapable of controlling the food supply or food prices. Wealth and connections dictated diet in German life. Chain stores, for example, diverted food items to outlets in wealthier neighborhoods where the management could demand higher prices.

One device developed by German society to deal with the growing food pinch was a set of artificial (or "ersatz") goods. Ersatz coffee might be a beverage made from burned barley or tree bark; ersatz butter a combination of artificial fats and water. During the "turnip winter" of 1916–17, a vast range of foods, which most Germans found unpalatable, grew out of the one available staple, turnips: turnip jam being one example.

Standing in a food line—known in popular parlance as "dancing the Polonaise"—became a feature of German life. Most Germans without financial means had the discouraging experience of standing in such a line, perhaps overnight. When at last they reached the food counter, they often found no goods remained to be purchased. In an obvious blow to war production, the food shortage caused munitions workers, especially women, to give up their jobs. They had learned it was impossible to put in the required hours in the factory and also find time to "dance the Polonaise."

Great Britain

In contrast to the decentralized—and consequently unsuccessful—system in Germany, Britain created a rationing system under central control. The office of Food Controller, occupied starting in June 1917 by the energetic and effective Lord Rhondda, took increasingly tight charge of the nation's diet. The government also sponsored a program designed to increase farm production, thereby reversing a trend in British agriculture that had gone on for decades. The production of grains instead of livestock became a by-word of the program; it was more efficient to use farmland to grow crops like wheat than to graze animals.

By government order, bakers used grain more efficiently in producing bread: More flour had to be squeezed from wheat kernels. In addition, barley, oats, rice, and potatoes diluted the amount of wheat that went into a loaf of bread. This adulterated "war bread" was a gray substitute for its peacetime equivalent. "I can't eat the stuff" and "Its very colour annoys me" were remarks recorded in one town in the English Midlands, and probably repeated all over the British Isles. Limits on beer production also helped save grain. By early 1917, such restrictions reduced the total of beer available to a little more than one-quarter of the prewar level.[8]

Voluntary rationing affected other foods starting in early 1917. Each member of the population was asked to observe limits on what he or she ate each week: 4 pounds of bread and cereals, $\frac{3}{4}$ pound of sugar, $2\frac{1}{2}$ pounds of meat. The Royal Society of London, the nation's leading scientific body, protested at once. The nation's leading scientific body had established a committee to aid the government in formulating food policy. The Society noted that poor working families were so dependent on bread that working-age men within them relied upon having up to 14 pounds a week.

The British government never rationed bread, and this comforted a population facing limits on most other foodstuffs. "It was also good psychology," Barnett has written, "offering the British public the reassurance that however bad things were in other countries a certain amount of normality still prevailed in Britain."[9] Rejecting rationing did not mean that the government avoided urging Britons to cut their bread eating. Food authorities revived a proclamation dating from the Napoleonic wars on limiting bread consumption. Anyone attending a religious service starting in early May 1917 heard an updated version of this classic appeal to the British population from his or her local spiritual leader. It was placed in 1,600 newspapers and appeared on placards in every post office.

Compulsory rationing of key items began under the auspices of local authorities at the close of 1917. At that time, food lines were forming outside grocery stores by five o'clock in the morning. This indicated how shortages of bacon, margarine, and cheese—customary elements in the working-class diet—were beginning to pinch. In December, a crowd of more than 3,000 lined up for margarine at a store in southeast London. Meanwhile, a newspaper article describing a six-course dinner available to the wealthy at The Ritz inflamed popular resentment over the food situation. It recounted a meal complete with smoked salmon and unlimited quantities of cream and cheese.

By July 1918, the government put in place a centralized system that directly controlled the price and distribution of much of the nation's food supply. Everyone in the country received a ration book controlling the individual's purchases of sugar, butter and margarine, lard, and meat.

For example, detachable coupons assured that one could purchase 4 ounces per week of butter or margarine along with 2 ounces of lard. Meat coupons allowed the purchase of about a pound of meat along with 4 to 8 ounces of bacon. Local rationing of items like tea, cheese, and jam continued depending upon the decisions of local authorities. By restricting the availability of meats and fats, the government pushed the entire nation to eat more cereals and potatoes. The new policy had a sharp impact on the eating patterns of the affluent. One well-off Englishman wrote a relative abroad that his family now had only a small portion of meat once a week. The poor, however, had a continued—possibly even an improved—chance to buy basic nutritional items. By substituting bacon, much of it from the United States, for uncured meat, margarine for butter, bread and potatoes for proteins like meat and cheese, they met their food needs.[10]

Improved wages for workers during the wartime boom provided the opportunity for food luxuries (what the British call "greed foods"). A grocer's son during the war later wrote how "the once deprived began to savour strange delights" in food choices. "One of our customers, wife of a former foundry labourer, both making big money now on munitions" inquired when the modest grocery store would start stocking such edibles as "[t]ins o'lobster" or "them big jars o' pickled gherkins!"[11] At the same time, restrictions on sellers could be painful. One grocer in a London suburb sold margarine at a higher price than the law allowed, stating "It is my shop, my margarine and I shall do what I like with it." The government penalized him with a whopping fine and a six-week prison term.[12]

France

In France, the first effort to regulate the food supply came at the local level. In Isère, for example, the prefects and mayors dealt successfully with surging food costs at the war's start. They appealed to local merchants not to raise their prices, publicized the names of violators, and threatened to use powers under the Penal Code to seize food from the shops. In Paris, fear of disastrous popular unrest over the price of bread led the authorities at once to invoke a law dating from 1791. With it they were able to maintain the 1914 price almost unchanged until the close of the war. Next, concern about potential disorder in the nation's capital led the government to put local military authorities in charge of bread supplies in Paris. Then, starting in 1916, the Ministry of War took sweeping powers over Parisian wheat stocks, flour mills, and bakeries.

French consumers encountered serious shortages and price increases in 1916. In response, the national government stepped in to set maximum prices for key goods. The authorities targeted, among other items, sugar, potatoes, milk, and coffee. Sugar rationing began in early 1917. As the nation's food situation slipped into crisis, the government placed more restrictions on the consumption and sale of meat, cheese, and bread. The price of bread at the national level was fixed, starting in July 1917, for a period of two years. In August 1917, the French Chamber of Deputies passed a sweeping law placing all the nation's food under government control. The following January, bread rationing began. Only adults in active occupations were permitted the 14-ounce daily allowance that approximated what the French ate in peacetime.

The United States

In the United States, the government avoided outright rationing, because that measure was unlikely to get popular support. Nonetheless, aspects of the food supply quickly came under official control. The key figure was the young engineer and mining magnate Herbert Hoover. From his London home, he had played a key role in providing foreign food to the hungry population of Belgium starting in the fall of 1914. Soon after the United States entered the war, President Woodrow Wilson appointed Hoover the director of the United States Food Administration.[13]

Hoover began a program based first of all on an appeal to the American people. With its abundant food supplies, the United States was in no danger of seeing its population go hungry. Nonetheless, there was a pressing need to send large quantities of food, especially wheat and meat products, to its European allies. This meant getting the American population to eat less and to eat differently.

In the summer of 1917, Hoover set out to link all American housewives to the work of the United States Food Administration. He hoped to get their promise to pursue a voluntary system of food control in their kitchens and dining rooms. Specifically, they were to pledge to lower their family's consumption of wheat and meat, buying less meat and serving it only in small portions. Housewives were to reduce their use of butter in cooking and to increase their family's consumption of foods like vegetables. Hoover made a call for American families to observe "wheatless" Mondays and Wednesdays and "meatless" Tuesdays, and additionally to observe "wheatless" and "meatless" meals at other times during the week.

In the fall of 1917, almost half the housewives all over the United States answered a knock on the door and greeted one of 500,000 women volunteers of the Food Administration. Dressed in a military-style uniform of white skirt and blouse with armband, these volunteers tried to convince America's homemakers to abide by Hoover's recommendations.

An American food program worker. Courtesy
of the Hoover Institution Archives.

Americans traveling by railroad or streetcar found themselves confronted by advertisements touting Hoover's program.

Using the power of law, Hoover required restaurants to limit the
amount of bread, butter, and meat they served customers. Following the
example of European governments, American authorities required mill-
ers to extract more flour from grain than was the practice in peacetime.
Bread and other baked goods made with wheat had to contain a substantial portion of flour from different grains. Government nutritionists
provided housewives with sample menus; one such book of menus covered three meals a day for an entire year.

In the South and the West, Hoover's program drew an especially
strong response. Average citizens learned that the enthusiasm of their
neighbors for food conservation could be dangerous to oppose. The
Oklahoma City municipal government declared by local ordinance that
failure to observe "wheatless Wednesday" was an act of sedition. When
the owner of a Birmingham, Alabama, restaurant refused to drop wheat

products from his menu, a mob of his fellow citizens ransacked his establishment.

Hoover promoted the slogan "Food will win the war" during the first year the United States fought in World War I. He employed the term less prominently from the summer of 1918 when it seemed embarrassingly inappropriate. By that time, large numbers of American troops found themselves dying on the battlefield in France, and it was clear that armed force was winning the war. As the United States produced a bumper crop that summer, Hoover also found it possible to end some of his demands for restricted consumption—for example, for wheatless days—in August 1918.

The efforts of the Food Director enjoyed some success. In affluent and middle-class families, his patriotic appeal to limit food consumption hit home. His campaign had a lesser impact on other groups. As the wartime economy boomed, families in the working class had far more disposable income than in the past. Many of these poorer families used their heightened earnings to heighten their food consumption. This meant buying more meat, often of better quality, than they had before the war. African American farm laborers in the southeastern states used the higher incomes the war brought them to replace dry salt pork with better cuts of cured pork.[14]

At the same time, the eating habits of many American groups contributed to achieving Hoover's aims. Italian American families were accustomed to stretching their meat consumption with such foods as pasta sauces. They often did not buy more meat merely because their incomes were higher. Some groups from Eastern Europe, like the Lithuanians, had no desire even in peacetime to eat white bread made from wheat. In wartime they were happy to consume their usual crusty breads made from rye.[15]

For a rich nation, the sacrifices for which Hoover called often meant little more than substituting one form of eating pleasure for another. The Chicago, Milwaukee, and St. Paul Railway presented its patrons with a menu designed to make "meatless Tuesdays" more than tolerable. No beef or pork would be available, but breakfast offered fresh fruit and juices, whitefish and mackerel, oysters, grilled chicken, and broiled squab.[16]

One measure undertaken during the wartime emergency led to a fundamental shift in American law. Starting in December 1917, the government began to restrict the alcohol content of beer and the amount of grain that could be used in brewing. Further restrictions followed. This wartime measure, enforced to reduce the strain on the food supply, became the legal starting point for postwar Prohibition.

THE PAIN OF DEPRIVATION

Germans especially experienced the force of food shortages during most of the four years of the war. The pain might take the form of persistent hunger sharpened by memories of recent abundance. As one German woman, a child in an affluent Berlin family during the wartime years, recalled: "Soon the quantity and quality of the food at our disposal declined so much that we were always hungry. After all, we were four lively, growing children and had by no means forgotten the meals we once enjoyed. . . . Cakes, whipped cream, chops, chicken, ham and lovely puddings became a tantalising memory." The constant need to ration oneself provided another woman who had grown up in wartime Germany with harsh memories: "When I went to school I remember that I had one loaf of bread per week. . . . I measured the loaf in so many centimetres and had a piece per day of perhaps 2 or 3 centimetres."[17]

The desperate search for food became a constant effort for most Germans. Standing in a food line, often for hours in harsh winter weather, became the norm for many German women. George Schreiner, an American newspaper correspondent in Germany, recorded a picture of one of these sad gatherings. "[A]mong the three hundred applicants for food there was not one who had had enough to eat for weeks. In the case of the younger women and children the skin was drawn hard to the bones and bloodless. Eyes had fallen deeper into the sockets. From the lips all color was gone."[18]

The quest for food in the countryside occupied Germans of all social classes. The well-off could afford to go during the week; the less affluent had to take time on weekends. All had to walk around negotiating with farmers for something to take back to the city. Even the leading Socialist politician Philip Scheidemann was subject to this humiliation. "Who would have thought that such a thing could ever happen," he declared. "I, who am buried in work, should be forced to spend time begging for a few pounds of potatoes along with women and children."[19]

The black market struck another blow at German morale. It had begun early in the war. By 1918, up to one-third of the total food supply in Berlin came from illicit sources. Buying food on the black market meant paying prices as high as ten times the peacetime level; those of limited means had no way to tap this source. Although more affluent Germans had this alternative way of getting food, the food came at a high psychological price. As Avner Offer has put it, "The constant recourse to the black market provoked outrage, humiliation and guilt." For the many Germans who prided themselves on their fidelity to the law, the need to break the law in order to feed their families was degrading in the extreme. So, too, was the need to sell off family treasures to raise money for exorbitant prices demanded. If one was willing to do it, but could not afford the high prices, "the illicit enterprise around them rankled even more."[20]

SOME RESULTS

In Germany, the strain on the food supply eventually became intolerable. By the closing year of the war, most of the population was malnourished. Some historians have contested the view that there was actual starvation, but there is no disagreement on the presence of extraordinary strains on the average German.

Food riots began in Berlin in October 1915. By the following summer, they were taking place from one end of the country to the other. The danger of such outbursts led the police to devote increasingly large resources to control them. The example of the March 1917 revolution in Russia became too relevant to ignore. A food line of desperate German housewives made up a dangerous nucleus of social discontent that seemed likely to explode. The widespread knowledge that Berlin, and possibly other major cities, contained an elite population that was spared the hardships of a food shortage heightened popular fury. The government's failure either to secure a steady food supply or to distribute it fairly undercut existing political authority in deadly fashion.

Extreme and prolonged hunger along with the other hardships of the war may have poisoned German life for decades. Peter Loewenberg has contended that the food shortages contributed to an emotional trauma that scarred German children of the wartime generation. Wartime deprivation had a "causal" relationship to the willingness of these individuals, as adults, to turn to radical figures such as Adolf Hitler in times of crisis.[21]

In Britain, France, and the United States, effective food control from above helped maintain a high level of national unity. Government competence in this crucial area promoted political loyalty and social cohesion that lasted to the end of the war. By distributing food efficiently and fairly, the authorities gave the poorer groups in British society, in particular, a better, more healthful diet during the final stages of the war than they had in peacetime.

NOTES

1. The best general treatment of Germany's food situation is in Roger Chickering, *Imperial Germany and the Great War, 1914–1918* (Cambridge, Eng.: Cambridge University Press, 1998); for Britain, see L. Margaret Barnett, *British Food Policy during the First World War* (Boston: Allen and Unwin, 1985); for the United States, see Harvey A. Levenstein, *Revolution at the Table: The Transformation of the American Diet* (New York: Oxford University Press, 1988); for France, see Michel

Augé-Laribé and P. Pinot, *Agriculture and Food Supply in France during the War* (New Haven: Yale University Press, 1927).

2. Barnett, *British Food Policy*, xiv, 30.

3. Levenstein, *Revolution*, 96, 101–2, 106.

4. Barnett, *British Food Policy*, 35–36.

5. Augé-Laribé, *Agriculture and Food Supply*, 39, 55, 63–68, 74.

6. P.J. Flood, *France, 1914–1918: Public Opinion and the War* (Houndmills, Basingstoke, Hampshire, Eng.: Macmillan, 1990), 120; Augé-Laribé, *Agriculture and Food Supply*, 35.

7. Quoted in Peter Loewenberg, "Germany, the Home Front (1): The Physical and Psychological Consequences of Home Front Hardship," in *Facing Armageddon: The First World War Experienced*, ed. Hugh Cecil and Peter Liddle (London: Leo Cooper, 1996), 555.

8. Trevor Wilson, *The Myriad Faces of War: Britain and the Great War, 1914–1918* (Cambridge, Eng.: Polity Press, 1986), 514; Barnett, *British Food Policy*, 105–6.

9. Barnett, *British Food Policy*, 112.

10. Ibid., 149, 151–52; J.M. Winter, *The Great War and the British People* (London: Macmillan, 1986), 216; Peter Dewey, "Nutrition and Living Standards in Wartime Britain," in *The Upheaval of War: Family, Work and Welfare in Europe, 1914–1918*, ed. Richard Wall and Jay Winter (Cambridge, Eng.: Cambridge University Press, 1988), 209–10.

11. Quoted in Winter, *Great War*, 240.

12. Wilson, *Myriad Faces*, 515.

13. The best treatment of Hoover's role as Food Director can be found in George N. Nash, *The Life of Herbert Hoover*, vol. 3, *Master of Emergencies, 1917–1918* (New York: W.W. Norton, 1996).

14. Levenstein, *Revolution*, 144–45.

15. Ibid., 143.

16. Ibid., 141.

17. Alyson Jackson, "Germany, the Home Front (2): Blockade, Government and Revolution," in *Facing Armageddon*, ed. Cecil and Liddle, 564–66.

18. George Abel Schreiner, *The Iron Ration: Three Years in Warring Central Europe* (New York: Harper and Row, 1918), 258.

19. Quoted in Laurence Moyer, *Victory Must Be Ours: Germany in the Great War, 1914–1918* (New York: Hippocrene Books, 1995), 214.

20. Avner Offer, *The First World War: An Agrarian Interpretation* (Oxford: Clarendon Press, 1989), 58–59.

21. Loewenberg, "Germany," in *Facing Armageddon*, ed. Cecil and Liddle, 559–60.

12

Women at Home

The major participants in the war soon discovered that they could not conduct such a conflict without the help of their nation's women. As men entered the army by the millions, their work remained to be done by others—and women were ready and willing to step up.

WOMEN ENTER THE WARTIME LABOR FORCE

Women made up a substantial part of the prewar workforce in all four key countries that fought on the western front. But women's roles had been restricted in a variety of ways. About 32 percent of British women worked outside their homes. The most common women wage-earners were domestic servants and workers in the textile industry. Most were single. The poorly paid and overworked domestic servant was likely to be a young woman, who would leave this dreary form of employment if she managed to marry. The textile worker tended to be older and better paid, a married woman helping to support her family. But her prospects of obtaining highly skilled positions, even in the industry where she was heavily represented, remained slim.[1]

In France, 39 percent of the nation's women and girls claimed a working occupation. Only 10 percent called themselves domestic servants, and the majority worked in some kind of industry or, more likely, in agriculture.[2] In the United States, some 24 percent of women held paying jobs outside the home. In that country, an advanced industrial economy and widening educational opportunities opened several areas of employment outside the factory, the farm, and the servants' quarters. Positions as secretaries, telephone operators, social workers, and teachers were within reach for some women from a middle-class background who were equipped with schooling beyond the primary level.[3] Still, the picture of opportunities for employed women remained mixed. "Women were . . . finding frequent employment in corporate offices, department stores, and urban telephone exchanges," as one authority has put it. But, "[t]he American labor force remained sex-segregated. Domestic and personal service still engaged the largest number of women workers, and the long-standing patterns of female employment in clothing and textile manufacturing overshadowed the use of women machine operatives in new industrial jobs."[4] The employment pattern for German women was similar, and some 25 percent of all German women worked for wages. In rural regions like Bavaria, the figure climbed to 35 percent.[5]

In all the belligerent countries that fought on the western front, women found that the war opened vast new opportunities for employment. In no instance did the total female workforce grow dramatically. But many women found it possible for the first time to move from poorly paid positions such as a domestic servant to more lucrative work. Novel opportunities such as openings in armaments factories appeared only after some delay. British, French, and German working women often had a spell of unemployment as peacetime jobs disappeared when their societies entered the war.

Everywhere, the garment trade and textile factories that employed many women in peacetime shrank in size. The small dressmaker found that her upper-class patrons were no longer interested in clothing themselves in the latest fashion. Many well-off families in Britain and Germany released their domestic servants, sometimes because they could no longer afford to keep them, sometimes as a sign of "doing one's bit" by embracing a more austere lifestyle. Women employed to gut and clean the catch brought in by British fishermen were laid off when the war at sea made it too dangerous for the fishing fleet to operate. But some British women soon found better jobs. The departure of men who volunteered in the closing months of 1914 increased the need for store salespeople and office clerks, and women stepped into their shoes. It was a sign of much greater wartime opportunities to come.

By mid-1915, the pace of military production coupled with the shortage of military-age men in the belligerent countries drew more and more women into the war factories. By 1916, the pressure for employers to accept—and even to seek—women workers grew sharply. The onset of conscription in Great Britain and the heavy manpower losses for both France and Germany at Verdun in 1916 created an unmistakable need for more women in the factories.

Women who entered war factories were often experienced workers from other areas of their nation's economy. Some left low-paid "women's positions" as laundresses and domestic servants. Others abandoned industries like textile manufacturing that had depended upon a large, female workforce. These new workers soon showed that they could do a variety of jobs once restricted to men. Nonetheless, the limits of change also became clear.

Many of the women who took on wartime jobs found themselves operating a machine of some sort. Doubts about women's ability to do complex tasks combined with the urgent need to increase the workforce as quickly as possible. Thus, relatively few women received extensive job training. Employers normally assigned a woman worker to a simple, repetitive task that resulted from breaking down skilled jobs into numerous components. The work of a highly trained male machinist might be fragmented into twenty or more steps, each of which a woman could learn to do quickly. Employers found—or at least believed—that women had a special aptitude for tasks involving careful, repetitive motions.

Meanwhile, the desire from trade union leaders to restore an old industrial order without women frequently received clear expression. In 1916, with the war's combat and casualties at a peak, Britain's *Factory Times* noted that females brought into industry throughout the war "were doing work that is not congenial or natural to a woman," and demanded that "we must get the women back into the home as soon as possible. That they ever left is one of the evil results of the war."[6] In the following year, the French metalworkers' union put it with equal force: "The systematic introduction of women into workshops is entirely at odds with the establishment and maintenance of homes and family life."[7]

France mobilized virtually all its young men, and women filled government and industrial jobs in huge numbers. Whereas no female had a civilian position as a secretary or bookkeeper for the army before the war, more than 130,000 women had such jobs by the start of 1918. Every woman who held a job in the iron and steel industries before the war was joined by nearly six more by the closing months of the war. Women workers in stone cutting and building tripled their numbers during the course of the conflict. Munitions plants quadrupled the number of their female workers in just the last two years of the war. At least some of the women in French armaments factories were engaged in skilled tasks. Even in 1915, they had a near monopoly on the tasks of inspecting finished munitions, and a few even had authority over male workers.

Women faced harsh conditions everywhere. One out of every three French women who worked in a wartime factory was required to fill a position on the night shift. Like their sisters in Germany and Britain, they found themselves deprived of the protection of prewar labor regulations, which had limited or prohibited employing women for nighttime work. Early in the war, some French employers even ended the practice of making Sunday a day of rest. But they dropped this drastic attempt to squeeze work from an exhausted employee as the industrial system became more organized for the war's requirements. Even so, the French government helped establish a system of thirteen days of labor, followed by a single day of rest.

On the other hand, by 1917 an experienced woman munitions worker in France could expect to earn twice the salary of a woman who worked in a clothing plant. A visitor to the Citroën munitions works in the spring of 1918 described with a mixture of admiration and surprise the working conditions for thousands of women there. In "ovenlike heat" they shaped bars of steel into hollow shells; riding electric carts, they carried lead ball bearings for shrapnel shells to the finishing room; there, in a workshop "immense like a railway station," they assembled the shells, filled them with shrapnel, wrapped and loaded them onto the factory's internal railroad.[8]

Many German women previously employed as domestics or garment workers entered the factories. Thus, as in the other belligerent countries, Germany saw only a modest increase in the total number of women working outside the home. During the war some women in Germany performed a kind of heavy labor British and French women were spared. The German woman working in an open mine, digging ditches, and even laboring on the Berlin subway illustrated the range of occupations women now filled. In the fall of 1914, urban women even received free railroad tickets so that they could help with the harvest.

For every German woman in the prewar metal and electrical industries, there were more than eight women workers by the closing months of the conflict. For every one in a chemical plant in early 1914, there were more than four by the fall of 1918. The need to increase production took explicit priority over other considerations. A woman in a German arms factory was expected to put in as many as fifteen hours in a working day; at night, she was required to labor for a twelve-hour shift. In testimony before a Reichstag committee in the third year of the war, a representative of the government conceded that German women worked in conditions endangering their health and their prospects for motherhood. But he insisted that such matters had a lesser priority than the flow of arms to the soldiers at the front. That echoed the view of a British magistrate in 1915 who refused to convict the directors of a munitions factory for keeping women at work for twenty-five or even thirty hours at a time. "The most important thing in the world today," the judge declared, "is that ammunition shall be made."[9]

But many women still saw their new opportunities as a step or two upward. A typical working woman in wartime Britain had probably labored as a household servant before August 1914. In her old role, she had put in an eighty-hour week for a modest wage. Compelled by cus-

tom to live with her employers, she had found herself under their supervision both in working hours and during her meager leisure time.
Under the watchful eye of homeowners who resembled unsympathetic
parents, she could not entertain suitors and had spent her solitary evenings in a bare servants' kitchen.

Women were wanted, she learned from the newspapers and government posters. Her earlier work experience, her education, and even her
age were of no concern so long as she was willing to go into an arms
factory. The Ministry of Munitions placed many war plants away from
settled areas in the southern part of Great Britain to avoid enemy air
attack. Shifting to a job as a munitions worker, the young woman likely
moved to remote locations such as Gretna in southern Scotland. She
worked with hundreds of other women and many men in an environment as different from her previous employment site as night from day.
Her pay doubled or even tripled, and, despite long wartime hours, she
had more leisure than at any time in her working life. She had found
lodgings with the help of a government agency, possibly in a workers'
hostel, possibly in a private rooming house. The factory authorities sponsored sports teams, theater groups, and other activities, but she was free
to seek out whatever other entertainment—like movie theaters and music halls—that the area might offer.

The nonmonetary cost of such employment could be substantial. Even
before the war, machinists and munitions workers ran the risk of injury,
and the risks now multiplied as working hours increased and the pace
of production quickened. This meant "fingers and hands crushed in the
powerful and heavy presses, clothing and limbs caught in the whirring
belts that drove the machines, burns and eye injuries from shards of hot
metal flying up from the lathe."[10]

For many women, work in munitions factories meant handling un-
healthy, even toxic substances. A woman who dealt with TNT faced the
likelihood of developing jaundice, becoming one of those whom the British dubbed "Canary Girls." In some British factories, TNT workers were
segregated. They even ate in special canteens, because everything they
touched became yellow. One TNT worker noted, "You'd wash and wash
and it didn't make no difference. . . . Your whole body was yellow."[11]
Many women worked in airplane factories where the varnish used to
cover the body of planes was extremely poisonous.

Workers in factories in southern England knew they were likely to be
visited by the enemy. The zeppelins first came in 1915, and they were
joined by German bombing planes as the war went on. Even without the
interference of the enemy, fatal accidents occurred. If a worker's plant
did not experience an accidental explosion, rumors informed her that
other, similar plants had. All governments stifled such news as dangerous to morale, but there was no way to keep many incidents secret.

Scottish working women await a visit from King George V. Courtesy of the Hoover Institution Archives.

Hamburg was the scene of at least one deadly explosion in a powder factory. In the Paris region, two known explosions and rumors of several more impelled workers to dub a particular war plant the "death factory." The explosion at a grenade factory in 1916 was too spectacular for the Parisian press to ignore. Newspaper reports spoke of thirty deaths, but observers claimed they saw more than 100 corpses being carried off in addition to a crowd of the gravely wounded. That same year, thirty-five British women were killed in a single explosion at a shell factory in Leeds. All told, at least 300 British women died in accidents at war plants.

The best jobs in a plant often went to women whose menfolk had been employees there. British and French women normally received their wages based on piecework rates lower than those given to men. Employers often "rewarded" women's high productivity by cutting back on the rate paid. Employers in all countries had a common excuse for paying women less than men: It was allegedly necessary to make expensive alterations to machines so that an average woman could operate them.

Employers also claimed that the need to provide separate toilets and dressing rooms for female workers constituted an economic burden justifying lesser pay. Many clung to a prewar view that women should be paid according to their needs rather than their worth. It was taken as given that, as an actual or potential spouse, a woman had fewer material needs than a male worker.

When a British woman got pay comparable to a man's, she soon learned this was not a tribute to ideas of equality. Rather it was at the demand of male-dominated trade unions, anxious that women be prevented from undercutting the wages of the men around them on the shop floor. To most women, it seemed that the majority of workers, men and women alike, were engaged in similar tasks. But in all the belligerent nations, women heard their employers claim that more highly paid male workers filled more demanding positions than women. Moreover, highly skilled men could make financial demands on the women around them. A woman might depend upon a male tool setter to arrange her machine for the next production run. This often meant donating a portion of her earnings to him.

Some well-off British women could pay fees to attend industrial training schools sponsored by the government and by the Women's Suffrage Society. By delaying their entry into the factory, they qualified for a demanding position. But many found that this did not mean they would be accepted as a skilled worker. Male workers might respond to the arrival of such women with sabotage, and friction with their male colleagues sometimes reached the level that our era labels "sexual harassment."

One skilled woman recalled that "over and over again the foreman gave me wrong or incomplete directions and altered them in such a way as to give me hours more work." Coworkers had more imaginative means of harassment: "My drawer was nailed up by the men, and oil was poured over everything through a crack another night." Even the unskilled women were enough of a threat to find obstacles put in their path. They sometimes found themselves trying to operate the oldest lathes in a machine shop, and they experienced long delays before a tool setter would agree to adjust their operating equipment.[17]

Women workers in Britain, like their male colleagues, labored under onerous legal restrictions intended to keep them at a given job. Without a "leaving certificate" provided by their employer, they could not take another position without a prolonged delay. This compulsory break in the work cycle meant weeks without pay. Infractions of work rules put many women in front of special munitions tribunals. These had sweeping powers to punish cases of indiscipline or even mistakes. A woman in a Coventry munitions plant carried a match into a restricted area and received a jail term of twenty-eight days.

Another wartime novelty in Britain was the female police officer. With the start of hostilities, several women's organizations recruited females to patrol the areas around military camps and, later, around munitions factories. They were instructed to enforce moral guidelines for the young and emotionally vulnerable women attracted to these areas. Hiring women police had been discussed before the war, but the government had not yet adopted the idea. These women acted in an unofficial capacity for the initial period of the war. Over time the government sanctioned their organizations, and, in 1916, they began to receive salaries from the state. The middle-class women who entered such work reflected society's efforts to limit the impact of the war. Their new role, paradoxically, also reflected the degree to which the war was bringing about change.

Another example of middle-class women setting boundaries for their presumably weaker social inferiors was the factory social worker or welfare supervisor. She appeared in British factories in 1915. The French, imitating Britain, placed such officials in some of their munitions factories in 1917. These French and British social workers looked after the welfare of the swarm of female workers drawn to the factories. At a minimum, this meant ensuring the safety and cleanliness of the workplace. But these officials often directed the hiring process itself as well as setting the rules for workers' hostels. The local welfare supervisor made a strong impression on young women who were told the gates to their residence would be locked at ten o'clock in the evening, that no men or alcohol were permitted inside, and that excessive attendance at the cinema was a moral danger.

Many women saw welfare supervisors as busybodies intruding on a worker's off-hours behavior. But these middle-class mentors provided welcome protection as well. They helped settle disputes over the money British and French workers earned in the war's piecework pay system. One British worker described her factory's chief supervisor as "ever so abrupt" but "she wouldn't have anything wrong in our factory. She was like a real old battle axe, you know, she'd fight for you."[13]

The German government took the same path when it promoted the role of factory nurses (*Fabrikpflegerinnen*) to look after the welfare of female workers. Their nursing duties included ensuring safety regulations inside the factory and visiting the sick. But they functioned as social workers as well. They ran hostels for women working away from their homes, and they helped women workers find child care and deal with the ever-present food shortages. Only 20 strong in the summer of 1914, the group increased its number to 752 at the time of the Armistice. They helped to look after nearly 800,000 women workers.[14]

Once the United States had entered the war in April 1917, American women found their services in demand. The flood of European immigrants that had traditionally solved the country's need for new workers had ceased with the outbreak of the war. In addition, military service drew millions of young men away from their customary employment.

As a result, novel opportunities for women opened up in both business and government. The young domestic worker who left to enter a war plant exemplified one such change. The young secretary from a small town in the South or Midwest who moved to Washington, D.C., to put her skills at the disposal of the government demonstrated another. The former waitress who now worked as a trolley conductor personified a third.

The greatest surge in employment opportunities came after draft calls went up in August 1918. Employers recruited women with large print advertisements in the nation's newspapers and through government employment agencies. As the shortage of workers became desperate, women in some areas found themselves the targets of imaginative hiring campaigns. The shortage of munitions workers in Bridgeport, Connecticut, in the war's closing months led employers to use airplanes to scatter recruiting literature from the sky. The result was a workforce with more women in formerly male jobs than anyone could have imagined before America's entry into the conflict. The number of women in the iron and steel industry more than tripled in the year and a half the United States engaged in hostilities.

Some women were fortunate enough to work for enlightened employers like the Dayton, Ohio, Recording & Computing Machines Company. There, they entered a carefully designed training program. It segregated women into those able to handle heavy machinery and those who could only do lighter work. The training staff consisted of women who had already succeeded as production workers and who could serve as reassuring role models.

Other women benefited from the efforts of female inspectors employed by the army's Ordnance Department. These energetic and idealistic officials encouraged companies like Bethlehem Steel Company to become model employers, training women to be skilled machinists instead of merely production workers. Bethlehem also broke the existing pattern of employment in the steel industry by instituting an eight-hour day.

Openings on the nation's railroads drew many women applicants. The government takeover of the railroad system at the close of 1917 made these jobs particularly attractive. The government authorized a generous pay scale, and women received the same wages as men. Most women railroad employees found themselves in unskilled clerical positions with no chance for advancement. But at least some women were trained for skilled work like adjusting accident claims, and others rose to supervisory—a few even to executive—positions. Railroad employment also offered rail passes and thus gave women unprecedented freedom to travel extensively in their spare time. Besides clerical work, there were numerous openings on the railroad for unskilled labor. African American

American women railroad workers. Courtesy
of the National Archives.

women, whom a segregated society put a step behind their white sisters
in taking advantage of wartime, filled many of those.

When American women entered the world of the roundhouse and the
machine shop, they encountered the same substantial resistance their
counterparts in Europe faced. Seen as interlopers in a male world, they
were also feared as a tool for management. Men were concerned that
their bosses would use women to break down skilled jobs into tasks less
qualified, cheaper workers could perform. Nonetheless, at least some
women spent the wartime months doing highly demanding work like
servicing engines.

As American women took new positions on the railroads, sexual harassment made its appearance. Women were fondled against their will
by foremen and supervisors in offices and rail yards from Montana to
Virginia. Men in positions of authority instigated many of the incidents,
and such abuses often went unrecorded. Nonetheless, the government's
operation of the railroads brought some incidents to light. The workers

themselves or, more often, female officials in the government's Railroad Administration filed complaints. In once instance, a manager in the Richmond office of the Chesapeake & Ohio Railroad was dismissed.

A visible role for women everywhere was that of streetcar conductor. From San Francisco to Berlin, whenever the population used public transportation, they saw women taking over this traditionally male occupation. Women began this work in the German capital as early as August 1914. Soon rumor had it that Germany's female conductors stabbed their formidable hatpins in the flesh of troublesome passengers to make them behave. Restricted to men before the war, a conductor's job endangered health and safety by exposing the body to bad weather and the vibration of the streetcar's motor. But, like other wartime openings, the job attracted applicants because of the high pay it offered. Hundreds of American women in twelve cities took jobs as conductors. One former American janitress more than doubled her income by obtaining a position on the local streetcar line.[15]

WOMEN AND THE FARM

In prewar France and Germany, women played a key role in working the land. Those French and German peasant women took on major responsibilities from the first days of the war. The mobilization in the summer of 1914 left it to women and children to bring in the harvest. During the years that followed, female workers continued to dominate the rural workforce, despite government promises to send men home at harvest time and to assign prisoners of war to farm labor. The effort to run a farm without the menfolk drove some to despair. One French woman recalled that her brother had taught her to plow before he left for the army. But, with a plow designed for a man, "I got the handle in the chest or face every time I hit a stone. For me plowing was the road to Calvary." Another, who tried to cultivate the family farm aided only by her fourteen-year-old brother, remembered the war years with deep bitterness: "We were often overwhelmed with fatigue and discouragement. In our conversations, in our ideas, we took voyages to free us from our misery."[16]

Women played a lesser although well publicized role in British agriculture. In contrast to France and Germany, Britain was able to maintain food production without a great influx of female workers. Rural males above and below the age of military service took up some of the slack created by wartime mobilization. Prisoners of war, British soldiers reassigned temporarily from military duties, and greater mechanization aided as well.

But some British women, many of them from the privileged classes, answered a government call to provide farm labor in the final years of the war by joining the Land Army. The Land Army gave a young woman an opportunity to leave home, to do useful manual labor on a farm, and thus to contribute to the war effort. The picture of a healthy English girl of twenty or so, dressed in a farmer's smock and wielding a hoe, was a compelling propaganda device. But only 48,000 signed on. Farmers were skeptical about what women workers from the city could contribute. The enthusiasm of many potential recruits faded when they found being a farm worker was little more than holding a position as a common laborer.

WOMEN AS A FOCUS FOR CRITICISM

Both public opinion and government authorities remained uncomfortable with the position of women in wartime society. Some women found themselves the scapegoats for the strains wartime placed upon everyone. During the first months of the war, many German women were stigmatized as undeserving "soldiers' wives." The allowances such women received were insufficient to support their families in many cases. Nonetheless, the meager financial support they received from the government and their right to rationed foodstuffs led other Germans, including women, to paint them as pampered individuals. Supposedly they lived well while contributing nothing to the war effort. One local official in December 1914 lamented how working-class women were spending large amounts of money on "sweets, finery and other luxury items" while "neglecting housekeeping and children, and, along with their children, are subsisting on bread, butter, and meat." Easy money, the absence of a husband's stabilizing influence, and the ability to remain idle, he noted, was leading to "grave social ills in working-class settlements."[17]

Sometimes the German husband's departure did reduce family expenses enough to permit the wife a bit more money than she had in peacetime. Moreover, the man's absence meant his wife was in direct control of the family's income for the first time. Criticism diminished as more of the male population entered military service and the term "soldier's wife" applied to greater numbers of women. Nonetheless, the effort in 1916 to increase government support to the spouses soldiers left behind inflamed attitudes once again.

The heroic French farm wife of 1914 suffered a change in her public image as the war went on. Increasingly, she was portrayed as a greedy profiteer selling scarce goods at exorbitant prices to helpless city dwellers. She also seemed to benefit financially from soldiers' loneliness and isolation from home. In the first months of the war, French soldiers praised their countrywomen near the front for providing them with food, drink, and temporary lodgings. As the war of movement turned into stalemate, the *poilu*, the French frontline soldier, viewed such women running a small shop or living room café near the battle zone as despicable parasites. Most damning of all, they appeared to many men in uniform as wishing the war to go on as long as possible.

Women in munitions factories sometimes faced vicious criticism as war profiteers. While men died in the trenches, the adult females in their families supposedly took their own generous earnings and spent them on frivolities. In France, a twisted version of reality in newspaper and magazine commentaries pictured munitions workers who wore diamond combs and silk stockings to work, gorged themselves on cream and pastries, and bought chickens and oranges—two symbolically scarce and expensive food items—without a thought about the cost. Rushing from the factory, the *munitionette* amused herself with an appointment at the hairdresser followed by dinner out and a visit to the movies. This female factory worker appeared in some accounts as a bawdy creature, drinking, smoking, cursing, and satisfying her sexual urges as if she were a man. Like her imaginary rural sister in the war zone, she supposedly hoped the war would go on forever. In Britain, gossip had it that the prosperous factory girl earned some of her wealth from selling her sexual favors in her free time, the so-called "extra shift."

Even volunteer nurses drew bitter comments concerning their motives and conduct. In France, they faced accusations of shopping around to be assigned to a "chic" hospital and viewing their service as an opportunity for adventure, "a sport, a new game, a more enthralling variation of flirtation and the tango." They allegedly refused to take orders, undermining the vital discipline of the hospital, and tried to minister only to handsome officers, preferably those who were lightly wounded.[18]

Governments looked with increasing unease at the role women were playing. The German government presided over the society with the most painful shortages faced by any of the belligerents. Its leaders worried about the behavior of women in the ever-present food lines. When German men were required to sign up for industrial service in 1916, the government considered putting the same burden on women. It held back, fearing the opposition such a step would provoke.

The authorities then discovered that many German women would not enter the factories voluntarily. In a world governed by the Allied blockade, even high wages gave women no guarantee of obtaining food for their families. And factory work made it impossible for them to stand in lengthy food lines seeking the means to feed their families. Only by guaranteeing women the status of heavy worker, with its accompanying right to a greater food ration, could the government draw some into the factory.

But even then the typical German housewife was reluctant to respond. Government allowances to the families of fighting men, combined with compulsory rent reductions and contributions from the military man's former employer, sufficed—if just barely—to meet the needs of a lower-class German family. Withholding a family allowance to compel a house-wife to work in a factory seemed too dangerous to risk: No one wanted to strike at the morale of numerous soldiers at the front by throwing their families into destitution. Many German housewives tried to balance the different burdens placed on them by working at home. Facing reality, military authorities provided homemakers with tasks that could be done in their own dwellings—for example, making sandbags and articles of clothing for the armed forces.

Many enemy prisoners of war worked in the German economy. The authorities saw sexual relations between German women and these for-eigners as particularly alarming. Evident in industrial regions, these ex-tramarital relationships were believed to be even more common in the countryside. Where prisoners worked as agricultural laborers, they were often loosely supervised and even welcomed into the local community.

To control women who showed so "little feeling for national con-sciousness," military and civilian officials cracked down with jail sen-tences and fines for women tried and convicted of consorting with the enemy. They also encouraged the nation's newspapers, at both the local and national level, to publish the names and locations of women who had dishonored themselves in this fashion.

Governments also had cause to worry about the role of women in strikes like those that swept the Paris region in the spring of 1917. In these walkouts, French women constituted a large percentage of the strikers, who were protesting their employer's attempt to lower piece-work rates. The first strikers got women from several other factories to join them, and they widened their complaints to demand an end to the war—or at least to conscript men who dodged the draft by pretending to be essential skilled workers. Police investigations of strike leaders fo-cused on their sexual behavior—the authorities assumed that a female worker's militancy or political interests were linked to an uncontrolled sex drive. At this very time, massive strikes erupted in Germany as Ber-lin workers—many of them women as well—protested a cut in the bread ration.

CONCERTED EFFORTS TO INCREASE THE BIRTHRATE

Women in Britain, France, and Germany found themselves the target of a campaign to boost their nation's birthrate. The campaign to fill empty cradles to counteract the carnage of the battlefield carried special weight in France. There the birthrate had been declining for a century prior to the outbreak of the war. France had seen the size of its popu-lation fall disastrously behind that of its German adversary between 1871 and 1914. A vocal group of doctors, social critics, and other members of the nation's elite had long called for an effort to reverse this trend. But the war seemed to intensify the crisis. Most of France's men of marriageable age found themselves away in the army. A chaotic system of military leaves determined when they could make brief trips home, and it began to work properly only at the close of 1915. As a result, whereas 594,000 infants had been born alive in 1914, the number dropped to barely half that in 1916.[19]

The sense of crisis entered the mind of the population at large. One feminist newspaper, whose editors had been outraged by these birthrate promoters' demands before the war, took a very different line by the second year of the conflict. In December 1915, it called upon women to accept the obligation of producing "children, lots of children to fill the gaps." Common forms of communication such as the picture postcard exhorted men to marry and encouraged soldiers to use their home leaves (*permission*) as the occasion to produce a "leave baby" (*un petit permissionaire*). Women were invited, with only slightly veiled language, to offer a warm welcome to their husband or boyfriend so that he could serve France during his leave at home by expanding the population. Although French society frowned on picturing pregnant women, wartime postcards approvingly showed Marianne, the female symbol for France, with full breasts and bulging stomach.[20]

Welfare supervisors entered French factories in 1917 in large part to protect the health of real and prospective mothers in the workforce. Government regulations now barred pregnant women from working at night, and the authorities enjoined employers to put expectant mothers on tasks like assembly work during which they could sit. Factories had to provide a nursing room in which infants remained during the worker's shift; a mother had the right to visit regularly to breast-feed her child.

Birthrate concerns were evident in prewar Britain as well. A declining birthrate here made remarks about "empty cradles" and "silent nurseries" common in discussions about the nation's future. During the course of the war, national policy led to a huge expansion in social welfare efforts to aid the family; the number of Great Britain's maternity and child welfare centers doubled in these years. A prominent female union leader in Britain called on women to put the care of their children first. Work in factories helped the nation, she admitted, "but a baby is more wonderful than a machine gun. I believe that the hand that rocks the cradle will still be a power when the other is only a hateful memory."[21]

Prominent Germans also told their nation's women that producing the soldiers of the future was their urgent duty. Germany's birthrate was not as low as that of France and Britain, but it had declined steadily since the 1870s. The war lent a tone of urgency to the ongoing discussion about this national trend. A leading socialist and Berlin university pro-

fessor claimed in 1915 that having babies was the "only female contribution to war and military power which equals" the wartime military
service men were expected to perform. To have children and fill the
population gaps left by the war was, he declared, "indispensable for our
national ascendancy." As for working women, he dismissed their efforts
as "irrelevant to national production but fatal for population growth."[22]
Women thus received a message that stood in direct opposition to the
recruiting posters and other means for drawing them into the factory.

A German woman of childbearing age found the government acting
to promote her pregnancy. The national government in Berlin urged action on local authorities. Soon, several German states prevented newspapers in their territory from publishing the addresses of couples who
had registered their intention to be married with the authorities. Thus,
a woman and her future spouse no longer received the catalogues of
contraceptives that formally engaged couples got prior to the war. She
could no longer find contraceptives displayed or advertised, and even
door-to-door salesmen were no longer permitted to peddle such devices.

Restrictions on the civilian use of rubber blocked German women from
buying female contraceptive devices that used the material, although her
sexual partner could still find rubber condoms—defined as a tool against
sexually transmitted diseases—without difficulty. Her doctor had likely
received government instructions to interpret more strictly the definition
of an abortion performed for medical reasons. Voluntary abortions remained illegal, with a mandatory prison sentence for any woman who
underwent one.

The government also offered positive inducements for pregnancy. A
prospective German mother found that she would receive a special maternity allowance. In 1915, it became possible for an unmarried woman
to get such support. Before the war, unmarried mothers had twice the
possibility of losing their new child in its first year of life than did married women. Thus, for many of the 180,000 children born out of wedlock
each year in Germany, government action contributed materially to the
difference between life and death.

Despite the pressures to produce more children, the wartime birthrate
in Germany fell below the 1914 level. In 1918, it was at the lowest point
ever recorded. When a Berlin physician surveyed 300 married couples
in 1916, he found that more than 200 were using birth control to prevent
pregnancy. Their motive was to promote the prosperity of their family
by limiting the number of children to support. Germany remained a
country in which coitus interruptus was the favored form of birth control
and abortion was common. Thus, government restrictions on the availability of contraceptives had little chance of achieving the goal of expanding the population.

Despite the wave of birthrate-related thoughts and actions, many in

German society viewed a pregnant woman with some discomfort. She could not contribute immediately to the war effort, but her need for nourishment meant a stronger claim on the constricted food supply. German women with large numbers of children found themselves the target of public suspicion. They allegedly consumed the food allocated for their offspring. Many German mothers of modest means found that the state would not underwrite their efforts to stay home. Even with the maternity allowance, family finances remained precarious. Going out to work, even at the cost of neglecting her children, was the only way for such a woman to make ends meet.

In France, both medical authorities and some in the general population insisted that a pregnant woman did not belong in a war plant. In December 1916, one of France's leading obstetricians, Dr. Adolphe Pinard, opened a bitter debate on the subject. One Parisian newspaper summarized his position with a striking headline that read "The Factory, Baby Killer." One of Pinard's supporters added that the factory was worse than the war itself: "It kills, but [it kills] the youngest, the weak, it kills the future."[23]

NEW FREEDOMS AND LONG-STANDING CHANGES

As women became mobile, independent of family supervision, and financially solvent, they seemed even during the war to be undermining national traditions. The expanded role of women in national life—and their growing visibility on the home front—sharpened the question of defining their postwar rights. It seemed likely, although hardly certain given the hardiness of gender traditions, that women would continue to play a great role outside their normal arena of the home. Nonetheless, men's attitudes toward a woman's place in society stood firm.

Despite the social disruption brought on by years of intensive warfare, females in the belligerent countries saw only limited changes in their status in the postwar years. Most women did not keep their foothold in the areas of the economy that had temporarily opened to them. Britain granted women the right to vote in 1918, as did Germany. The United States followed in 1920. But in France, the franchise remained out of reach until 1944.

Many women who had found employment in the industrial system were compelled to leave at the war's conclusion. Women workers had been a common feature of the French economy before the war, and their overall numbers did not grow markedly over the years 1914–18. The Armistice saw their new role in war-related industries shrink back to prewar levels by early 1919. Overall, the percentage of women in the French workforce began a long decline after the Armistice.

In some areas of the various economies, changes, albeit limited, became permanent. The British and French metals industry gave wartime opportunity for women, then imposed massive layoffs following the Armistice. But companies in both countries began to hire women once again after 1919. The period between World War I and World War II saw the number of women workers here double over the levels reached before 1914. Nonetheless, women remained restricted to relatively unskilled positions, and their pay lagged behind that of male workers. The number of German women in the chemical and metals industries surged temporarily during World War I. Over the longer range, from the start of the century to the mid-1920s, the total size of the women's contingent in this work force grew—but only modestly. On the other hand, French and British women who took on office work in banks and insurance companies during the war changed the composition of that workforce in a permanent fashion.

British women found the doors closed to them when the government set up job-training programs after the war. Offered a position in a laundry or as a domestic servant, a woman risked losing her employment benefits if she turned it down. The government would not accept a claim that working in a war plant had given her a new occupation. By January 1919, the British popular press was openly scoffing at women who balked at becoming domestic servants. "When are munitions girls to grow tired of their holiday?" one asked. Another sneered at women who were taking "a holiday at the National expense."[24] Nonetheless, British women who went back to being servants often did so with a new attitude toward domestic work. Many refused to live with the families employing them, and they avoided working in a large household with its highly structured and tightly disciplined hierarchy of servants.

Most American women lost the working opportunities that had opened up in wartime. Only a handful of the hundreds of women streetcar conductors were able to keep their positions. On the railroads former male workers returning from military service got their old jobs back, displacing women in the process. Local managers manipulated job classifications and seniority rules to force out much of the female workforce. The master mechanic for the Pennsylvania Railroad in Harrisburg stated bluntly that he wanted men to be "reinstated for the good of all and women should lend a willing obedience to that fact."[25]

In the political sphere, change did come. Women had made a major, perhaps vital contribution to the war effort in each of the western front belligerents. In Britain in 1914, prospective women voters had found the leaders of their movement putting aside the goal of suffrage in the interest of backing the war effort. Suffragist leaders took positions of outspoken hostility toward the country's opponents. The National Union of Women Suffrage Societies, despite the objections of some of its leaders, rejected efforts to contact women in Germany. It also refused to question the need to fight the war to a victorious conclusion.

By 1917, there was a growing likelihood that at least some British women would win the vote. Paradoxically, the right of men to vote helped reopen the issue of women's suffrage. Military service put many men in conflict with the British election law's residency requirements. The law had to be changed to protect their rights to the franchise, and this seemed the logical moment to bring at least some women into the electorate.

The role women had played in the war effort had received favorable, even glamorized coverage in the press. This served to temper the opposition against giving at least some women the vote. So too did the fear of public disorder as exemplified in revolutionary Russia. Many in Britain recalled how militant women like members of the Pankhurst family had disrupted the prewar domestic scene. The country had been devastated by a variety of wartime losses, and there was a pressing need to restore domestic calm and public order. Many of the leaders of British society thought a prerequisite for achieving that calm was to avoid a renewal of the public, sexual confrontations that had abated only in August 1914.

Opponents of giving women the vote revived old arguments and mixed them with supposed lessons from the present. Speakers in the House of Commons in March 1917 began by following traditional lines. They conjured up a picture of flighty and naïve women casting their votes in ignorance, "necessarily inexperienced voters liable to be swayed by the arguments of hysterical agitators" to vote in foolish ways. But they put this in the context of the war. Opponents of women's suffrage declared that there were masses of pacifists "among the millions of women who without political experience it is proposed to enfranchise," and such females would favor a hasty peace with an undefeated Germany. They attempted to diminish the impact of the woman working in the factory or on the streetcar by noting that, whatever their contributions, women were not being asked to risk their lives in the same way that millions of men were required to do.[26]

But many in Britain saw women as warriors on the home front, and contrary arguments did not sway those grateful for what women had done to win the war. Parliament decided the "woman question" by granting at least some women the right to vote in the spring of 1918. This was something less than political equality. The vote went only to women who had reached the age of thirty, thus excluding younger women despite their contribution to the war effort. A woman voter also had to meet the requirement of being a home-owner, either in her own right or as the spouse of a home-owner. Thus, many poorer women aged thirty or over had no way to gain the franchise. By contrast all men over the age of twenty-one who could meet a brief residency requirement got the vote in 1918. Moreover, by giving the vote to men as young as nineteen if they were military veterans, the government made sure that the new female voters would still be outvoted by the male electorate. Only the electoral reform of 1928, lowering the voting age of women to twenty-one and subjecting them only to the same residency requirement as men, created an equitable system.[27]

American women also received the vote in the aftermath of the war. The example of militant British suffragists helped to revive the movement for women's political rights in the years before the United States entered the war. So too did the success of women in winning the vote in several American states. Important leaders of the women's movement, notably Carrie Chapman Catt, pledged their support to the war effort, knowing that "the ability of suffragists to plead their cause successfully would depend in some measure on whether they too had joined in the national war effort."[28]

In wartime, women filled visible posts in the Department of Labor and the Ordnance Department as well as on the Women's Committee for National Defense. That body worked to mobilize American women for food conservation and selling war bonds. These public roles in the war effort strengthened women's claim to participate fully in the nation's political life. The explicit American war aim of spreading democracy abroad also buttressed calls to extend the vote to women at home.

The House of Representatives passed the suffrage amendment in early January 1918. At this point, the influence of President Woodrow Wilson took on crucial significance. Wilson had never shaken off "a rather patronizing approach to women" derived from his upbringing in a traditional southern family. Even though he had never warmly embraced women's suffrage as an issue, the enthusiasm of his intelligent and independent-minded second wife and his three daughters toward giving the women the vote had probably made an impression. Moreover, the 1916 Democratic platform had endorsed women's suffrage. And now, in wartime circumstances, Wilson did so as well.[29] He appeared personally before the Senate on September 30. He noted that the average American now believed "that democracy means that women shall play their part in affairs alongside men and upon an equal footing with them." The war, Wilson added, could not have been fought by America or its allies "if it had not been for the services of the women."[30] Even so, it took the convening of the new Senate in 1919 to pass the amendment, and it was ratified only in July 1920.

The war years had raised the issue of extending political rights to France's women. Several proposals indicated that male political leaders felt some discomfort in simply denying all women the vote. Perhaps, some politicians suggested, the relatives of deceased soldiers could be given the franchise and thus exercise it in the name of a man who had died for France. In any case, the contribution of women to winning the war was too obvious to dismiss out of hand. Nonetheless, opponents argued that Frenchwomen had not been motivated by selfish goals like obtaining the franchise when they donated their time and sweat to the task of defeating Germany. Rather, their contribution to the war effort had been the fruit of their patriotism. Thus, there was no sacrifice that called for an official reward. In all, French politicians of all stripes felt a growing discomfort at overthrowing a voting system that excluded women.

Fear that women would form a decisive voting bloc manipulated by the Roman Catholic Church made some French politicians hesitate. Others declared that motherhood, not politics, should be the first thought and concern for a woman in the peacetime era. The bodies in the French National Assembly split over the issue. The Chamber of Deputies passed a woman's suffrage bill in 1919 by a wide margin of three to one only to have it delayed by the Senate. That body finally defeated the bill in 1922. By that time popular gratitude for the women's role in the war had faded, and the arguments about Church influence over women voters and the need to emphasize women's roles as mothers prevailed in the Assembly's upper chamber. An analysis of the Senate vote in 1922 shows that every political group now opposed giving women the vote, including many on the political left. As one scholar has put it, "Though each opponent gave his own particular reasons, none wanted to share political power with women. Political participation by women would blur gender lines more than war had done."[31]

The war years had brought talk at the highest levels in Germany about changing that country's complex system of voting rights. The election laws not only excluded women but gave excessive weight to wealthy men at the expense of those of lesser means. In 1917, the Emperor himself had promised a new political system. Nonetheless, women received the right to vote only in the turmoil of revolution in mid-November 1918 when the Social Democrats came to power as Germany fell into defeat.

NOTES

1. Gail Braybon, *Women Workers in the First World War: The British Experience* (London: Croom Helm, 1981), 24–32.

2. Colin Dyer, *Population and Society in Twentieth Century France* (London: Hodder and Stoughton, 1978), 12, 17–18.

3. Kendrick A. Clements, *The Presidency of Woodrow Wilson* (Lawrence, Kans.: University Press of Kansas, 1992), 16–17.

4. Maurine Weiner Greenwald, *Women, War, and Work: The Impact of World War I on Women Workers in the United States* (Westport, Conn.: Greenwood Press, 1980), 12.

5. Ute Daniel, *The War from Within: German Working-Class Women in the First World War*, trans. Margaret Ries (Oxford: Berg, 1997), 38–45.

6. Quoted in Braybon, *Women Workers*, 176.

7. Quoted in Gail Braybon, "Women, War, and Work," in *World War I: A History*, ed. Hew Strachan (Oxford: Oxford University Press, 1998), 155.

8. Laura Lee Downs, *Manufacturing Inequality: Gender Division in the French and British Metalworking Industries, 1914–1939* (Ithaca, N.Y.: Cornell University Press, 1995), 15–16.

9. Quoted in Braybon, *Women Workers*, 115.

10. Downs, *Manufacturing Inequality*, 76.

11. Quoted in Angela Woollacott, *On Her Their Lives Depend: Munitions Workers in the Great War* (Berkeley: University of California Press, 1994), 82.

12. Downs, *Manufacturing Inequality*, 98.

13. Ibid., 165.

14. Ute Daniel, "Women's Work in Industry and Family: Germany, 1914–1918," in *The Upheaval of War: Family, Work and Welfare in Europe, 1914–1918*, ed. Richard Wall and Jay Winter (Cambridge, Eng.: Cambridge University Press, 1988), 279.

15. Greenwald, *Women, War, and Work*, 155.

16. Quoted in Margaret H. Darrow, *French Women and the First World War: War Stories of the Home Front* (Oxford: Berg, 2000), 183.

17. Quoted in Ute Daniel, *The War from Within: German Working-Class Women in the First World War*, trans. Margaret Ries (Oxford: Berg, 1997), 28.

18. Darrow, *French Women*, 147–48.

19. Dyer, *Population and Society*, 49–51, 55–56.

20. Monique Huss, "Pronatalism and the Popular Ideology of the Child in Wartime France: The Evidence of the Picture Postcard," in *The Upheaval of War*, ed. Wall and Winter, 329–54. The picture of a pregnant Marianne is on page 347.

21. Quoted in Richard Soloway, "Eugenics and Pronatalism in Wartime Britain," in ibid., 381.

22. Cornelie Usborne, " 'Pregnancy is the Woman's Active Service': Pronatalism in Germany during the First World War," in ibid., 389, 397.

23. Darrow, *French Women*, 206–8.

24. Quoted in Braybon, *Women Workers*, 187–88.

25. Greenwald, *Women, War, Work*, 129.

26. Susan Kingsley Kent, *Making Peace: The Reconstruction of Gender in Interwar Britain* (Princeton, N.J.: Princeton University Press, 1993), 87–89.

27. Charles Loch Mowat, *Britain between the Wars, 1918–1940* (Chicago: University of Chicago Press, [1955]), 5–6, 343; also A.J.P. Taylor, *English History, 1914–1945* (New York: Oxford University Press, 1965), 93–94, 115–16.

28. Eleanor Flexner, *Century of Struggle: The Woman's Rights Movement in the United States*, rev. ed. (Cambridge, Mass.: The Belknap Press of Harvard University Press, 1975), 294.

29. Clements, *The Presidency of Woodrow Wilson*, x, 159.

30. Quoted in Flexner, *Century of Struggle*, 321–22.

31. Bonnie G. Smith, *Changing Lives: Women in European History since 1700* (Lexington, Mass.: D.C. Heath, 1989), 398.

PART III

RESULTS AND THE WAR'S END

13

Bereavement

Despite its huge scale, World War I resembled all wars in one sad respect. It left a trail of death and grieving. Men in uniform who had
survived so far had to confront the death of their comrades in arms.
Governments had to find ways to announce the occurrence of an insup-
portable tragedy to those at home. Friends and loved ones had to think
about the prospective death of the men to whom they were bidding
good-bye. And when tragic news came, as it often did, they had to find
the inner strength to cope with it. Even as the war continued, the belligerent societies that were losing so many of their young men began to
search for a way to commemorate those who had died.

FATALITIES

The most convincing totals combine those known to have died with
those missing and presumed dead. Each of the European countries that
fought on the western front lost a significant portion of its young men.
The United States suffered grievously given its relatively brief participation in the great actions of 1918. The four countries together lost a
total of approximately 4.25 million men.[1]

Large numbers of American forces fought only for a brief period, and
this kept the losses of that country light compared to other nations. The
western front belligerent with the largest population had a final overseas
death toll between 76,000 and 83,000. Some 50,000 died in combat or as
a result of their wounds; most of the remaining fatalities in the AEF died

of disease, the principal ailment being the influenza epidemic that struck during the final part of the war. Influenza deaths of soldiers in the United States at home elevated the total death toll of men in uniform to about 112,000.

The European belligerents saw great gaps created in their populations. Millions of healthy young men were drawn into the struggle, and almost one in six of them perished in the war. Including those listed as missing and colonial forces as well, France ended the war with just under 1.4 million fatalities. Virtually all those deaths came in connection with the fighting on the western front. Germany's two-front war brought a total given variously as 1.7 million dead to just over 2 million dead. Britain's military efforts spread over several continents. Over 6 million served in uniform, but some 570,000 (the vast majority of its 750,000 dead) came from fighting on the western front.

France and Germany had large armies engaged from the start of the war, and each experienced heavy losses in the early fighting. Four hundred thousand French servicemen died during the first four months of the war. Even before the great 1916 bloodletting began at Verdun, the nation had lost a million of its sons. Fighting offensive actions on both the eastern and western fronts, Germany also incurred its worst losses during the first months of combat in 1914: Fully half of the field army of 1.5 million men was killed or injured. In that year, the western front alone saw the demise of 116,000 German soldiers, four times the entire German death toll in the victorious Franco-Prussian War of 1870–71. Unlike France, Germany stood on the defensive in the west in 1915 and found its casualties diminished accordingly.

Ninety percent of the men in the small expeditionary force of five divisions Britain sent to the Continent in 1914 were casualties by the close of the year. Britain's land forces first suffered losses comparable in total numbers to those of Germany and France at the Battle of the Somme in 1916. At that time Kitchener's new armies came on to the scene in large numbers. Those hideous losses were matched in the comparably bloody and futile offensive at Passchendaele (the Third Battle of Ypres) in the fall of 1917. Germany's casualties escalated when it took the offensive, first against Verdun in 1916, then in the gambler's throw of the spring of 1918 when it tried to separate the French and British armies and win the war outright before American troops could arrive.

In some countries, elevated social groups lost a startlingly large number of young men. Privileged status in peacetime created a heightened danger in war. Educated young men from the upper levels of society provided a disproportionate number of ground combat officers. The number of young men from England's elite universities, Oxford and Cambridge, who failed to survive the war gives grim testimony to that generalization. The entering class at Oxford in 1913 lost 31 percent of its members. One French lycée, attended by the nephew of a cabinet minister, lost twenty-six out of twenty-seven members of its senior class by Christmas 1914. Only the one class member excused from military service due to illness remained alive.[2]

Across the battle line, the students at the Kaiser Wilhelm Gymnasium, an elite Berlin secondary school, likewise died in large numbers. They volunteered in the patriotic fervor of the war's early months and had their baptism of fire in Flanders at the First Battle of Ypres in October–November 1914. They lost large numbers of former students in 1915, and their casualties surged again in May 1916. Some 20 percent of the school's student body and alumni perished in the war.[3]

The fate of Edward Revere Osler personalizes such losses. The son of the era's most prominent physician, the Canadian-born William Osler, Revere was born in the United States in 1895. As his name indicates, on his mother's side he was a direct descendant of Paul Revere. Being the only child of relatively old parents, Revere was, in the words of Osler's biographer, adored and worried over "as though he were the only boy ever to grow up in the world."[4] When his father capped a brilliant career in the United States by accepting the position of Regius Professor of Medicine at Oxford, the family moved to Britain in 1905. Revere was educated at a famous British boarding school, but he needed special tutoring to qualify for Oxford.

After a single term at the university, the eighteen-year-old student tried to enlist as a private in a socially exclusive regiment. The family pulled strings to get him assigned to a hospital unit instead, but he persuaded them to help him join an artillery unit by the close of 1915. His mother had no doubt of the danger: Visiting a circle of seven Oxford acquaintances in May 1916, she learned that two of their boys had been killed, two wounded, and one taken prisoner; seven more were still serving on the western front. Three months later, she reacted with desperation to the losses on the Somme, noting, "The Casualty lists are so horrible now it makes one ill to look in the papers and one's friends are in trouble in every direction."[5] Revere survived for another year and reached his twenty-first birthday despite the danger of serving as an artillery lieutenant. His good fortune ended during the Battle of Passchendaele on August 29, 1917, when he was wounded in the chest, abdomen, and thigh from a nearby shell burst. Two of William Osler's distinguished colleagues happened to be serving in the area, but, despite their efforts, the young man died the following morning.

Enlisted men made up the vast majority of the combatant armies; they died in larger numbers than did officers. British army figures show that only 4 of every 100 infantrymen who died in combat held commissions. Similarly, in the German army only 3 percent of some 2 million dead were officers. But 23 of every 100 German officers died compared to only

14 out of every 100 enlisted men. The task of junior officers—to lead men into battle—explained the disparity. As the first to climb from the shelter of a trench and the first to cross no man's land, such young men were in deadly peril. Thus, approximately 96 percent of the officers who died in the German army were captains or lieutenants.

Within the British army, the percentage of officers killed versus enlisted fatalities varied during the war's stages. But officers always lost a greater percentage of their numbers than did the enlisted men. From the fall of 1914 to the fall of 1915, 14.2 percent of the officers fell compared to 5.8 percent of the enlisted men. From the fall of 1917 to the fall of the following year, 6.9 percent of the officers died compared to 4 percent of the "other ranks." French figures likewise show that the dangers of being an officer outweighed those of serving in the ranks.

In several countries, soldiers from rural areas went to their deaths in greater numbers than those from the cities. The majority of the German population now lived in cities, but exemptions to serve in industry kept large numbers in urban areas away from enemy fire. In France, the rural population still outnumbered those in the cities. Military districts in agricultural regions such as Orléans and Limoges provided a disproportionate share of the young men lost to the war, and the average peasant stood a far greater chance of dying in uniform than his urban counterpart.

The young suffered disproportionately. In Britain, the greatest danger presented itself to men at the age of twenty. Men whose ages ranged from seventeen to thirty-seven had a likelihood of perishing in these bloody years between two and eight times the peacetime norm. Within the age group thirty-eight to forty-six mortality rates rose less starkly, and British men above that age actually increased their life expectancy. The chance of being killed in action faded from one in seven for those below the age of twenty-five to one in twenty for those older than forty. Single men stood a greater chance of dying than the already married: Two out of every three German fatalities were bachelors, and the marriage prospects of German women suffered accordingly. In 1919, there were only three German men for every four women in the age groups most likely to marry.

Service in the forces of one country offered greater danger than in others. One in ten men of the British forces in uniform died, but one of every six men serving in the French forces did; the grisly larger number applied to the German military as well. In marked contrast, Americans faced a rate of fatalities at less than 3 percent (27 out of each 1,000) for those serving in the armed forces. Service in different branches of the military made a vast difference. Only one of every two men serving in the British army could be expected to pass through his military service without being killed, wounded, or taken prisoner. One out of eight soldiers was killed. In the navy, on the other hand, only one man in sixteen failed to survive the war; in the air service (the Royal Flying Corps, which became the RAF) only one in fifty died. The casualties among actual aviators, however, were far higher due first to the danger of a fatal accident during training followed by the perils of aerial combat.

THE DEVASTATED FAMILY

The death of any individual in the course of the war struck the lives of many others: a fiancée, family members, friends. The nineteenth century had brought a significant decline in the death rate for the young, and families now linked death with the elderly and the infirm. In Britain, the death rate fell from 22 per 1,000 around 1870 to only 13 per 1,000 on the eve of the war. The death of a child was becoming an unusual family tragedy rather than a common one. A male's life expectancy of forty years around the middle of the previous century swelled to fifty-two years in 1910. Similar figures can be found for France, although the decline in infant mortality was a more gradual one. Sudden, violent death, especially for young adults in Western Europe had become a rarity.[6]

In France, there had been a decline in the observance of conventional religion, as well as open conflict between secularists and devotees of Roman Catholicism. These trends undermined traditional practices in mourning the dead. In England, as well, elaborate funerals and prolonged periods of formal mourning declined in popularity. Nonetheless, cultural along with religious traditions remained potent. They favored a "good death" in the family home with loving relatives gathered at the bedside. They called for a burial service, and the ability to bid farewell to the physical remains of a loved one provided most families with solace at their loss.

But now deaths of young adults took place violently, in unimaginable numbers, and within a brief time frame. Young men died far from home, often with their bodies unrecoverable if not completely destroyed. Individual families suffered multiple deaths or the death of an only son. The impact can be gauged, or at least imagined, by considering specific, prominent families on both sides of the battlefront.

The family experience of Anthony Eden, a future British prime minister, suggests the pain the war could inflict. In the first months of fighting, Eden's older brother John, a professional army officer, died in combat. In 1916, his younger brother Nicholas, only sixteen, went down with his ship at the Battle of Jutland. A fourth brother had the good fortune—although he might not have viewed it as such—of being interned in Austria-Hungary for the duration of the conflict. In addition, Eden's brother-in-law was badly wounded, and his uncle was captured after the enemy downed his plane.

Friedrich Ebert was a leading figure of Germany's Socialist Party (the SPD). When he assumed the post of prime minister in November 1918, his predecessor reminded him of the grave responsibility of directing Germany's future. Ebert replied that the death of two of his sons in battle left him in no doubt about the heavy burden that he was to undertake.

The scions of prominent military families fell in the line of duty. Their willingness to go into combat almost certainly drew upon the example set by their fathers and their sense of family tradition. Germain Foch, the only son of General Ferdinand Foch, was killed in fighting near the Belgian frontier during the first weeks of the war; Foch's son-in-law died in the same locale on the same day. The French leader received the tragic news only three weeks later during the aftermath of the Battle of the Marne. Lieutenant Michael Allenby, the only child of General Edmund Allenby, died when a shell splinter penetrated his helmet at Nieuport near the Belgian coast in July 1917. General Erich Ludendorff had no natural children, but two of his three stepsons, Franz and Erich Pernet, both aviators, died on the western front. Franz was shot down in September 1917; Erich in March of the following year. Rudyard Kipling, no soldier himself but the literary spokesman for the British army, pulled strings to get a commission in the Irish Guards for his only son. John Kipling, barely eighteen, died at the Battle of Loos in September 1915. And sometimes families contributed even more heavily to war's casualty lists. General Eduard de Castelnau lost one of his three sons at the start of the fighting in 1914; the remaining two perished later in the conflict.

Far more families from the everyday levels of the population suffered grievous losses. By the closing months of 1915, a year in which French forces suffered their worst casualties, more than four-fifths of the *communes* in the Isère region of southern France had lost at least one of their male citizens in combat. By the war's conclusion, one of the local villages with 400 inhabitants had to accept the fact that thirty of its young men would never return.

German mothers bidding good-bye to departing troop trains in 1916 were often dressed in mourning clothing from an earlier loss. The *New York Times* correspondent in Germany reported in January 1916 that visitors to a Berlin home commonly encountered a bereaved mother who presented them with pictures of several of her sons, starting with the youngest, and stating for each, "He has fallen."[7] The American soldiers arriving in France found the rural villages where they trained filled with widows and bereaved mothers all wearing black.

The Coster and Shaw families of England offer grim examples of that country's sacrifice. Four of the five Costers from Watford never returned from the fighting; one of them died shortly before the Armistice ended the killing on the western front. Between 1916 and August 1918, the Shaw family of Kent lost all five of the sons who participated in the war.

The Kiekebusch family of Berlin saw one son die on the western front in the war's first months; his elder brother survived two years of combat starting in Flanders in May 1916 only to perish on the first day of Ludendorff's final offensive in the spring of 1918.[8]

THE ANTICIPATION OF DEATH

By the start of 1915, the huge casualty lists gave a fearful indication that a soldier departing for the battlefront might never return. Many families and circles of friends probably avoided a discussion of this grim reality with the men in uniform. But others felt compelled to broach the subject and to discuss it at length.

In England, Vera Brittain and her fiancé Roland Leighton had a year before Roland's death to ponder the issue. Despite his poor eyesight, he contrived to enlist, to obtain a commission, and to get assigned to the 11th Sherwood Foresters in late November 1914. In the spring of 1915, he left for France. In letters and face-to-face conversations, the two young people, neither yet having reached the age of twenty, considered such questions as whether death in combat was preferable to a peaceful demise. They discussed whether a vague sense of heroism should make a young man risk his life. On one occasion Roland promised the young woman that, if he died at the front, he would try to reach Vera somehow. Even in death he wanted to assure her his love for her still survived.

More commonly the two painted a happy future together. He knew he would return, he assured her. She told him that their relationship had given both of them a glimpse of happiness. She did not believe it would end with "a vision of the Promised Land only to be told we were never to enter it." But such forced optimism fell on hard times. "Every ring at the door suggested a telegram," she later wrote, "every telephone call a long-distance message giving bad news." She dreamed of her young man's death and wrote to assure him that whatever happened he would live in her heart. She had hopes of having his child so that she would have "something of Roland's very own, something of himself to remember him by if he goes."[9]

Brittain received word of her fiancé's death the day following Christmas 1915. She had carefully arranged a leave from her work as a volunteer nurse and was preparing to greet him when he returned from France. Instead, she received the dreaded phone call. It told her that, even as she was performing her last duties for her patients, Roland had been fatally wounded. Soon afterward, she received letters of condolence from his colonel, his fellow officers, his servant, and the unit's Catholic priest. To satisfy her need to know as many details as possible, a fellow officer visited the doctors who had treated Roland at a casualty clearing station.

Brittain recorded her stunned and painful reaction to the news. Numbed and disoriented, she gazed at the English Channel and—still unable to grasp the reality of his death—worried about the rough passage Roland would have crossing over for this leave. Finding roses in a shop reminded her of those he had given her shortly before. A worm on a sidewalk forced her to contemplate how his body was decomposing in the earth, and, six months later, the comfort of a mild spring day shocked her into realizing she might "not be keeping faith with him."[10]

NOTIFICATION OF A LOSS

Families received tragic news in several ways. In France, the local mayor received news that a member of the community in military service had died. He had the grim responsibility of communicating the message to the casualty's family. Members of the community watched with alarm as this local official walked the streets looking for one particular house. In some areas, he passed the painful task to the local mail carrier, now often a woman. In Britain, the families of dead and missing officers received the word via telegram. The Scottish music hall star Harry Lauder received grim news on January 1, 1917. "I could not bring myself to open the telegram," he later recalled, because he knew what it contained. "God! the agonies I suffered that bright New Year's morning.... My only son. The one child God had given us."[11] In June 1918, the dreaded sound of the front door-knocker alerted Vera Brittain and her father to the telegram informing them that Vera's brother Edward had been killed in Italy.

Families of Britain's dead and missing enlisted men were informed by letter. It was the practice in the British army to return letters addressed to soldiers who had lost their lives. The letters were marked with the harsh statement "killed." They sometimes reached the senders even before an official notice of the death came for the next of kin. Parcels addressed to the dead soldier were opened and their contents shared out among members of his unit.

Because of the distance between home and battlefield, letters sometimes arrived that had been written by a loved one before his death. Theodore Roosevelt's son Quentin wrote several such letters only hours before leaving for the aerial mission in which he was killed. They reached the Roosevelt estate at Sagamore Hill, New York, shortly after the family had been informed of his death. The recent messages from the dead young man only deepened the existing gloom and despair.

Frequently, bereaved families received a letter from a loved one's superior officer, and sometimes from his army comrades and even those under his command as well. Superior officers customarily tried to comfort the family using a number of conventional themes. The deceased serviceman had died instantaneously without excessive pain. He had always been diligent in performing his duties, and he was liked by his comrades and respected by the men below him in the military hierarchy. His superiors had always been able to rely upon him, and death took place at a moment when he was displaying his soldierly qualities of bravery and devotion. Letters from comrades-in-arms were likely to be frank and disturbing in presenting the actual facts of a death in combat.

A British family could expect to receive their loved one's belongings. The parents and sister of Roland Leighton, Vera Brittain's beloved, got Roland's garments, including the ones in which he received his fatal wound. A damp and muddy tunic and khaki vest showed where a bullet had entered, and the bloodstains left by the dying young man were visible. The breeches were cut open, evidently by someone in the medical service who had tried to render aid.

A common reaction to the tragic news, like that Vera Brittain exhibited, was a sense of numbness, sometimes followed by hysteria or disbelief. A young French mail carrier who delivered word to families recalled that her fellow villagers "reacted differently of course. Some received the news hysterically, but most reacted with a kind of numbed shock, as if they had expected it in some way."[12]

The violent death of a loved one on a distant battlefield often made the remains unavailable, even if combat had left the body intact. Often there was no body, even if eyewitnesses could confirm that the man had been killed. Families receiving word that a loved one was missing and presumed dead often reacted by seizing upon any element of ambiguity in the message. For two years, Rudyard Kipling and his wife clung to the belief that their son John, whose body had never been found, might still be alive. One mother in rural England insisted until her death ten years after the war that her son had not been killed. She firmly believed that, when his amnesia had been cured, he would return to his home. The widow of the writer Edward Thomas, killed in France in the spring of 1917, accepted his death, but, in the mid-1930s, she rushed into a London crowd with the certainty that she had just caught a glimpse of him.

THE ACT OF MOURNING

Any family stricken by news of a loved one's loss faced a psychological trauma, and the individuals affected numbered in the millions. One estimate declares that, in Britain alone, approximately "three million ... lost a close relative in the First World War, a substantial number in a population of under 42 million." Beyond that there were those close enough to an individual to attend his funeral if it had been possible to hold one, those who had lost "a cousin, uncle, son-in-law, a colleague, a friend or a neighbor."[13] Thus, the entire population felt the gaps in those whom it had known personally.

In the fall of 1914, the artist Käthe Kollwitz and her husband, a Berlin physician, received the terrible news that their son Peter had been killed in Flanders. She declared to one friend that she felt "a wound that would never heal," and she passed word of her loss to another friend with a sad, oblique phrase: "Your pretty shawl will no longer be able to warm our boy." Kollwitz, like many other bereaved parents, spent hours sitting in her son's empty room where she claimed she could still feel his presence.[14]

The despairing mother immediately took up the idea of creating a sculpture as a memorial to her son. But, as the war proceeded, she was tormented by her changing attitude to the conflict as well as her personal loss. Willing if not enthusiastic to see her son leave to fight for the Fatherland in 1914, by 1916 she became convinced the war was "only madness." Thus, she faced the heavy burden of believing Peter had died in vain. Only in 1925 was she able to take up the final version of the sculpture—two grieving parents—and she completed it in 1931.[15]

Relatives or close friends in the military could sometimes visit the site of a loved one's death. But for most family members such journeys had to be deferred until after the war. Even then the physical strain of reaching a remote battlefield could be enormous, witness Vera Brittain's journey to the Italian village north of Vicenza where her brother had been killed by an Austrian sniper in the summer of 1918.

The distinguished Bickersteth family—Samuel Bickersteth was the vicar of Leeds—lost their only son during the bloody first day of the Battle of the Somme in July 1916. Morris Bickersteth was initially reported missing, but later inquiries established that he had been killed by artillery fire. His body lay somewhere in a stretch of no man's land that changed hands repeatedly over the remaining years of the war. The young man's mother found some solace in attending the June 1918 memorial service at her son's public school, Rugby, and she "communed with [her] darling" by sitting near the dormitory house in which the young man had lived only a few years before.[16]

A privileged figure like British cabinet minister Bonar Law could console himself with a wartime visit to his son's military unit. After losing one son in the Middle East in April 1917, Law received word three months later that the eldest of his three surviving sons had been shot down in France. A colleague described the pit of sorrow into which Law fell: "The second bereavement ... came as a terrible, almost overwhelming blow. ... For the moment he was incapable of work, and could only sit despondently, gazing into vacancy."[17] He found some solace by traveling to France and visiting his son's squadron. The old gentlemen sat for hours in the cockpit of a plane similar to the one in which

James had lost his life. The ailing Theodore Roosevelt mourned the death of his youngest son Quentin, who had also died in aerial combat over France, by sitting alone in the rocking chair in which he had held all his children, murmuring the boy's nickname, "Poor Quinikins! Poor Quinikins."[18]

MILITARY MEN FACE LOSSES

The steady loss of friends and comrades, as well as members of one's own family, drained the energy and vitality from men in uniform. Herbert Sulzbach first encountered bereavement within his family circle. Before the war had gone on for a month, his brother-in-law, a naval doctor, perished in an early sea battle. Sulzbach found it almost impossible to say good-bye to his stricken sister, because "she finds the sight of me in uniform too painful." As the war ended its third year, the young German artillery officer lamented his fellow young volunteers of 1914, of whom "few are now left alive," and the death of his closest friend in the spring of 1918 made an indelible impression on him although "you keep moving on and on, and on."[19]

Even when the dead were not friends but fellow members of a unit, the steady losses struck to the heart. James Dunn, a British army doctor, saw his battalion repeatedly shattered and rebuilt. After two and a half years, only two officers and some 40 enlisted men of the original 800 remained present. Another medical officer recalled the strain he felt as his battalion suffered casualties and replaced them with strange faces: "Seven colonels came and went. I could never school myself to grow indifferent to these gaps." The psychological wounds stirred and tormented him three decades later.[20]

A combination of patriotism and a renewed sense of duty and determination aided some in the military. Down to the close of the war, Captain Henri Lécluse expressed his sadness at the loss of his fellow soldiers but coupled it with a determination to fight on to victory. Coming across the grave of a lone German isolated in a French military cemetery, however, Lécluse was filled with a mixture of emotions. He stood in the small Lorraine graveyard in the winter of 1916 and hoped that the man's fate was a preview of what would befall the Kaiser Wilhelm II, the German warlord. But he could not help feeling sympathy at the death of a fellow soldier.[21]

The constant loss of comrades led some soldiers to express a mixture of relief and callousness. Relief that another had died while you survived was a predictable reaction to the drain on a military unit. But callousness and indifference shocked even those who felt these emotions. And, while the war stretched on, men in uniform defended themselves psychologically by putting aside sympathy for the dead. As one French soldier, the future cabinet minister Georges Bonnet, put it in 1917, experience had "notably hardened hearts." Living with the constant reality of death eventually dried up all the tears one had to give. "Our brothers, our best friends, have been killed. Grief has become so common that it ends by becoming normal," and in such circumstances, "pity died in our hearts."[22] A young English officer put the idea in similar fashion: "The dead, even our friends were not unduly mourned. There was, in our unconscious mind, the feeling, 'better them than me.' "[23]

BURYING THE DEAD, REMEMBERING THE DEAD

No one entering a combat zone could be certain his remains would receive the decent burial that was the peacetime norm. Many bodies were blown into unrecognizable fragments by heavy artillery, many sank into the mud of no man's land or rotted on the barbed wire. Hundreds of thousands received only a place in a mass grave. In sorting through grave sites at quieter moments in the war, searchers sometimes discovered friend and foe buried in a single hole.

Some soldiers lived long enough to reach a hospital in the rear. Many found their resting place in one of the large cemeteries that sprang up near those medical centers. British authorities created several near the Channel coast. There, after every major offensive, the bugles signaling a soldier's funeral could be heard more than twenty times a day, and a single chaplain was expected to preside over as many as sixteen of those gloomy ceremonies between sunrise and sunset.

During the course of the war, the deeply emotional problem of how to bury the masses of the dead on the battlefield inevitably emerged. Should their bodies be left in the original graves, or should they be gathered together in military cemeteries at the front? Some argued that the bodies should be returned to families for burial and remembrance in home communities. There remained the grisly, complicating fact that many of the dead could not be found and conclusively identified. Soldiers on both sides of the battle line were expected to wear identity discs to aid authorities in keeping track of casualties. But this proved only partially successful. The force of combat shattered many corpses, destroying identity discs, and obliterating any possibility a body could receive more than a place in a mass grave. Some fighting men failed to obey the order, or some lost their discs. When bodies sank into the mud of a battlefield like the one at Passchendaele, the identity disc also disappeared.

From the first months of the war, British Red Cross official Fabian Ward took on the task of finding the graves of British servicemen lost in action and recording the location. By 1916, his organization was incorporated into the army with Ward commissioned a lieutenant colonel.

King George V of Britain visits war graves. Courtesy of the Hoover Institution Archives.

Eventually, he rose to the rank of brigadier general. Ward negotiated with the French and then the Belgian government to provide cemetery sites for British dead. By the war's close, Ward had taken the lead in establishing the Commonwealth War Graves Commission. Chartered by the British government, it included representatives from public and private life. The Commission undertook to look after the cemeteries in the postwar period. Even during the war, Ward's organization had begun to disguise the barrenness of some of the mass resting places with grass and shrubs. The cemeteries soon featured the results of loving and expert English gardening.

The United States Army established a Graves Registration Service in the Quartermaster Corps in August 1917. Staffed largely by men who could no longer serve as combat soldiers, it followed advancing American units and sought out unburied bodies. Its members also reburied fallen fighting men who had received only a hasty interment in the midst of battle. Recording a soldier's burial site made it possible to transfer the remains to a permanent cemetery at some future time.

In March 1918 the American Secretaries of War and the Navy decided to bury all dead abroad for the time being. But they also determined to return the bodies to the United States at some point in the future. At the close of the conflict, families of the deceased received an inquiry from the government. They could choose between a resting place abroad for the remains or interment in a National Cemetery in the United States. More than two-thirds—some 46,000—chose to have their family member's body returned home, but that left some 30,000 remains in Europe. As a result eight permanent American cemeteries were established, one in England, one in Belgium, and six in France. The largest, the Meuse-Argonne Cemetery holds the remains of 13,724 American dead of whom 458 are unidentified. In all, 3,100 American wartime casualties could never be found or identified.

In France, the issue of where to put the country's huge number of battle corpses stood unresolved until after the war. While hostilities continued and in the immediate postwar period, the government resisted the call to let families take the bodies of loved ones for burial in their home communities. For the time being, most were placed in graves near the combat zone. But some families refused to accept the decision, hiring private firms to find and exhume the body of a loved one. Because military cemeteries were government institutions, the tensions between church and state in France emerged in full force. Staunchly Catholic families felt a duty to bring their sons and husbands home to parish graveyards and hence to their religious roots. The final decision, reached in September 1920, permitted French families to claim bodies and to return them to a home community for burial. The state stood the expense involved, and some 300,000 of the dead returned to their homes in this way.

By contrast, Britain decided to bury all its dead at the front, although some well-connected families were able to bring their deceased members home. Germany had little choice in the matter of how to treat its war dead. They lay in burial sites in Belgium or France, and the postwar German government received only grudging permission to construct memorial cemeteries for them.

Unlike previous conflicts, the war had drawn much of a nation's male population into military service. Now, all the belligerents on the western front moved in unprecedented ways to commemorate each of the fallen. Individual graves in a military cemetery with an inscription identifying the remains stood as the desirable norm. Many of the dead received such a resting place in France and Belgium. A memorial to those whose remains had not been recovered presented a different challenge. The postwar selection of an unknown soldier to be honored as a representative of the missing was one solution. By Armistice Day, 1920, Britain and France had chosen their Unknown Soldier. France placed him in Paris at the Arc de Triomphe; Britain laid him to rest in Westminster Abbey. The United States followed a year later, placing its Unknown Soldier in Arlington Cemetery near the nation's capital. In addition, governments or private organizations set up memorial structures near the battlefields on which the names of the missing were inscribed. Edward Luytens's famous Monument of the Missing of the Battle of the Somme at Thiepval listed 73,000 names. At Verdun a private organization gathered the bones of those who could not be identified in a giant ossuary.

Another way to honor the dead was to visit their burial place or, if that was unknown, the region in which they had spent their last days. All the victorious powers, some sooner than others, subsidized trips to the battle zone for bereaved families. The latest were the Americans. Starting in May 1930, with an initial contingent of 234, the first of more than twenty groups of American mothers left the United States to visit their sons' graves in France. Congress had just appropriated $5 million to fund the trips. The phenomenon of postwar battle tourism allowed large groups to visit once desolate and battered locales like Ypres. In a surprisingly short time, however, the processes of reconstruction made battle zones look more normal than tourists anticipated.

The desire to contact lost loved ones led to a resurgence of Spiritualism in several countries. A minor religious cult prior to the war, Spiritualism claimed that the dead were still present among the living, and contact with them was possible. Especially in Britain in the 1920s, many people participated in séances, which supposedly allowed them to communicate with the war dead.

Some families of means like Britain's Lord and Lady Wemyss came to terms with their loss by publishing a private memorial volume. The Roosevelts displayed the twisted axle from Quentin's downed plane in a place of honor in their home. When anonymously mailed photographs of his corpse arrived at Sagamore Hill, the family ignored the malice of the sender, placed the pictures lovingly in scrapbooks, and sent copies to relatives. Some parents persisted in referring to their lost children as if they were still alive. In receiving a peerage in 1919 for his services during the war, General Allenby reminded his wife that it was "Michael's birthday. He is 21 today."[24]

NOTES

1. Figures and information for the American losses can be found in Edward M. Coffman, *The War to End All Wars: The American Military Experience in World War I* (New York: Oxford University Press, 1968), 363; see also Harvey A. DeWeerd, *President Wilson Fights His War: World War I and the American Intervention* (New York: Macmillan, 1968), 392. For French losses, see Jean-Jacques Becker, *The Great War and the French People*, trans. Arnold Pomerans (Leamington Spa, Eng.: Berg, 1985), 330–31. For German losses, see Richard Bessel, *Germany after the First World War* (Oxford, Eng.: Clarendon Press, 1993), 6, 9–10; also Laurence Moyer, *Victory Must Be Ours: Germany in the Great War, 1914–1918* (New York:

Hippocrene, 1995), 333–34, and Robert Weldon Whalen, *Bitter Wounds: German Victims of the Great War, 1914–1939* (Ithaca, N.Y.: Cornell University Press, 1984), 38–43. For British losses, see J.M. Winter, *The Great War and the British People* (London: Macmillan, 1986), 66–99; also Denis Winter, *Death's Men: Soldiers of the Great War* (London: Penguin, 1978), 254–261.

2. J.M. Winter, *Great War*, 97; Barbara Tuchman, *The Guns of August* (New York: Macmillan, 1962), 439.

3. Adrian Gregory, "Lost Generations: The Impact of Military Casualties on Paris, London, and Berlin," in *Capital Cities at War: Paris, London, Berlin, 1914–1918*, ed. Jay Winter and Jean-Louis Robert (Cambridge, Eng.: Cambridge University Press, 1997), 69–71, 81–82.

4. Quoted in Michael Bliss, *William Osler: A Life in Medicine* (Oxford: Oxford University Press, 1999), 397.

5. Ibid., 424, 428.

6. David Cannadine, "War and Death, Grief and Mourning in Modern Britain," in *Mirrors of Mortality: Studies in the Social History of Death*, ed. Joachim Whaley (New York: St. Martin's Press, 1981), 193; Thomas A. Kselman, *Death and the Afterlife in Modern France* (Princeton: Princeton University Press, 1993), 16–17, 24.

7. Moyer, *Victory*, 166; also, *New York Times*, January 26, 1916.

8. Denis Winter, *Death's Men: Soldiers of the Great War* (London: Penguin Books, 1978), 255; Gregory, "Lost Generations," in *Capital Cities*, ed. Winter and Robert, 87.

9. Vera Brittain, *Testament of Youth: An Autobiographical Study of the Years 1900–1925* (New York: Macmillan, 1933), 136, 142–43, 234.

10. Ibid., 241; on disbelief at the news, see John Hinton, *Dying* (Harmondsworth, Middlesex, Eng.: Penguin Books, 1967), 180.

11. Quoted in David Cannadine, "War and Death," in *Mirrors of Mortality*, ed. Whaley, 213.

12. Quoted in P.J. Flood, *France, 1914–18: Public Opinion and the War Effort* (Houndmills, Basingstoke, Hampshire, Eng.: Macmillan, 1990), 91.

13. Adrian Gregory, *The Silence of Memory: Armistice Day, 1919–1946* (Oxford: Berg, 1994), 19.

14. Quoted in Jay Winter, *Sites of Memory, Sites of Mourning: The Great War in European Cultural History* (Cambridge, Eng.: Cambridge University Press, 1995), 108–10.

15. Ibid.

16. Quoted in Pat Jalland, *Death in the Victorian Family* (Oxford: Oxford University Press, 1996), 377–78.

17. Quoted in Cannadine, "War and Death," in *Mirrors*, ed. Whaley, 214.

18. Edward J. Renehan, Jr., *The Lion's Pride: Theodore Roosevelt and His Family in Peace and War* (New York: Oxford University Press, 1998), 198.

19. Herbert Sulzbach, *With the German Guns: Four Years on the Western Front, 1914–1918*, trans. Richard Thonger (London: Leo Cooper, 1973), 25, 124, 178.

20. Keith Simpson, "Dr. James Dunn and Shell-shock," in *Facing Armageddon: The First World War Experienced*, ed. Hugh Cecil and Peter Liddle (London: Leo Cooper, 1996), 511.

21. Henri de Lécluse, *Comrades in Arms: The World War I Memoir of Captain*

Henri de Lécluse, Comte de Trévoëdal, edited by Roy E. Sandstrom; translated by Jacques F. Dubois (Kent, Ohio: Kent State Press, 1998), 119–20.

22. Quoted in Antoine Prost, *In the Wake of War: 'Les Anciens Combatants' and French Society*, trans. Helen McPhail (Providence, R.I.: Berg, 1992), 21.

23. Quoted in Cannadine, "War and Death," in *Mirrors*, ed. Whaley, 204.

24. Brian Gardner, *Allenby of Arabia: Lawrence's General* (New York: Coward McCann, [1966]), 223.

14

The Armistice and Demobilization

The war came to an end at eleven o'clock the morning of November 11, 1918. It had affected all the inhabitants of the belligerent countries in one fashion or another. Such universal involvement in the conflict meant that millions of civilians and millions more in uniform greeted the Armistice with rapt attention. Only in a cold and exhausted Germany, where the Armistice coincided with an ongoing political revolution, did the day resemble those just preceding.

Just as governments had faced the unprecedented step of mobilizing huge numbers for the war, they now faced the equally unprecedented problem of sending home the massive forces that existed in November 1918. For the Germans and the Allies alike, the pressures to reduce the size of their military systems mounted. In the aftermath of the Armistice, men hoped to return home as soon as possible.

THE ARMISTICE

Anyone who read a newspaper in the first days of November knew that the two sides were exchanging messages pointing toward armistice negotiations. Then, on November 7, word came to civilians and soldiers alike that the war was about to end. Possibly planted in the Paris office of French intelligence by the Germans, the rumor spread widely and gave rise to joyous celebrations, especially in the United States. When it proved to be a mistake or a hoax, the letdown was harsh. Disappointed revelers in New York City's Times Square tore up newspapers that announced the real situation and vandalized nearby store windows.

Meanwhile, Field Marshal Ferdinand Foch, the Allied commander-in-chief, urged French, British, and American troops to continue their offensives. In the face of this energetic action by the Allies, the Germans fell back in good order, conducting a fighting retreat that cost lives on both sides. There was one notable sign that German soldiers were growing aware that their task was futile: As German units retreated, they left numbers of their wounded in place to be treated by the superior medical resources the Allies could muster.

Unit commanders on both sides received the news of the real armistice on the morning of November 11. Captain Harry Truman, commanding a battery of National Guard field artillery, later recalled that he had received orders to withhold the news from his men until the actual moment of the cease-fire. His guns fired their last shot at fifteen minutes before eleven. Many units continued active and dangerous operations, and American infantrymen attacking in the Argonne Forest like Lieutenant Francis Austin of the Twenty-eighth Division were mortally wounded in the hours leading up to the war's ending. Meanwhile Germans like the men of the 425th Infantry Division whom the clock still identified as the Americans' enemies perished in combat. On Armistice morning they launched a counterattack against American units that had just crossed the Meuse. One courageous German officer came within yards of the American lines before a bullet to the head cut him down.

Some units continued to fire until the last minute—and beyond. Zealous senior officers on the Allied side issued firm orders to pursue the enemy vigorously until eleven o'clock. Some isolated units missed the word of the cease-fire entirely. Engaged in fierce combat, their commanders had no communication with the rear or no opportunity to read the messages that were arriving. These forces continued to strike against their opponents even as the guns became silent in most sectors.

Thus, combat ceased in an uncertain, fractured manner. But the silence of the guns at eleven o'clock that Monday morning was a signal for most soldiers on both sides of no man's land to raise their heads from concealment, first tentatively, then more confidently. Many moved across the barren stretch of land separating the two sides to meet their erstwhile enemies and to share rations and cigarettes. Germans who wanted to fraternize and beg cigarettes sometimes received a hostile reception. One reporter for the *Saturday Evening Post* observed American units demanding that the Germans leave at once. He remarked that "American temper, at this stage . . . with the enemy guns not yet cold and their own dead not yet buried, was not of the sloppy, sentimental kind that embraces a recent foe."[1] More often, the two sides met amicably, if cautiously.

FÊTES DE LA VICTOIRE
14 Juillet 1919

A French victory parade, 1919. Courtesy of the Hoover Institution Archives.

Souvenir-hungry Americans traded cigarettes and chocolate bars for German army pistols.

Civilians in cities and small towns stretching from France to the West Coast of the United States and on to Australia and New Zealand went into the streets to celebrate. School children enjoyed a holiday everywhere. Parisians had received an early hint of the end of hostilities. On the evening before the Armistice, the police ordered the blue paint— camouflage against air attack—removed from the city's street lamps. On November 11, the people of the French capital danced in the streets of the city's center. Some, in tribute to their American ally, called on their best English to sing "Yankee Doodle Dandy," widely understood by the French to be the American national anthem.

In London, the bells of Big Ben pealed for the first time since the summer of 1914. Joyous crowds took over Trafalgar Square for a wild celebration that lasted for three days. One British soldier home from France later described the scene there as the crowd "danced round and round all night long, singing 'Knees Up, Mother Brown,' and other fragments from English folklore. Whooping, the crowd seized omnibuses and . . . played catch with [policemen's] helmets."[2]

The American celebration began on the East Coast early in the morning. Authorities lit up the Statue of Liberty for the first time since the country had entered the war, and impromptu parades marked the day in thousands of communities. On the West Coast, word of the impending

Armistice arrived around midnight, and the first celebrations began in the dead of night. Shipyard workers in Long Beach, California, left the night shift to join victory parades.

Some young Americans who were inducted into the army on the morning of November 11 received their discharges within a matter of hours. Industrialist Henry Ford ordered his plants to stop war production immediately and to start to turn out the tractors that would be needed in a peacetime economy. That evening, opera singers Enrico Caruso and Louise Homer, performing *Samson and Delilah* at New York's Metropolitan Opera, appeared during intermissions to sing the national anthems of the victorious nations.

For many in those victorious countries, prayer, either formal or spontaneous, was the appropriate response to the news. In England, Birmingham Cathedral provided three special worship services during the day. Across the Atlantic, Evangeline Booth, the leader of the Salvation Army, gathered 400 members of her organization on the steps of the New York Public Library to thank God for an end to the fighting.

In Germany, news of the Armistice reached a population in a depressed, troubled state of mind. The government had admitted defeat, and the nation found itself in the midst of an ongoing political revolution. The sailors' mutiny in the High Seas Fleet had sparked political unrest in both the military and civilian population. Soldiers' Councils now dictated policy for many military units, and the overthrow of the monarchy gave birth to a shaky republican government. At the local level, Workers Councils—or sometimes Soldiers and Workers Councils— sprang up to take control.

There was only scattered violence in Berlin. But rebellious military units bearing red armbands challenged the new government, and red flags symbolizing revolution were on display everywhere. The threat of civil war hung in the background, and the German capital was no place to find the exhilaration evident in London, Paris, and New York. Berliners were cold, weary of the war, and hungry. Keeping up a normal routine was all most of them could manage, and, on November 11, "as the world went delirious with joy, most Germans went back to work."[3] Stores remained open for business, and public transportation operated on a normal schedule. Princess Evelyn Blücher, the English-born wife of a German aristocrat, remarked during the day of the Armistice on "the disciplined and orderly way in which a revolution of such dimensions has been organized, with until now the least possible loss of life."[4]

In all the civilian populations, the memory of loved ones who had perished in the conflict darkened the joy at the news of the Armistice. Some families had no chance to absorb knowledge that the fighting had ended; grim tidings continued to arrive on November 11. In Shrewsbury,

England, the parents of poet Wilfred Owen, a decorated British officer, received a telegram at noon, one hour after the good news of the end of the war, announcing his death in combat precisely a week before.

Some soldiers at the front greeted the arrival of Armistice hour with weary thanks and a sense of relief, others with jubilation. But all noticed the onset of quiet: The artillery fire that had given the war much of its gruesome character suddenly ended. One American enlisted artilleryman recalled that "everything then went dead. Not a sound. It was the funniest feeling I ever had in my life." An American officer who commanded an artillery unit likewise noted, "The silence is oppressive. It weighs on one's eardrums."[5] Another change that all noticed came with the arrival of evening. Vehicles now used their headlights, and campfires burned freely. That same evening, German forces set off huge quantities of flares and rockets. In part celebrating the end of the war, the Germans were destroying war supplies they could not carry home and did not wish to surrender to the Allies.

THE DEMOBILIZATION

Ironically, the losers in the war were the first to see their homeland. The Armistice terms dictated a rapid German withdrawal from foreign territory. Long before a sizable number of Americans or Englishmen got home, the entire German army on the western front left the territories it had occupied, crossed the French or the Belgian border, and entered Germany.

The American victors in the war hailed from the richest and least battle-torn nation on the winning side, but they were far from home and short of ways to transport large numbers across the Atlantic. There was often an extended wait before the doughboys and their families saw each other again. Meanwhile, most German soldiers were reentering civilian life.

Most British and French troops abroad did not require a long trip to reach the homeland. But their governments still faced the difficult question of how best to release millions of men from the military. Both the British and the French governments needed to stabilize economies distorted by war—and the French needed to repair massive wartime damage as well. Should a soldier receive a high priority for demobilization based upon the economic talents he could bring to the civilian world? Or ought men to be allowed to doff their uniforms depending on how long they had served? Strikes and other disturbances in the remaining British and French armed forces penalized those leaders who chose a policy unpopular with the soldiers.

THE AMERICANS

Some American soldiers went home immediately. Late arrivals who approached the coast of France when the Armistice was signed did not get permission to land; instead, they found their transports turned around and headed westward for the United States. But almost a quarter of a million in the newly formed American Third Army marched through France and Belgium in the wake of the retreating German forces, and, on December 1, entered western Germany to take up occupation duty in cities like Trier and Coblenz.[6]

Secretary of War Newton Baker rejected out of hand a French request that American soldiers be used to help in reconstruction work. Thus, American soldiers in Europe found themselves kept artificially busy with drills and training courses. Nonetheless, the average doughboy now found army discipline harder to accept than ever despite being surrounded by unprecedented numbers of military policemen. Starting in early 1919, the army emphasized an extensive sports program to sop up excess energy. Through the auspices of the YMCA, both American officers and enlisted men entered British and French universities, and a special AEF university was set up in Beaunne, France. Army officers like Lieutenant Colonel Theodore Roosevelt, Jr., stimulated in part by the hope of counteracting the troops' boredom and declining morale, worked to create a postwar veterans' organization. The future American Legion had its origins in a conference of officers held in Paris during February 1919 followed by a larger gathering of both officers and enlisted men in March.

In 1917 and 1918, most Americans had crossed the Atlantic in British ships. British vessels were now occupied in repatriating British troops, most from France but some from distant parts of the globe. The ships were also carrying troops from remote parts of the empire like Australia home. Thus, Americans in uniform had to cool their heels until they could be assigned a place on board an American vessel, civilian or military. Some returned on converted cargo vessels; others were crammed aboard warships.

The news an American unit had been ordered home led to predictably wild parties. These were likely to be matched by raucous celebrations just before departing. When the men reached the United States, and prepared to be mustered out of the service, parades were the order of the day. More than 500 parades took place by the close of June 1919. The 165th Infantry regiment, formerly the "Fighting 69th" of the New York National Guard and made up of men of Irish descent, arrived too late to parade on St. Patrick's Day as many hoped for. But in late April this unit of the Forty-second "Rainbow" Division staged a memorable march in full battle gear and steel helmets from the southern tip of Manhattan to 110th Street. Four months later, the First Division, the one remaining American combat division in Europe, left France for home. Last to come home, its soldiers had been the first arrivals of the growing American Expeditionary Force two summers earlier.

Between the Armistice and mid-April, 1919, the American armed forces discharged an average of 4,000 men daily. Only one man in five from the hugely expanded military ranks of wartime was still in service by midsummer 1919, and barely 100,000 remained in Germany. By fall, the number there dropped to only 11,000. The rapidly shrinking American army provided every discharged soldier with $60 and a ticket home from his mustering out center. He also received permission to keep his uniform, one coat, and one pair of shoes. Many American homes in the postwar period had a helmet and gas mask on display. They were souvenirs of military service that men who had served abroad were permitted to keep.

THE GERMANS

The German demobilization began even before the Armistice. By summer 1918, the country's declining military fortunes were obvious, and tens of thousands of men avoided returning to duty after receiving leave at home. Others feigned illness or deliberately lost pieces of equipment to prevent being restored to their units. The neighborhoods around railroad stations witnessed violent episodes as soldiers vandalized shops and fired off their weapons.[7]

The terms of the Armistice gave Germany fifteen days to remove its troops from France, Belgium, and Luxembourg, as well as from Alsace-Lorraine. With the orders to cease fire, some German units specializing in engineering and bridge construction got instructions to start the march home at once. Others quickly demobilized themselves in dramatic fashion. Just before eleven o'clock, German troops near the Dutch border crossed into neutral Holland after casting away their weapons on the German side of the frontier.

The emergence of Soldiers' Councils signaled the partial overthrow of army authority. General Hermann von Kuhl, the ranking commander at Spa, had to obtain a pass from these rebellious soldiers in order to enter his own headquarters. During the retreat through Antwerp, drunken enlisted men assaulted officers. Epaulettes, one of the visible symbols of an officer's authority, were torn off and presented to the local prostitutes.

Most units retreated in good order under the control of their officers, even if those leaders had removed their insignias of rank. Army directives called for covering between fifteen and twenty-five miles per day. Unlike the advance westward in 1914, there were no trains to transport German troops. Meeting the schedule imposed by the Allies meant weary marching for twelve-hour stretches, and units moved eastward both during the daylight hours and at night. In the end, it took about six weeks for the bulk of the armed forces to reach the homeland from the western front, with the last contingents arriving in mid-January 1919. Though most men traveled with their unit, as many as one out of every three took off alone to find his own way home.

Herbert Sulzbach ended his war in Belgium, and the day following the Armistice he saw Belgians raising their nation's flag to taunt the German occupying forces. The Belgian people rang the local bells to welcome the French troops who were moving in behind the withdrawing Germans. Sulzbach expressed the thought of many Germans lucky enough to survive their western front ordeal. He noted that "you do get filled with a feeling of happiness to be going home for good, and an inexpressible thankfulness as well that in all these years, in all those countless battles and actions, absolutely nothing has happened to me."[8]

Units entering German territory in November found a warm welcome in many locales with flags on the houses and cheering crowds. Soldiers were offered flowers, food, and cigarettes. In Frankfurt, 100,000 citizens greeted returning contingents of the Fifth Army. Marching through Bonn, Sulzbach recorded that "the narrow streets were packed with civilians who cheered us like anything" and, moving eastward, in village after village "we get a joyous welcome everywhere, all the village children run after us and take us to the next village."[9] Apparently spontaneous, the urban demonstrations were encouraged by official agencies like the Prussian War Ministry in order "to make the day of their return to the *Heimat* a lasting memory for the soldiers."[10] But in some cities and especially in smaller towns and villages, the greeting was muted. Marching with his regiment through Cologne, one soldier noted the silent crowds and the indifferent gaze of the leaders of the city's new revolutionary government. In the midst of festive welcomes, Sulzbach noted local women breaking into tears at the thought of sons and husbands who would not be returning.

The German military authorities planned for an orderly demobilization of the armed forces. Men were to march with their units to their home garrison, there to be released from service. The oldest were to return to civilian life first, and among them workers considered economically essential, such as coal miners, were to have the highest priority. Each former soldier was to receive civilian clothing and money for transportation home. Finally, the army expected to provide everyone with a gratuity of fifty marks, roughly what a civilian worker earned in a week.

Sometimes the procedure worked, and numerous men entered civilian life in the planned fashion the authorities favored. More often, the system collapsed or was ignored. Some units disintegrated once they had crossed the German border. Many that remained intact did so because their members relied on the military system for food and pay. Soldiers sold weapons to civilians and plundered local stores to obtain civilian clothing. Individual officers discharged their men and sent them to the nearest railroad station to find their own way home. Soldiers' Councils set up discharge offices and transferred numerous men back to civilian status. Major cities like Berlin were soon filled with wandering ex-soldiers, unemployed and disease-ridden.

But there were many veterans of the war who did not enter civilian life at this time. Hundreds of thousands of Germans ended the war as prisoners, many of them after landing into Allied hands during the final German retreat in 1918. Even the most fortunate German war prisoners returned only in the fall of 1919, a year after the Armistice. These men, released from British and American captivity, were followed by their counterparts from French prison camps who had been put to work on reconstruction projects. They saw Germany again in the first months of 1920. In all these cases, the government organized festive crowds to greet their return.

THE FRENCH AND THE BRITISH

A French soldier soon learned that he would be released from military service based upon his age, how long he had served, and the length of his combat experience. In general, those conscripted first would be released first. He was probably grateful to the government for rejecting the call of French labor leaders to use a different standard. Union chiefs had argued unsuccessfully for demobilization based upon the country's economic needs. In such a scheme, a soldier who could provide crucial assistance to the country's economic recovery would have had a high priority regardless of his length of time in uniform.[11]

Nonetheless, France cushioned the economic blow of massive demobilization and assured itself a large army until the peace was signed. It staggered the release of its men in uniform. Starting in early December, men between the ages of fifty and fifty-two were released. Every ten days, the next youngest group was permitted to go home. By early April, the half of the army above the age of thirty-two—more than 2 million men—was back in civilian life. Younger soldiers had to wait until the peace was signed in June 1919 before their age groups were released, and the last of them reached home in October, almost a year after the Armistice.

British soldiers initially received different and, for many, more discouraging news.[12] The government looked first to economic recovery, and it released men who could make a substantial contribution to industry's transition to peacetime status. The government hoped to follow a complex scheme that gave the highest priority for release from the service to the economically useful. Men who were slated to serve in demobilization centers got first preference. Next after these "demobilizers" were "pivotals," men whose services were essential to the coming economic transition. Right after the fighting stopped, a hasty amendment to the plan made coal miners the most essential group to be sent back to civilian life. Within two days after the Armistice, coal miners began to reunite with their families and to take up their old jobs. Thousands reentered civilian life by the start of December.

The government could argue that the policy made good sense for the nation. Releasing large numbers of men indiscriminately from military service would only swell unemployment. On the other hand, targeted discharges would stimulate industry and create jobs for all. And the government was willing, although only within the established categories, to favor married men, men who had served for long periods, and those who had faced extensive combat.

But the scheme was an easy target to criticize. For one thing, it was cumbersome, requiring the classification of millions of men into one of twelve categories for officers or into one of thirteen for those in the ranks. More important, to the average soldier, this approach was outrageously unfair. A man who had served for years in the trenches would have to wait; men conscripted at the close of the war, who had long been deferred because of their occupations, were to be first in line to reenter civilian life. A man able to arrange a job in advance of his release had priority over someone less lucky or less well connected. There was even worse news for British soldiers in supply and transport units; they learned they had the lowest priority for a return to civilian life. Their labor was required for supporting the remaining units of the army.

Men in uniform demonstrated their discontent in frightening fashion. Leave trains were vandalized, and even the privileged miners defied army discipline on their way home. In the supply and transport units at Le Havre in early January 1919, the threat of a strike—itself a sign of shaky discipline—pushed military leaders to permit men in some specialties to be demobilized. That same month, soldiers in army trucks mounted demonstrations near government centers in London. Displaying signs with slogans like "We won the war. Give us our tickets" and "We want civvie suits," they helped force the nation's political leaders to reverse course.

British military men now obtained their discharges based upon the length of time they had served. A man who had been wounded at least three times also ranked high on the priority list regardless of his time in uniform. Some 900,000 were still needed for occupation duty in western Germany, but the remaining 2.6 million soldiers received their releases at a rapid pace as 10,000 a day exchanged their uniforms for "civvie suits." Even so, moving most of the army back to civilian life took almost a year. Men received a discharge payment and a ticket home, as well as a special demobilization bonus, as high as £40. Demobilization benefits also included an unemployment benefit; the individual did not have to contribute to it, and it covered him for twenty weeks during the year after he left service. Few of those lucky enough to come home in 1919 needed it, since they found a temporarily booming economy with plentiful jobs.

The brief postwar boom in Britain faded by the start of 1920 to give way to decades of stagnation and unemployment. In Germany, Allied armies of occupation sat on the left bank of the Rhine as well as on three spacious zones to the east of the river. Meanwhile, the relatively peaceful German revolution of November 1918 had given rise to bloody civil war.

The economic difficulty facing one of the conflict's victors was a sign of the troubling legacy the great war had produced. So too was the deeply resented presence of foreign troops in the German homeland. Finally, there was the domestic political upheaval convulsing Germany, the principal loser of the conflict. Taken together, these developments pointed to a dark and bitter future.

NOTES

1. Quoted in Stanley Weintraub, *A Stillness Heard Round the World: The End of the Great War, November 1918* (New York: E.P. Dutton, 1985), 207.

2. Quoted in ibid., 265.

3. Laurence Moyer. *Victory Must Be Ours: Germany in the Great War, 1914–1918* (New York: Hippocrene Books, 1995), 313.

4. Quoted in Weintraub, *Stillness*, 400.

5. Quoted in ibid., 202, 204.

6. On American demobilization, see Edward Coffman, *The War to End All Wars: The American Military Experience in World War I* (New York: Oxford University Press, 1968), 356–60; also, Byron Farwell, *Over There: The United States in the Great War, 1917–1918* (New York: W.W. Norton, 1999), 267–72, 285–88.

7. On German demobilization, see Richard Bessel, *Germany after the First World War* (Oxford: Clarendon Press, 1993), 69–90; also Moyer, *Victory Must Be Ours*, 329–36.

8. Herbert Sulzbach, *With the German Guns: Four Years on the Western Front, 1914–1918*, trans. Richard Thonger (London: Leo Cooper, 1973), 250.

9. Ibid., 254.

10. Quoted in Bessel, *Germany after the First World War*, 84.

11. On French demobilization, see Joshua Cole, "The Transition to Peace, 1918–1919," in *Capital Cities at War: Paris, London, Berlin, 1914–1918*, ed. Jay Winter and Jean-Louis Robert (Cambridge, Eng.: Cambridge University Press, 1997), 209–10;

also, John Horne, *Labour at War: France and Britain, 1914–1918* (Oxford: Clarendon Press, 1991), 355–57.

12. On British mobilization, see Stephen Richards Graubard, "Military Demobilization in Great Britain following the First World War." *Journal of Modern History* 19, no. 4 (1947): 297–311; also Horne, *Labour at War*, 355–57.

Selected Bibliography

WRITING ABOUT THE WAR

More than eight decades have passed since the war's conclusion, but the examination of this grandiose and horrifying event continues. New directions in research and new controversies make clear how this complex subject continues to fascinate. There follows a consideration of only a few of the many paths historians have taken.

Did Europeans go to war enthusiastically, even joyfully? The pictures of frenzied crowds bidding farewell to soldiers leaving for the front seem to confirm that many welcomed the war. Recent scholarship has presented a more nuanced picture. The research of Jean-Jacques Becker indicates that, at least in rural France, people greeted the war—and went on to bear it—as a harsh duty forced upon them. Jeffrey Verhey has presented a subtle picture of Germans at many social levels reacting ambiguously to the outbreak of the conflict.[1]

Books of comparative social history, tapping the talents of many specialists, have allowed us to see the various belligerent peoples side by side as they coped with problems ranging from mobilizing their young men to heating their homes. The outstanding works in this genre are Richard Wall and Jay Winter's *Upheaval of War* and Jean-Jacques Becker and Jay Winter's *Capital Cities at War*. Another valuable collection, although with essays of more varying quality, is Hugh Cecil and Peter Liddle's *Facing Armageddon*.[2]

A vital, new line of inquiry has approached the way in which people from the belligerent countries remembered the war. The mass graves of previous wars with no indication of their inhabitants' identity gave way to carefully planned cemeteries containing individual graves. Massive monuments displayed a careful listing of the names of the missing. Every community sought to remember its war dead—who had for the most part been drawn from the ranks of the average citizen—with some kind of memorial. A tradition of remembrance, including vast war cemeteries, begun in the United States after the Civil War, now became the norm for the European countries that fought on the western front. Works like Jay Winter's *Sites of Memory*, Adrian Gregory's *Silence of Memory*, George Mosse's *Fallen Soldiers*, and Daniel Sherman's magisterial *The Construction of Memory in Interwar France* explore how the people and communities who survived the war tried to come to grips with the memory of immeasurable loss.[3]

The study of women in the war has moved the spotlight away from the battlefield in some respects. But it has also added to our understanding of the combat soldier. Women were drawn into the conflict in innumerable ways, ranging from service in uniform and work in war plants to mourning the loss of the men they sent to the fighting fronts. Following the path marked two decades ago by Gail Braybon, scholars like Laura Downs both have considered women's experiences in the factory world many entered for the first time, and have explored whether this newly central economic role for women proved lasting or liberating. Susan Zeiger has presented an incisive look at American women serving with the AEF, and Ute Daniel has explored the experience of Germany's working-class women. Margaret Darrow has offered a valuable examination of women in various roles in wartime France, including the sometimes hostile view of them that combat soldiers displayed. Belinda Davis's study of women in World War I Berlin shows the difficulties the authorities had in dealing with this segment of the city's population. In introducing and editing an examination of wartime societies in the twentieth century, Margaret Higonnet has offered the stimulating view that the war changed the roles of men and women but the size of the gap separating the status of the two sexes remained fixed.[4]

Another new turn has been to consider the role of the average soldier in diminishing the carnage of the war. Numerous books like Leon Wolff's *In Flanders Fields* have condemned stupid and stubborn "brass hats" for sending men to die in hopeless attacks for unworthy objectives. Tony Ashworth has explored the way in which units created or maintained quiet on much of the front during the times when the great battles were not taking place. By tacit mutual agreement, the Germans on one side of the battlefield and their opponents on the other held their fire, shot only on predictable schedules, and otherwise avoided inflicting casualties on their foes. In a different fashion, Leonard Smith's study of a single, distinguished French infantry division has shown how the men in the ranks took some control of battles to limit casualties. As he points out, all attacks logically should have ended in victory or in 100 percent casualties. In fact few did, and this was due to the influence the soldiers themselves were willing to exert. The French army mutiny in the spring of 1917 was simply the largest example of soldiers who remained loyal to their country and their commanders but who refused to sacrifice their lives in hopeless military ventures.[5]

Was the war an exercise in futility? Did the generals fail to learn anything as the conflict proceeded? Books such as Paddy Griffith's *Battle Tactics of the Western Front* and Albert Palazzo's *Seeking Victory on the Western Front* point to the growing sophistication of the military and its leaders in the final two years of the war. The technical problems of trench warfare, these authors suggest, found solutions as those in authority came to understand the conflict they were fighting. Better tactics combined with better technology, especially in the British Army, to bring a long-awaited but deserved victory.[6]

Such a view was likely to be unconvincing to the soldier suffering through the bloodbath at Passchendaele in the final months of 1917. A view that leaders understood the war better and fought it with greater skill seems to pertain, at best, to the final year of the conflict. And here, apart from the continuing heavy casualties, the question remains whether it was skilled Allied leadership, or vast Allied numbers, or perhaps just Germany's exhaustion from attrition that decided the issue.

A soldier at Passchendaele or any number of other bloody encounters would likely find even more controversial the views of Correlli Barnett in *The Collapse of British Power*. Brian Bond has recently taken up the same position.[7] In a compelling chapter, "Covenants without Swords," Barnett presents three important themes to draw from the war. First, it was a conflict undertaken for appropriate political reasons, namely to defend British interests against dangerous German aggression leveled at France and Belgium but eventually imperiling Britain. Second, the horrors of the war have been overemphasized. It was Englishmen from privileged and sheltered backgrounds who wrote the war memoirs that began to appear at the close of the 1920s. These writings gave a picture of suffering and hardship that looked far different—that is, were more tolerable—to men of working-class origins who made up the mass of the armed forces. Finally, such a view of the war had a disastrous impact on British foreign policy when Adolf Hitler's Germany raised new threats in foreign affairs in the 1930s.

One issue of particular interest to an American audience is the assessment of the AEF's performance on the battlefield. The view Americans long favored was presented by General John Pershing in his memoirs, published in 1931. Pershing lauded both the skills of his soldiers and subordinate commanders and pointed to the great role they had played in bringing the war to a conclusion. European leaders like Georges Clemenceau and David Lloyd George had contested that view while the conflict still raged. It was to their advantage to diminish America's military role in the war in order to diminish America's influence at the peace conference. By the last decades of the twentieth century, American scholars like David Kennedy were contesting Pershing's view. They stressed the raw character of the American units that fought in France, as well as the often uncertain leadership those units received. Unskilled American units contributed to the overall victory by pinning down portions of the German army while the French and especially the British army conducted the war-winning offensive.[8]

Most recently, Mark E. Grotelueschen's *Doctrine under Fire* has proposed a more sophisticated alternative. Grotelueschen, a professional officer as well as a historian, shows how some AEF divisions developed formidable fighting skills. The Second Division, the particular target of his investigation, became a crack military unit, skilled in taking the war to the enemy and successful in reaching its objectives.[9]

John Eisenhower's *Yanks*, like *Doctrine under Fire*, examines the middle ground of military operations, the war fought by majors and colonels. Discussions of leadership at the highest level came immediately after the war, aided by the publication of the memoirs of senior commanders. Soon afterward, the view from the bottom of the military ladder—junior officers and men in the ranks—appeared. Eisenhower, like Grotelueschen, brings the experience of a professional army officer as well as the talents of the historian to the question of how specific operations were planned. How did regiments and battalions, the basic tools in the senior commander's arsenal, maneuver in order to achieve the generals' objectives?[10]

World War I has long served as the background for important works of fiction, witness the writing of Ernest Hemingway and Erich Maria Remarque. By the mid-1930s, C.S. Forester took the literary examination of the war in a new direction with his superb psychological dissection of a senior British military leader in *The General*. Two recent authors who have enriched our understanding of the war through imaginative and forceful novels are Pat Barker and Sebastian Faulks. Barker's trilogy—*Regeneration*, *The Eye in the Door*, and *The Ghost Road*—slices through multiple layers of British society during the war with psychological insight. Its characters inhabit haunting scenes ranging from the battlefield to the psychiatric hospital to the prison confining conscientious objectors. Equally impressive is Sebastian Faulks' *Birdsong*. One of Faulks' achievements has been to link the prewar world—his early scenes take place in the still peaceful locale that was to become the Somme battlefield in 1916—to present-day characters discovering the agony their ancestors experienced.[11]

NOTES

1. Jean-Jacques Becker, *The Great War and the French* People, trans. Arnold Pomerans (Leamington Spa, Eng.: Berg, 1985); Jeffrey Verhey, *The Spirit of 1914: Militarism, Myth, and Mobilization in Germany* (Cambridge, Eng.: Cambridge University Press, 2000).

2. Richard Wall and Jay Winter, eds., *The Upheaval of War: Family, Work and Welfare in Europe, 1914–1918* (Cambridge, Eng.: Cambridge University Press, 1988); Jay Winter and Jean-Louis Robert, eds., *Capital Cities at War: Paris, London, Berlin, 1914–1919* (Cambridge, Eng.: Cambridge University Press, 1997); Hugh Cecil and Peter Liddle, eds., *Facing Armageddon: The First World War Experienced* (London: Leo Cooper, 1996).

3. Jay Winter, *Sites of Memory, Sites of Mourning: The Great War in European Cultural History* (Cambridge, Eng.: Cambridge University Press, 1995); Adrian Gregory, *The Silence of Memory: Armistice Day, 1919–1946* (Oxford: Berg, 1994); George Mosse, *Fallen Soldiers: Reshaping the Memory of the World Wars* (New York: Oxford University Press, 1990); Daniel Sherman, *The Construction of Memory in Interwar France* (Chicago: University of Chicago Press, 1999).

4. Gail Braybon, *Women Workers in the First World War: The British Experience* (London: Croom Helm, 1981); Laura Lee Downs, *Manufacturing Inequality: Gender Division in the French and British Metalworking Industries, 1914–1939* (Ithaca, N.Y.: Cornell University Press, 1995); Susan Zeiger, *In Uncle Sam's Service: Women Workers in the American Expeditionary Force, 1917–1919* (Ithaca, N.Y.: Cornell University Press, 1999); Ute Daniel, *The War from Within: German Working-Class Women in the First World War*, trans. Margaret Ries (Oxford: Berg, 1997); Margaret H. Darrow, *French Women and the First World War: War Stories of the Home Front* (Oxford: Berg, 2000); Belinda Davis, *Home Fires Burning: Food, Politics, and Every-*

day Life in World War I Berlin (Chapel Hill: University of North Carolina Press, 2000); Margaret Randolph Higgonet, et al., eds., *Behind the Lines: Gender and the Two World Wars* (New Haven, Conn.: Yale University Press, 1987).

5. Leon Wolff, *In Flanders Fields: The 1917 Campaign* (New York: Viking, 1958); Tony Ashworth, *Trench Warfare, 1914–1918: The Live and Let Live System* (London: Macmillan, 1980); Leonard Smith, *Between Mutiny and Obedience: The Case of the French Fifth Infantry Division during World War I* (Princeton: Princeton University Press, 1994).

6. Paddy Griffith, *Battle Tactics of the Western Front: The British Army's Art of Attack, 1916–1918* (New Haven, Conn.: Yale University Press, 1984); Albert Palazzo, *Seeking Victory on the Western Front* (Lincoln, Nebr.: University of Nebraska Press, 2000).

7. Correlli Barnett, *The Collapse of British Power* (New York: William Morrow, 1972); Brian Bond, "British 'Anti-War' Writers and Their Critics," in *Facing Armageddon*, ed. Cecil and Liddle.

8. David M. Kennedy, *Over Here: The First World War and American Society* (Oxford: Oxford University Press, 1980), 202–5.

9. Mark E. Grotelueschen, *Doctrine under Fire: American Artillery Employment in World War I* (Westport, Conn.: Greenwood Press, 2001).

10. John S.D. Eisenhower, *Yanks: The Epic Story of the American Army in World War I* (New York: Free Press, 2001); also, Grotelueschen, *Doctrine under Fire.*

11. C.S. Forester, *The General* (London: Michael Joseph, 1953); Pat Barker, *Regeneration* (New York: Dutton, 1992), *The Eye in the Door* (New York: Dutton, 1994), and *The Ghost Road* (New York: Dutton, 1996); Sebastian Faulks, *Birdsong* (New York: Vintage, 1997).

ADDITIONAL USEFUL WORKS ON WORLD WAR I

The titles listed here are key books on the subject, many of which have been cited in the notes. More specialized works can be found in the notes for individual chapters.

Augé-Laribé, Michel, and P. Pinot. *Agriculture and Food Supply in France during the War.* New Haven: Yale University Press, 1927.

Barnett, L. Margaret. *British Food Policy during the First World War.* Boston: Allen and Unwin, 1985.

Becker, Annette. *Oubliés de la Grande Guerre: Humanitaire et Culture de Guerre: Populations Occupées, Déportés Civils, Prisonniers de Guerre.* Paris: Éditions Noêsis, 1998.

Bessel, Richard. *Germany after the First World War.* Oxford: Clarendon Press, 1993.

Bland, Lucy. "In the Name of Protection: The Policing of Women in the First World War." In *Women in Law: Explorations in Family and Sexuality*, edited by Julia Brophy and Carol Smart. London: Routledge and Kegan Paul, 1985.

Brittain, Vera. *Testament of Youth: An Autobiographical Study of the Years 1900–1925.* New York: Macmillan, 1933.

Brown, Malcolm. *Tommy Goes to War.* London: J.M. Dent, 1978.

Bull, Stephen. *Arms and Armor.* New York: Facts on File, 1996.

————. *Stormtrooper: Elite German Assault Soldiers*. London: Publishing News, 1999.

Cahalan, Peter. *Belgian Refugee Relief in England during the Great War*. New York: Garland Publishing, 1982.

Cannadine, David. "War and Death, Grief and Mourning in Modern Britain." In *Mirrors of Mortality: Studies in the Social History of Death*, edited by Joachim Whaley. New York: St. Martin's Press, 1981.

Cecil, Hugh, and Peter Liddle, eds. *At the Eleventh Hour: Reflections, Hopes and Anxieties at the Closing of the Great War, 1918*. London: Leo Cooper, 1998.

Chickering, Roger. *Imperial Germany and the Great War, 1914–1918*. Cambridge, Eng.: Cambridge University Press, 1998.

Cobb, Richard. *French and Germans, Germans and French: A Personal Interpretation of France under Two Occupations, 1914–1918/1940–1944*. Hanover, N.H.: University Press of New England, 1983.

Coffman, Edward M. *The War to End All Wars: The American Military Experience in World War I*. New York: Oxford University Press, 1968.

Cushing, Harvey. *From a Surgeon's Journal, 1915–1918*. Boston: Little, Brown and Company, 1936.

Dyer, Colin. *Population and Society in Twentieth Century France*. London: Hodder and Stoughton, 1978.

Eksteins, Modris. "War, Memory, and the Modern: Pilgrimage and Tourism to the Western Front." In *World War I and the Cultures of Modernity*, edited by Douglas Mackaman and Michael Mays. Jackson, Miss.: University of Mississippi Press, 2000.

Ellis, John. *Eye-Deep in Hell: Trench Warfare in World War I*. New York: Pantheon, 1976.

Farwell, Byron. *Over There: The United States in the Great War, 1917–1918*. New York: W.W. Norton, 1999.

Ferrell, Robert. *Woodrow Wilson and World War I, 1917–1921*. New York: Harper and Row, 1985.

Feuer, A.B. *The U.S. Navy in World War I: Combat at Sea and in the Air*. Westport, Conn.: Praeger, 1999.

Flexner, Eleanor. *Century of Struggle: The Woman's Rights Movement in the United States*. Rev. ed. Cambridge, Mass.: The Belknap Press of Harvard University Press, 1975.

Fredette, Raymond H. *The Sky on Fire: The First Battle of Britain, 1917–1918 and the Birth of the Royal Air Force*. New York: Holt, Rinehart and Winston, 1966.

Freidel, Frank. *Over There: The Story of America's First Great Overseas Crusade*. Revised ed. Philadelphia: Temple University Press, 1990.

Gavin, Lettie. *American Women in World War I: They Also Served*. Niwot, Colo.: University Press of Colorado, 1997.

Graubard, Stephen Richards. "Military Demobilization in Great Britain following the First World War." *Journal of Modern History* 19, no. 4 (1947): 297–311.

Gray, Edwyn A. *The Killing Time: The German U-boats, 1914–1918*. New York: Charles Scribner's Sons, 1972.

Grayling, Christopher. *A Land Fit for Heroes: British Life after the Great War*. London: Buchan and Enright, 1987.

Grayzel, Susan R. *Women's Identities at War: Gender, Motherhood, and Politics in Britain and France during the First World War.* Chapel Hill: University of North Carolina Press, 1999.

Greenwald, Maurine Weiner. *Women, War, and Work: The Impact of World War I on Women Workers in the United States.* Westport, Conn.: Greenwood Press, 1980.

Haber, L.F. *The Poisonous Cloud: Chemical Warfare in the First World War.* Oxford: Clarendon Press, 1986.

Hallas, James H. *The Doughboy War: The American Expeditionary Force in World War I.* Boulder, Colo.: Lynne Rienner Publishers, 2000.

Haythornthwaite, Philip J. *The World War One Source Book.* London: Arms and Armour Press, 1992.

Higgonet, Margaret R., ed. *Nurses at the Front: Writing the Wounds of the Great War.* Boston: Northeastern University Press, 2001.

Hogg, Ian. *The Guns, 1914–1918.* New York: Ballantine Books, 1971.

Holm, Jeanne, Maj. Gen., USAF (Ret.). *Women in the Military: An Unfinished Revolution.* Rev. ed. Novato, Calif.: Presidio Press, 1992.

Horne, Alistair. *The Price of Glory: Verdun, 1916.* New York: Harper and Row, 1962.

Horne, John. "Immigrant Workers in France during World War I." *French Historical Studies* 14, no. 1 (1985): 57–88.

Horne, John, and Alan Kramer. "German 'Atrocities' and Franco-German Opinion, 1914: The Evidence of German Soldiers' Diaries." *Journal of Modern History* 66, no. 1 (1994): 1–33.

Jackson, Robert. *The Prisoners, 1914–1918.* London: Routledge, 1989.

Jalland, Pat. *Death in the Victorian Family.* Oxford: Oxford University Press, 1996.

Keegan, John. *The First World War.* New York: Alfred A. Knopf, 1999.

———. *The Price of Admiralty: The Evolution of Naval Warfare.* New York: Penguin, 1989.

Kent, Susan Kingsley. *Making Peace: The Reconstruction of Gender in Interwar Britain.* Princeton, N.J.: Princeton University Press, 1993.

Ketchum, J. Davidson. *Ruhleben: A Prison Camp Society.* Toronto: University of Toronto Press, 1965.

Kocka, Jürgen. *Facing Total War: German Society, 1914–1918.* Translated by Barbara Weinberger. Leamington Spa, Eng.: Berg Publishers, 1984.

Levenstein, Harvey A. *Revolution at the Table: The Transformation of the American Diet.* New York: Oxford University Press, 1988.

Liddle, Peter H. *The Airman's War, 1914–18.* Poole, Eng.: Blandford Press, 1987.

———. *The Sailor's War, 1914–1918.* Poole, Eng.: Blandford Press, 1985.

———. *The Soldier's War, 1914–1918.* London: Blandford Press, 1988.

Longworth, Philip. *The Unending Vigil: A History of the Commonwealth War Graves Commission, 1917–1984.* Rev. and updated ed. London: Leo Cooper, in association with Secker and Warburg, 1985.

Macdonald, Lyn. *The Roses of No Man's Land.* London: Michael Joseph, 1980.

———. *To the Last Man: Spring 1918.* New York: Carroll and Graf. 1998.

———. *1914–1918: Voices and Images of the Great War.* London: Michael Joseph, 1988.

McPhail, Helen. *The Long Silence: Civilian Life under the German Occupation of Northern France, 1914–1918*. London: I.B. Tauris, 1999.

Middlebrook, Martin. *First Day on the Somme: 1 July 1916*. New York: W.W. Norton, 1972.

———. *The Kaiser's Battle: 21 March 1918: The First Day of the German Spring Offensive*. London: Allen Lane, 1978.

Mosse, George. "Shell Shock as a Social Disease." *Journal of Contemporary History* 35, no. 1 (2000): 101–8.

Moyer, Laurence. *Victory Must Be Ours: Germany in the Great War, 1914–1918*. New York: Hippocrene Books, 1995.

Offer, Avner. *The First World War: An Agrarian Interpretation*. Oxford: Clarendon Press, 1989.

Panayi, Panikos. *The Enemy in Our Midst: Germans in Britain during the First World War*. New York: Berg, 1991.

Porch, Douglas. *The March to the Marne: The French Army, 1871–1914*. Cambridge, Eng.: Cambridge University Press, 1981.

Pound, Reginald. *Gillies: Surgeon Extraordinary*. London: Michael Joseph, 1964.

Prost, Antoine. *In the Wake of War: 'Les Anciens Combatants' and French Society*. Translated by Helen McPhail. Providence, R.I.: Berg, 1992.

Renehan, Edward J., Jr. *The Lion's Pride: Theodore Roosevelt and His Family in Peace and War*. New York: Oxford University Press, 1998.

Roberts, Mary Louise. *Civilization without Sexes: Reconstructing Gender in Postwar France, 1917–1927*. Chicago: University of Chicago Press, 1994.

Roshwald, Aviel, and Richard Stites, eds. *European Culture in the Great War: The Arts, Entertainment, and Propaganda, 1914–1918*. Cambridge, Eng.: Cambridge University Press, 1999.

Sarnecky, Mary T., Colonel, USA (Ret.). *A History of the U.S. Army Nurse Corps*. Philadelphia: University of Pennsylvania Press, 1999.

Schneider, Dorothy, and Carl J. Schneider. *Into the Breach: American Women Overseas in World War I*. New York: Viking, 1991.

Schulte, Regina. "The Sick Warrior's Sister: Nursing during the First World War." In *Gender Relations in German History: Power, Agency and Experience from the Sixteenth to the Twentieth Century*, edited by Lynn Abrams and Elizabeth Harvey. Durham, N.C.: Duke University Press, 1997.

Shephard, Ben. *A War of Nerves: Soldiers and Psychiatrists in the Twentieth Century*. Cambridge, Mass.: Harvard University Press, 2001.

Simkins, Peter. *Kitchener's Army: The Raising of the New Armies, 1914–1916*. Manchester, Eng.: Manchester University Press, 1988.

Spector, Ronald H. *At War at Sea: Sailors and Naval Combat in the Twentieth Century*. New York: Viking, 2001.

Speed, Richard B., III. *Prisoners, Diplomats, and the Great War: A Study in the Diplomacy of Captivity*. New York: Greenwood Press, 1990.

Strachan, Hew, ed. *World War I: A History*. Oxford: Oxford University Press, 1998.

Terraine, John. *To Win a War: 1918, The Year of Victory*. London: Sidgwick and Jackson, 1978.

Tuchman, Barbara. *The Guns of August*. New York: Macmillan, 1962.

Van Emden, Richard. *Prisoners of the Kaiser: The Last POWs of the Great War*. London: Leo Cooper, 2000.

Wedd, A.F., trans. and ed. *German Students' War Letters*. New York: E.P. Dutton, [1929].

Weintraub, Stanley. *A Stillness Heard Round the World: The End of the Great War, November 1918*. New York: E.P. Dutton, 1985.

Westman, Stephen, M.D., F.R.C.S. *Surgeon with the Kaiser's Army*. London: William Kimber, 1968.

Whalen, Robert. *Bitter Wounds: German Victims of the Great War, 1914–1939*. Ithaca, N.Y.: Cornell University Press, 1984.

Williams, John. *The Other Battleground: The Home Fronts: Britain, France and Germany, 1914–1918*. Chicago: Henry Regnery, 1972.

Wilson, Trevor. *The Myriad Faces of War: Britain and the Great War, 1914–1918*. Cambridge, Eng.: Polity Press, 1986.

Winter, Denis. *Death's Men: Soldiers of the Great War*. London: Penguin Books, 1978.

Winter, J. (Jay) M. *The Great War and the British People*. London: Macmillan, 1986.

Woollacott, Angela. " 'Khaki Fever' and Its Control: Gender, Class, Age and Sexual Morality on the British Homefront in the First World War." *Journal of Contemporary History* 29, no. 2 (1994): 325–47.

———. *On Her Their Lives Depend: Munitions Workers in the Great War*. Berkeley: University of California Press, 1994.

Zabecki, David T. *Steel Wind: Colonel Georg Bruchmüller and the Birth of Modern Artillery*. Westport, Conn.: Praeger, 1994.

Zieger, Robert H. *America's Great War: World War I and the American Experience*. Lanham, Md.: Rowman and Littlefield, 2000.

WORLD WAR I WEB SITES

Art of the First World War. http://www.art-ww1.com. A Web site containing a collection of 110 paintings produced by fifty-four painters from countries that fought on both sides in the war.

British Army in the Great War. http://www.1914–1918.net. A Web site giving a detailed description of the major units of the British army and the battles in which they participated.

The Great War and the Shaping of the Twentieth Century. http://www.pbs.org/greatwar/. A companion Web site for the 1996 PBS documentary (see the Documentary Film list). It features critical reviews of the television production, interviews with historians of World War I, maps, and an interactive timeline.

Hellfire Corner. http://www.fylde.demon.co.uk/. A Web site devoted primarily to the British army in World War I, featuring information on visiting the battlefields today, cemeteries and memorials, and individuals who served in the war.

Navies of World War I. http://www.naval-history.net/NAVAL1914–18.htm. This Web site gives a wealth of information on all of the maritime powers that participated in the war. It includes a list of the major vessels in each nation's fleet, significant naval battles and campaigns, and the ships lost.

Photos of the Great War. http://www.ukans.edu/~kansite/ww_one/photos/

greatwar.htm. A growing collection of photographs of individuals and events from the war, the site presently contains almost 1,900 images.

U.S. Army Official War Artists. http://www.worldwar1.com/dbc/artists.htm. A Web site describing and illustrating the work of eight artists commissioned by the United States Army to record its activities in battle and in the rear areas of the western front.

DOCUMENTARY FILM LIST

The Battle of the Somme: 1916 (color, 94 minutes). Films for the Humanities and Sciences, 1994. An examination of one of the war's bloodiest battles featuring the accounts of individual participants and present-day views of the locales where combat took place.

Cavalry of the Clouds (color, 38 minutes). Films for the Humanities and Sciences, 1988. An account of Great Britain's airmen and their personal experiences on the western front.

Good-bye Billy: America Goes to War, 1917–1918 (black and white, 25 minutes). Cadre Films, 1972. A poignant, impressionistic account of the American war effort both at home and on the western front.

The Great War and the Shaping of the Twentieth Century (color, 8 hours). PBS, 1996. An extensive treatment of all aspects of the war with commentaries by a number of leading historians.

This Generation Has No Future: The Great War (color, 52 minutes). *Europe: The Mighty Continent* series. BBC, 1974. A factually detailed account of the war stressing the role of the European participants. It includes informed and colorful commentaries by historian John Terraine and English actor-playwright Peter Ustinov.

Verdun (black and white, 30 minutes). *Legacy* series. WNET, 1965. An account of the year-long battle between French and German forces in 1916 including the personal experiences of those in the ranks as well as a consideration of the generals' intentions.

Index

About the Author

NEIL M. HEYMAN is Professor of History at San Diego State University and Adjunct Professor of Strategy and Policy, United States Naval War College. He is a specialist in modern European history and military affairs. He has written two earlier books on World War I, *Biographical Dictionary of World War I* (co-author with Holger H. Herwig; Greenwood, 1982), and *World War I* (Greenwood, 1997). Professor Heyman is also the author of *Russian History* (1993) and *Western Civilization: A Critical Guide to Documentary Film* (Greenwood, 1996).